LUMMOX
NUMBER ONE

The Favorite Poems Issue

Edited by RD Armstrong

LUMMOX NUMBER ONE

©2012 LUMMOX Press

All rights revert to the contributors upon publication.

All rights reserved. No part of this book can be reproduced without the express written permission of the editor, except in the case of written reviews.

ISBN 978-1-929878- 38-3

First edition

PO Box 5301

San Pedro, CA 90733

www.lummoxpress.com

Printed in the United States of America

Acknowledgements

Some of these poems have been previously published; all credits are cited at the end of each poem or poems. The Editor-in-Chief gratefully acknowledges the wisdom of all the previous editors who saw the value in these poems.

Cover art by **Claudio Parentela**

"Poetry is important, the poet is not"

Octavio Paz

EDITOR-IN-CHIEF
RD ARMSTRONG

ART DIRECTOR
CHRIS YESETA

PUBLISHED BY
LUMMOX PRESS
P.O. BOX 5301
SAN PEDRO, CA 90733-5301
WWW.LUMMOXPRESS.COM

SUBMISSION GUIDELINES

Micro and flash fiction, novel extracts will be considered but it must be high quality material, inquire before sending. Essays on poetics, biographies, and the craft of writing, along with well written rants will also be considered, along with interviews. Articles that are topical in nature will be considered as well. Additionally, art work will be considered as long as it is conducive to a B&W format. Mostly, LUMMOX is about poetry, so send your best.

The Guidelines:

Send 3 poems via email. Poems should not exceed 60 lines (including blank lines—single spaced) and should not be formatted. Previously published poetry is fine, just let us know where. Please attach a 3 sentence bio (bios that are a paragraph long will be edited).

Reading period for the annual issue will be from May 1st to August 1st 2013. Please send subs via poetraindog@gmail.com in the message window (attachments will not be opened, unless I know you). If snail mail is necessary, then send to LUMMOX c/o PO Box 5301, San Pedro, CA 90733-5301

Ad Rates:
- Full Page (6″x8″)—$200; • Half Page (6″x3.875″)—$150;
- 1/4 Page (2.875″x3.875″)—$80; • 1/8 Page (2.875″x1.875″)—$45.
- Friends of LUMMOX get 25% off all ad sizes.

TABLE OF CONTENTS

TABLE OF CONTENTS

AN INTRODUCTION TO LUMMOX NO. 1

A Little Background…

IN OCTOBER OF 1995, A LITTLE magazine was born. The LUMMOX Journal started out as four pages stapled together with crude graphics and sad little scribblings by a guy known as Raindog. It then became a larger format "magazine" with crude graphics and the sad scribblings of other guys *and* Raindog. There were articles, interviews and a smattering of poetry. Next it evolved into a smart looking little digest sized journal with great graphics, better interviews, better articles and it stayed that way for eleven years. The LUMMOX Journal came out monthly for eight of those eleven years, and bimonthly for the last three. At its most popular it had 180 subscribers… that's all. It was made for a discerning audience and was highly recommended by its readership. But at the end of the day, it was a 'little' magazine. It never did enjoy the type of success that other L.A. mags of the day had…like Flipside, or Caffeine, or even Next…magazine. Of course none of them lasted for eleven years either.

I put out the LUMMOX Journal because I thought it would be interesting to learn about the creative process of the artistic mind. It was a hobby of sorts. I had a nice little gig as a handyman going and that paid the bills, allowing me time to run the LUMMOX Journal (and publish the Little

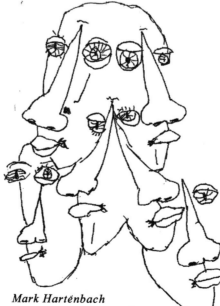

Mark Hartenbach

Red Book series). From the beginning I knew that the LJ had to pay for itself, which it did. I had no delusions about it ever becoming a big enough concern to where I could quit my "day job" and just publish a magazine and some poetry collections…but things change and eventually, long after I had tucked the LJ in for the rest of my life, I found myself relying more and more on the income that printing poetry books was bringing in (especially when I couldn't rely on the handyman trade anymore). *The LUMMOX Press had become my meal-ticket.*

Eventually, when things weren't going that well at the press, I found myself missing putting out a magazine…but not the deadlines of a monthly (which were pretty brutal). So, I hit on the idea of a yearly journal. But not a small magazine like before, I wanted something BIG. Something with some heft to it. Something with a name as big as the first issue, hence LUMMOX was born.

I wanted LUMMOX to represent a cross-section of what was going on in the small press across the country and around the world. I didn't quite get the world involved as much as I would have liked but I think I got a pretty good sampling from the US. In order to do this, I invited "Guest Editors" (poets whom I knew to be connected to a certain region, Doug Holder, for example, who hails from the Boston area; or poets that are associated with a school of poetry that might never be a part of something like this, such as Ed Nudelman's group) to invite 8-10 of their favorite poets to send in 3-4 of their favorite poems. The editors would then select 1-2 poems from each poet, and write a brief essay about why they thought these guys were important to the canon of twenty-first century poetry and send it to me. I invited fifteen thinking maybe eight would be interested... thirteen said yes! One dropped out, leaving twelve Guest Editors. Well, that would have been one volume already except I had already accepted another seventy-five submissions!

So, there you have it! I wanted a big issue and I got a big issue, no, I got a giant issue! I think that this is just the tip of the iceberg, too. There is so much well written poetry out there, so many MFA programs in creative writing, so many people learning how to express themselves through poetry...it's all a good start as far as I'm concerned. But it *is* just a good start. Writing poetry is at least a two part operation: craft & soul...writing a poem that is technically sound, like playing a guitar lick well, can be accomplished if one practices on a daily basis. But putting one's heart and soul into said poem or guitar lick, well that's another job altogether. That takes another kind of practice...it's called life experience.

There is a lot of gimmicky poetry (what I sometimes call 'cute' or 'precious' poetry) being written these days...poems that use buzz words or cliché to elicit a visceral reaction, for example. Or clever poetry that uses language twists and double entendre to please the ear. These are extreme examples but they represent the boundaries within which I worked while selecting most of the poems for this anthology...I say most because I let the guest editors make their selections autonomously (some of their choices don't reflect my tastes, but it gives the reader a greater cross-section to work with). That said, I have never been a big fan of "artsy" poetry and I have tried my damnedest to keep it out of this first anthology. My emphasis in this anthology is on the *POETRY*. Everything in this issue is concerned with moving the craft forward...expanding the scope of poetry beyond regions, beyond types, beyond the limitations of the "norm".

Now to the theme of this anthology: Favorite Poems. The theme breaks down into two different parts...favorite poems by favorite poets *and* the poem (not the poet) as artifact.

Octavio Paz once wrote, "poetry is important, the poet is not!" Steve Goldman and Michael C. Ford both address this topic in the essays section near the back of this book. Both are disgusted with the shift from the poem as a vehicle of expression to the poem as a means to promote the glory of the poet. This is something that has also been on my mind for a long time, how we have shifted from a community mind set to a cult of personality...where the individual is king, where everyone is a hero (I can only speak for the US here, it may not be so elsewhere in the world). It does remind me of Orwell's 1984...where everyone believes the propaganda that they are free and that their part is crucial in the balance of things, while in reality, they are slaves to the great corporate machine. But I digress.

The thing is, because poets are human, they are susceptible to the frailties of the flesh. And since poets try to "lay it on the line" as much as possible, there is bound to be some friction amid different factions of the poetry community. Here in the L.A. basin, it seems as if the poets of various sections of town are always in conflict with each other. Mostly the source of the L. A. friction is ego. Perhaps it's because of the connection to the entertainment industry... everyone wants to either be a star, have their 15 minutes of fame, or hang out with famous people. Because of this egotism, the poet has become iconic, superseding what is really important, namely the poem. It's out of balance.

I have, in this first issue, attempted to push the poet behind the poetry. There are only a few instances where the poet is honored (such as the TRIBUTES section, where we honor the dead, as in the case of Tony Moffeit's reflections on the late Kell Robertson). For the rest of the issue the poem is the focus.

But we cannot forget the poet altogether, since without the poet there would be no poetry, so the order in which the poems appear is based on the first name of the poet responsible for the poem or poetry group. This may sound like an odd approach, and it may well be (I have been under the influence of low blood-sugar and lack of sleep trying to put this puppy to bed), but it was obvious to me at the time I conceived it. Only time will tell.

I would like to thank the following people for their help with this inaugural issue: first and foremost, my friend and colleague Chris Yeseta who has been with LUMMOX since '96 and who is the genius behind all of the design and layout. Next the guest editors: Biola Olatunde, Don Kingfisher Campbell, Doug Holder, Ed Nudelman, Georgia Santa Maria, Jaimes Palacio, Jane Crown, Jane Lipman, Joe Shermis, Marie Lecrivain, Mike Adams and Ryan Guth. They brought a wonderful glimpse into the poetry of their interests, their regions and their souls. I am grateful that they have joined in the making of this book with such vigor. And finally, I thank the rest of the poets, whose contributions have further enriched my life and by doing so, will hopefully enrich your life too.

God bless the small press, possibly the last bastion of free speech left.

RD Armstrong
Sept. 18, 2012
Long Beach, CA

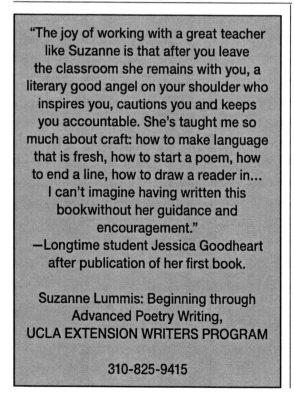

"The joy of working with a great teacher like Suzanne is that after you leave the classroom she remains with you, a literary good angel on your shoulder who inspires you, cautions you and keeps you accountable. She's taught me so much about craft: how to make language that is fresh, how to start a poem, how to end a line, how to draw a reader in... I can't imagine having written this bookwithout her guidance and encouragement."
—Longtime student Jessica Goodheart after publication of her first book.

Suzanne Lummis: Beginning through Advanced Poetry Writing,
UCLA EXTENSION WRITERS PROGRAM

310-825-9415

TRIBUTES

POETRY IS EVOLUTIONARY. IT INSPIRES others to pick it up and move it forward. Were it not for poets, we wouldn't have the poetry that inspires us. So when a poet dies, we honor the writer of the lines that have inspired us. Here are a few of those poets who have inspired many, some more than others…

FOR SCOTT WANNBERG

Scott Wannberg was one of the most unique people I ever met. He was always "on", in fact I don't think he even had an "off", at least not until his death in Oregon (and even then, he might have still been rapping when the EMTs took him away, but just very quietly). He was born and then 58 years later he died. In between he did a lot of cool stuff including going to San Francisco State, working at Dutton's Books for 28 years, befriending anyone and everyone, hitching a ride with the Carma Bums and generally becoming the darling of all media worldwide! When he died, I had no idea that he would be taken away from me completely and forever…at least I still have my menories.

THE VOICE OF THE MOUNTAIN
for Scott Wannberg

The mountain comes to Mohammed
And this time the mountain speaks.
And a stream runs off of the mountain
And it burbles and rollicks and purls over rocks
And it tinkles and tingles
And it never stops, it never stops.
And the stream is the voice
And the voice is the stream
And there are poems in the stream
And jive and parodies and jokes
And play-jewels of words
And there are movies in the stream that is the voice of the mountain
And Bogey can't get it together with Lauren
And Sam does play it again
And Clark doesn't give a damn, Scarlett
And Marlon leers over the bars of his chopper
And the Duke, most often in the Marines
Exhorts more adolescents to gallant slaughter
And Tom Joad hops the 20th Century Limited to Metropolis
And Gary and Cary and Jimmy and Edward G. and George C
And Judy and Veronica and Betty and Ginger and Raquel
And all the others are there in the chorus of the burbling stream
Trying to love
And Seven Are Saved In the Wake of the Red Witch
And it is a many splendored thing of terse encounters of the close kind.

And there are layers in the stream
Within the stream is noise

And in the noise are the movies
And in the movies is the voice within the voice
For the mountain sees the sadness and the lack of dancing
And song and the smog and the sad, sad irony.
And the featured films are Wm. H. <u>Heart</u> in The Great Train Robbery
And Melina planning The Great Jewel Heist
Which is really what it's all about
And one layer deeper is The Coming Attraction
The Great Earth Robbery
As yet in production, nascent in the rock,
Which the mountain himself, Mt. Wannberg
May direct.
And that is all your reporter is able to tell of layers.
But O God, O Yes
It's all in Technicolor and Dolby Sound
The Prophet decked out as Bob's Big Boy
But my man's all right
He doesn't care
Because what the hell
We're all Frankenstein
One way or another
And the mountain is walking, sputtering
Toward Mohammed.

Steve Goldman
Venice
Circa 1972-74

FOR BILL JONES

Billy Jones was an artist, poet and emotional expatriate born in Camden, New Jersey in 1935 where Walt Whitman died. He quit high school, joined the Marines, then went back to school on the GI Bill majoring in American Literature at LA State. He migrated to Australia from Stockholm in 1967. In addition to his previously published poetry collections and numerous exhibitions, he kept a journal of drawings, paintings, poetry and every day events since June 28, 1975. Started as a hermit on the riverbank in a she-oak grove at Mary Smokes Creek five weeks after his then girlfriend, Diane Kelly, was killed in a car accident, he was working on volume 167 (ME & MY GANG OF ALTER EGOS) when he died ---100,000 pages, 4500 illustrations. Overall title: THE ILLUMINATION OF BILLY BONES. Billy joined Diane on July 3, 2012.

"Billy Jones is well known to poetry lovers in his adopted country, and by some of the art world there, but he is also known in his country of birth. He is a no-borders man. His love of life startles me into joy. Even a serious illness brings him poems and wisdom and art. Even his fears take wing and fly over beauty."

Ann Menebroker, poet

"A unique American expatriate poet in Australian outback w/a soul as fine as a dingo dog & as big as the universe & as beautiful & wild as a Van Gogh sunflower"

Fred Voss, poet

FOR LEONARD J. CIRINO

"When I think of the poetry of Leonard Cirino, I think of dignity and integrity. He knows madness up close, and he knows discipline and seclusion, as well as love and tenderness. He is devoid of self-pity, looks death square in the eye, and writes of nature, the cosmos and his dog with equal authority.

He is a classical poet in a world gone mad with idiom."

John Bennett

Tribute to LEONARD J. CIRINO Part I

It was spring 1991, and my business partner and I were on our way to Caspar, CA, to stay with his friend, Leonard Cirino. The plan was to spend the night at Leonard's place just up the street from the Caspar Inn, and then get up in the morning and get going on our magazine, *The Steelhead Special*. But first, he tells me, it is important to spend some time with Leonard, get to know him a bit, before immersing ourselves into the Mendocino county poetry scene.

"He'll talk to ya, he will," Crawdad declared, "stay up all night long and tell ya things that will make your head spin and your heart swim."

I nodded, genuinely interested, and listened carefully as he told me of adventures had from staying up late and listening carefully to what Leonard could tell ya if ya

Norman J. Olson

gave him the chance. I decided right then I would give just that; one of those moments I realized I had much more to gain from listening than from saying anything besides "Tell me more...."

Little did I know that I would spend many hours in the next 20 plus years doing exactly that; listening to him describe experiences and express opinions on the beats and the government, the grant junkies and the penal system, and wax poetic over the curve of a woman's thigh and the height of man's humanity. It was a ride.

Years later I had a job distributing alternative press magazines in Mendocino county. By that time Leonard had his place in the Pygmy Forest in Albion. I would make the loop through Boonville, come to the coast and stay in Leonard's loft once a month, getting the opportunity to listen to Leonard's vivid descriptions of the world into the wee hours as part of the rhythm of my life and his. Sometimes we would jam, me on guitar, him on blues harp, connecting musically in our own unique way. It was a wonderful friendship, and had a profound affect on how I perceive the world.

Leonard became a key part in the making of *The Steelhead*, contributing poetry, making print bill loans, and providing me with the emotional support and courage to contend with the personalities and obstacles that one meets on such a venture. It could not have been done without him.

Years later he moved to the town I lived in, Eureka, CA, to live with his mother Marjorie. They shared a beautiful house in a nice neighborhood while Leonard volunteered at the Environmental Center and wrote poetry through the night and the occasional article for the Times-Standard by day. Marjorie and

Leonard later moved to Springfield, OR, to be with the love of his life, Ava.

Missing his presence in my life, I began to trade correspondence with him regularly; it was often the high point of my creative flow for the day. He sent poems several times a week, each one providing my mind with images and visual experiences that came no other way. It worked that way for me right up to the last few reminisces I received shortly before he passed.

The following poems are a small sampling that sat in my e mail inbox for a year. These ones touched me as much as any of several hundred others he sent, or I read in one of his books, or I heard him read out loud in public...

Joe Shermis

Joe Shermis lives in a small basement apartment five blocks from Humboldt Bay in Eureka, CA. He has graduated from both colleges in the area, helped to raise some children into fine adults, cared for numerous cats, and has published The Steelhead Special since 1991, managed a hippie store since 2008.

In the Kingdom of the Blind
The One-Eyed Man Is King

With thirteen teeth, one eye, and little hair left,
he sits and ages. He stands only for peace,
freedom, justice. At midnight he begins work
and listens for crows, crickets, his totems the turtle
and owl. He works while others sleep and ciphers
their dreams on paper. At eight a.m. he yields
to rest and dreams of his own lost: his mind,
his daughter. Distraught, he turns and tosses off
another cup of coffee, a cigarette, a small meal.
Hoping for sleep, against hope he wills his body
to relax. His legs and feet ache, stomach churns.
He's had a good night-- three or four poems,
a hundred pages absorbed. By ten he drifts off,
rises at two or three. Pleased, he tosses covers,
puts on shirt, brushes teeth, begins a new day.

Song of Songs

Grown women still want soft tongues
across the stretch of imagination
with lip to lap resuscitation.
Oh labia my love, of star and moon,
limb and stone, my wish for rising hips.

Breath, unfold your mist
across my mouth, the autumn come,
soil wet with mothers' gloom:
beasts and humans all curved
and formed like earth's unknowns.

Redwoods
after Ron Rash

It's wise to know a memory
deep and historical as water,
called down from the sky to nest
among leaves where the wind slopes
and stirs the leaves, thinks of roots

in the past, back to the time of Christ,
when this clearcut was a grove, limbs
large and sensate, fertile and strong.
It's the vanquished who have the last say,
knowing their absence will go on forever.

Advice

You need to get away from your garden. Go to the forest,

scrape through the trees and get to the mountain. Stay

a while. Then drop down to the rivers and plains, arrive

at the ocean and listen.

Muddy Water

...I'd rather drink muddy water
and sleep in a hollow log...
As sung by Aretha Franklin

It would be late summer or early fall
but I'd rather drink muddy water
and sleep in a hollow log than sip cognac
and rest in a feather bed. I'd sauté chanterelles
with a little butter. The muddy water is a myth,
but inside the hollow base of an old growth
redwood would do fine. I'd have the stars
and moon for a lamp, a bag for warmth,
the soil to curl up and lay my body on,
fresh air, and limbs that lean down and whisper.
Not much to ask in this world of trifles and baubles.

Poem Without an S

I get knocked down hard
into the well, the deep
pit of water where the earth,
the mud and the live live on.

Here and there I notice
one thing after another,
rock, lichen, hammer tapping.
Wound upon caring, I think
I belong to the rich growth.

What more can be done
than to crawl, to gather
leaf and branch, mouth them,
let them ripen on my tongue.

The Ultimate Poem Must Be Unknown

In one hand he holds the equation for sediment,
in the other, the temperature of the fly.
Like all faiths, one is constant to the believer,
while the other varies in ranges of the thermometer.

He has waited weeks for a small epiphany
of this sort, and respects the dissimilarities
of his subjects. If all things were basic
he could find a balance, but on the scale
of one to ten he realizes they are equally true.

Fat Chance, Lady Luck

He thought it contained
to his liver. But they said
it had gone wildfire.

***

Still have fourteen teeth
since the last eleven years,
some pain, but can chew.

***

Bald for forty years,
Ava thinks I'm still

handsome.
That's enough for me.

***

English hard to do.
In Spanish even more so.
Try Japanese think.

***

Thinking of life past,
having burnt many bridges.
joy, grief, abundance.

Pax
after Ales Debeljak

My solitude is an ornament of precision.
The deception happens when I open
a skull and there is only waste inside.

Crippled by mysterious thoughts I linger
on the steps heading to the Vatican.
The numerous saints speak to me in tongues,
their voices chanting, pox, pax, pox.

When I wake by the side of a stream
the soldiers crowd around me.
One asks if I had a bad dream. I answer,
Not until I woke up. He laughs, grabs
his rifle and walks off to the woods.
I am alone again, and happy for at least that.

Self-Portraits

In his sixty-ninth
year, pot bellied, stove chest caved
in, bald, with half his
teeth left and a good deal of
extra weight, he's beautiful.

***

His strength gone, without
stamina, he rests on couch,
broke down recliner.
Just deduces the inner,
mystically contemplative.

***

Quiet, quite often
alone, he prefers his jazz
straight ahead, unlike

what he calls whitebread music.
For folk, blues, it's acoustic.

***

Presently reading
Richard Wright's, Haiku--it's fine.
Written in the last
eighteen months of his life, I
find I can relate deeply.

Leonard J. Cirino

*Leonard J. Cirino (1943-2012)
was the author of nineteen chap-
books and seventeen full-length
collections of poetry since 1987
from numerous small presses.*

*He lived in Springfield, Oregon,
where he was retired and worked
full-time as a poet. His 100 page
collection, **Omphalos: Poems
2007** was published in 2010 from
Pygmy Forest Press. A 64 page
selection, **Tenebrion: Poems 2008**
is from Cedar Hill Publications, in
2010. His collection, **Homeland,
Exile, Longing & Freedom**
was published by AA Press in
2011. His full-length collection,
Chinese Masters, is from
March Street Press, 2009. His
last collection, **The Instrument
of Others** was published by
LUMMOX Press, 2012.*

LEONARD
an elegy

and so you are gone now
the creeping malaise of cancer
cutting you down in just five weeks
at 68 you are the greatest poet
I had ever the privilege to know
eschewing the academics in one hand
the confessonalists on the other
every time it was Christmas
you would treat yourself—a gift!
reading The Collected Poems of Wallace Stevens
Stevens segueing into—"no things but in ideas"
as opposed to William's "no ideas but in things"
tracing it back to the divergent paths
taken by Plato and Aristotle
you loved the translations of foreign poets
to those of your native tongue—

the early to middle Chinese, the French surrealists,
the Russians during the brutality of Stalin,
the Middle Europeans, the Spanish Poets
enduring their civil war,
the Ancient and Modern Greeks—

your Pygmy Forest Press
was a Mecca for emerging poets
surely the two books you did for me
were a testimony to your talent as an editor

your dear mother who was in her late 80's
apparently outlived you
whom you took care of 24/7 for years

and Ava your true love
12 years together
what will become of her
will her tears be around
watering the fertile ground
falling on fresh soil
will anything ever grow without you
Leonard—you were a master gardener

cutting and pruning words to fit
into your complex forms, your unique modalities

why you haven't won the Pulitzer Prize
in your lifetime is beyond me

even a Pushcart denied

now you have gone to your Calandra
your dearest daughter
whom you did away with
when she was a small child
in the throes of your schizophrenia
doing what the command Voice
told you to do
tearing an eye in retribution

I know she has forgiven you
a joyous reunion I am sure of

but I must now speak
man to man
poet to poet

because this legacy
is for you
my beautiful beautiful friend
only for you

Terrance Oberst

Terrance Oberst *has published over 70*
poems in various magazines, journals
and anthologies, as well as four books of
poetry; "Returning" *(Mulberry Press, 1994),*
"Transcendencies" *(Pygmy Forest Press,*
2000), "Kinship Patterns" *(AuthorHouse, 2005)*
and "SUN" *(Pygmy Forest Press, 2008).*

LEONARD CIRINO Part II

The best editorial experience of my life was coming together with Leo to write my own book. He taught me much by way of understanding structure, humility, forgiveness, perseverance and in general was a friend I could count on for clarity in my poetic and private life. We corresponded and worked on several projects together for several years up until his death in 2012.

Jane Crown

Song of Myself

I dreamt before I slept,
swallowed before I ate,
was I always late?

I drank before my thirst,
cut before I thought,
I'm learning what is taught.

I've aged before my years,
lost hair and teeth by thirty,
now I'm going on seventy.

Lean before I was husky,
overweight by sixty,
I'll trim down by seventy.

Hoping to make eighty,
but that's about all,
I'm five feet eight inches tall.

I drowned before I jumped,
sank before I swam,
it's happening all over again.

All Things

All things body, flesh; all things decay,
even the most enormous stone.
The minutes, hours, days, years, eons delay,
but even mountains have crumbling bones.

The bucket is suddenly empty
for Leonard

Ghost dog dreams
Chasing / being chased
The old demons
Unrelenting
Last / lost hours
Agitation and fear
Disorientation
Haunted by
Old dreams / nightmares
Not crazy but insane enough
Terror in an old dog's eye
As in life – so in death
No going out gently
Midnight at 3 pm
Old dog terrors
Ghosts returning
100 unfinished dreams
1000 unfinished thoughts
10000 unformed words
You face the end
Unblinking
The last rattling breath

No grand ideals left
Only the growing cold
The room filling with
A slow creeping fog
Moments / memories winking out
Madness takes the wheel
You veer off the main road
Heading off into the undiscovered country
No one can go with you this time
Your vision clouds over
Your words undone

A rippling image of the moon
In a leaky old bucket
A painful cry of a distant animal
A sudden cold wind rises from the land
You turning to face creation
The image of the moon
Suddenly stilled
The bucket empty

RD Armstrong

F. n. WRIGHT

Fred (F. n.) Wright died on the same day as Leonard Cirino. Fred did not ride off into the sunset on his hog like I think he would have preferred, nor was he given a Viking funeral, which I'm certain he would have really dug, for sure. But no, Fred died in his trailer; his daughter came out from Illinois cleaned it out and took her dad home. He was a Vietnam vet, an unrepentant hell-raiser and outsider who left Illinois at the age of 16 and never looked back. Fred wrote some novels, The Whorehouse, the best-known. Fred wrote poems too and had some chapbooks published. I met him in his final years. We were phone buddies, since my beater was too unreliable to make it up to his trailer in the Santa Monica Mountains. I miss him. *rd*

FOR DONNA GEBRON

Donna Gebron was born in Long Beach and raised in the shadow of Hollywood's magic under the quiet, incandescent light of the southern Californian sky. Among her influences she counted her children, her cats, wild gardens, Puccini and Hendrix, Matisse and Marilyn, Watts and Blake, Grandfather's Treasure House and the rambling spirits within. She worked as a nurse and believed that Medicine is an art, and considered her colleagues as guides, shamans, ancient healers and often, angels. She had two chapbooks published by Vinegar Hill Books (Pink & Naked in the Ultra-Violet Life - 1996 and Shakti Catechism - 1999).

A Friend Passes Away While I'm Bird Watching At Bolsa Chica

To birds, time is a circle, the day comes around again,
the same patterns of light, the same cycle
of fish, fly, sleep; the year
loops, and the Western Grebe,
the Pintail Duck, and the Coot
return to the wetlands.

To humans, time is a line,
like the solid silver horizon.
It starts by the shore -- over there! -- and ends
with a poet's final fading breath
this sunny morning.

To the water, time is a vibration.
The ebb and flow of its tides
mere ripples on its eternal, shimmering surface.
The ocean spreads out infinite before us.
The pelicans soar over it,
the humans watch.

And to the spirit? Does it know
that eternal surface? Does it know a space
outside of time? A space where eternity
is not just all time,
but no time at all?

The birds circle,
the ocean shimmers,
I walk straight back to my car.

G. Murray Thomas
Previously published in My Kidney Just Arrived
(Tebot Bach, 2011)

G. Murray Thomas has been an active part of the SoCal poetry scene for over 20 years. He has performed throughout the L.A. area and beyond. He was the editor and publisher of Next... Magazine, a poetry calendar/news magazine for Southern California. News Clips & Ego Trips, *a collection of articles from Next..., was just published by Write Bloody Press. His most recent book of poetry is* My Kidney Just Arrived, *published by Tebot Bach in 2011. His previous books are* Cows on the Freeway *and* Paper Shredders, *an anthology of surf writing. He has also published five chapbooks, and has been widely published in various literary magazines.*

FOR MAX PETRAKOS aka Baxter Daniels

Max Petrakos grew up in the Los Angeles poetry scene, he performed at open mics with his original poetry and stand up comedy as young as 7 years of age. He won awards for animation and wrote scripts for films and He created the website Internationalwordbank. org, and filmed local poets for two years. He was working on his first novel when he was killed by a drunk driver in June 2012…he was 13 years old.

This is a poem from Max Petrakos, aka Baxter Daniels   2012

I Am From

I am from guitar
From Paper and Pen
I am from Humble and Warm
I Am From
Bamboo Shoots and Palms
who's long gone limbs I remember as if they were my own
I Am From
Angry and Hair
From Mary and Anthony
From Loud and Laughter
And too much T.V. and Nachos
I Am From "Quiet Down" and "Do It Yourself"
I Am From Comedy Central
I Am From L.A. and New York
From the time my mom almost set the house on fire
(On accident, of course)
and countless awards on the wall
and in my head

Max(Baxter) Petrakos
1/4/99 - 6/2/12

No, Thank YOU!

My brother's son lives with me - he's 13
and he says "thank you,' for the strangest things
half way through his video watching,
before he is done dinner
he will come into the kitchen and say
"Thank you, Auntie" and hug me...

Yesterday, it happened again, he was on the couch
and he just got up and came into the kitchen and said
"Thank you , Auntie."

I said, "No... Thank you,
for loving me, being my friend, being here now
for growing up in my life, for being silly and funny
and not putting the seat down ever
for laughing hysterically at *South Park*
and explaining *Family Guy* to me
for telling me your story ideas
and rap verses
and asking me permission for your friends to come over

Thank you,
for being the son I didn't have
the love that will last forever
the laughter I will remember for a long time

Thank you
for reminding me life is silly and wonderful
and poignant, movies are in your dreams
laughter is at every corner
and life
life that came from the crazy
parents
who where children when they brought you to this earth
so bad that it was good for me
good that they could not handle your big brown eyes
the bright smile
the questions about the universe
they missed you
as they got high
and looked for love in all the wrong places

they missed you
and I found you
it was my pleasure to grow with you
So , no Max
don't thank me,
No, Thank YOU!

Bren Petrakos

__Brenda Petrakos__' works have been published in various journals and publications including, Red Fez, Poetic Diversity,Duke University Press, Houston Literary Review, her books : Stories From The Inside Edge, *and* Country Fixins *were published by Sybaritic Press. Her original Screenplay, "Stanley" is currently in development.*

Billy Jones

FOR ANDRE LEVI

André A. Levi was born September 4, 1959, and grew up in the Minneapolis-St. Paul area. She obtained a Ph.D. in Sociology from The Ohio State University and taught briefly at SBCC (Santa Barbara City College). She also worked at the Karpeles Manuscript Library and Museum. One of her poems appeared in the anthology *A Bird Black as the Sun* (Green Poet Press, 2011). A chapbook of twelve of her poems, edited and published by David Starkey and Ron Alexander, appeared Oct. 7, 2012. André died of melanoma on September 11, 2012.

Five Wishes Party
for Andre Levi 1958-2012

As she gets skinnier
she gets more luminous.
Playful wit shines
through the bridge of her nose.
Eyes big as lamps elucidate her speech.
Wordplay dances. Puns abound.

Moon moves through lace curtains.
Music reflects off the furniture.
Hangings bedeck the bedroom.
Earrings adorn the bathroom.
Cat curls round the kitchen chair.
Bubbles rise from blue glasses.
Everything's getting lighter,
rising to meet the setting moon.

We're all lunatics at once,
cackling at morbid jokes.

She wants her ashes mixed
with those of her dead cats,
shaken, not stirred,
then scattered in the redwoods.

I wish we could take her to Florence,
shine her light on all that painting,
illuminate the architecture.
She'd blink through round black spectacles
at ancient owls, pull her bowstring to her ear,
let fly at mythic deer, her women all around.

I wish she could write herself to Athens,
dream her way to Rome,
read her way to Thrace with me.

One day, when all our molecules mix,
when we're uploaded to other matrices,
maybe I'll hold her hand again.
We'll run like mad sandpipers
in sound, healthy, pain-free bodies
down to the gleaming strand.

Jan Steckel

Jan Steckel's first full-length poetry book, The Horizontal Poet *(Zeitgeist Press, 2011), won a Lambda Literary Award. Her chapbooks* Mixing Tracks *(Gertrude Press, 2009) and* The Underwater Hospital *(Zeitgeist Press, 2006) also won awards. Her writing has appeared in* Yale Medicine, Scholastic Magazine, Bellevue Literary Review, Red Rock Review, Redwood Coast Review *and elsewhere, and has been nominated twice for a Pushcart Prize.*

Raindog

SPOTLIGHT ON NEW MEXICO

POETRY IN ALBUQUERQUE, NM
by Georgia Santa Maria

MY CHOICE OF "FAVORITE" POETS IS, FOR the most part, simply that. It is difficult within the Albuquerque poetry "Scene" to choose only 10, as there are so many wonderful and interesting writers. When starting to compile this list, I began with a list of 32 and whittled it down to 10. Those chosen were all poets who are not only terrific in their own writing skills, but poets who inspire others. They are poets who are full of generosity and encouragement, who share their own work with the community and who have all helped the community grow and become marvelous in its variety and strength of expression.

I also wanted to pay tribute to this amazing variety of writers, men and women, old and young, well known and new, of broad backgrounds. There are native New Mexican and transplant writers, who have brought their previous experience with them. All are wonderful, and enrich our experience as a writing community in Albuquerque.

Kenneth P. Gurney is a wonderful poet with numerous publications. He began in the upper mid-west as a visual artist and transitioned to poetry in mid-life. His work has a gentle, sensual and playful quality. He is imaginative, and his work is often surreal. Also, it is deeply connected to the natural landscape. He addresses the existential big questions through imagery that is both classical and mundane: Delphi and the tennis shoe partner up in the same passage. Kenneth started and has edited the "Adobe Walls Anthology" since 2009. He has the best taste in poetry of anyone I've ever known, and his choices are always inspiring.

Robert Reeves is both an intellectual heavy-weight and a fan of pop-cultural rebellion. His work is playful, often funny, and sometimes bitingly satirical and self-deprecating. One of his most recent collections is of poems based on all of the Beatles' song titles, which he has then taken in every surprising and improbable direction imaginable. He likes experimenting with challenging ideas.

Sari Krosinski's work is always intriguing, and sometimes intensely personal. She is fearlessly honest, sometimes funny and always interesting. Hearing her read is always a treat to look forward to. The first time I heard her read, it was a piece about a mythological deity come down to live with an ordinary family in Brooklyn, riding the subway and complaining about human proclivities. In her book "Yossele" written with her husband, Bob Reeves (above), the story is told from the point of view of a Golem, a mythological character, who has outlived his usefulness to the community he has protected. Her work combines the earthy with the ethereal.

Dee Cohen is an amazingly gifted writer, both of poetry and short fiction. I admire her simplicity of language, her ability to give significance to the simplest of daily experience. She is also a great story teller, and her work often tells a tale or opens up a mystery within the most mundane of scenes. She is a fine photographer, and it is this photographic quality that her writing has--the attention to detail, that gives her work real power of expression.

Mitch Rayes is another Albuquerque treasure. His work is subtle and often funny, as well as profound. He uses simple language and every-day imagery to ask the important questions. He is a modest and quiet person, who is extremely generous with other poets, opening his home and work-space for weekly "East of Edith" readings and other events. While he is giving everybody else a space to showcase their work, it is often his work that is the highlight of the evening.

Johannah Orand is an amazing new writer. She often sends out new poems to friends, and I am lucky enough to be on her list. Everything I have ever read of hers has just knocked me out. She is wonderful. I haven't been able to hear her read often, as she doesn't regularly attend the usual reading venues. But her work is as good as any you will ever hear, deeply powerful and touching. Her language is rich and textured, and always original. I hope to see her work opened up to the appreciation it deserves.

Larry Goodell is not only a New Mexico treasure, but one for the world of Poetry as well. He has fantastic tales to tell of the early Beat Poets in New Mexico and elsewhere. His sense of humor is a national treasure. He is funny, and he is witty, frequently about the ridiculousness of politics and public policy. He relishes the absurd. His poetry is deeply human and connected to the values of love in the natural world.

Merimee Moffitt is another former child of the counter-culture. A marvelous writer, she speaks to the complexity of human relationships, politics and family. Her imagery is as rich as her famous corn-chowder, and as wonderful. Her work's power lies in the textures of a life really and honestly lived. While much of her writing is political, the politics are never theoretical or impersonal. She writes passionately and knowingly from her own life and experience. She is a dedicated teacher who has mentored many of Albuquerque's younger poets, and a deeply caring and compassionate person. Her work is both tough and tender.

Levi Romero is an authentic *"Norteno"* New Mexican voice with a richness fed by a cultural history going back to a century before Jamestown. In 2012 he was named New Mexico's Centennial Poet, in honor of the 100th anniversary of statehood. Levi writes in both Spanish and English, being equally fluent in both languages, but using them to express different emotional and historical contexts. His work is intensely personal and textured, reflecting on his life growing up in a small farming village near Taos, and the values of family, and tradition. He is also a successful urban 21st Century man, and this duality gives his work a deep and interesting perspective.

Richard Wolfson's work is filled with densely packed abstract expressionist imagery, magical, complex and thought provoking. He is also wonderfully absurd, combining ideas and images that no other person would ever think to do. Most recently he has been writing and performing stand-up comedy, and his humor and intellect are marvelous. It is like Salvador Dali meets Rodney Dangerfield. He is a treasure, and he always makes me think until my head hurts.

GSM

KENNETH P. GURNEY

I Counted Fifty-Two at Seven a.m.

My dad lined up all the mourning doves
on the telephone wire.

They do it, now, of their own accord,
but my dad taught them to do it in the beginning.

Some of their cooing announces this fact
as they assemble—it is in the contract.

But there are only five more years on the copyright
after it passed from my dad to me.

And then the mourning doves are free of us, of the announcement,
of any legal obligation to give us a cut of their seed.

You may have thought the first amendment right
to peaceful assembly covers the mourning doves,

but that is an inalienable *human* right
protected by the Bill of Rights and the mourning doves

live without a constitution that protects them
in any manner our courts recognize.

Yes, mourning doves long ago learned to gather,
to flock, and converse and envisioned the common good,

but they learned lining up on the telephone wires
from my dad when he was five years old,

living on a farm, just outside of Earlville,
which is just outside of Mendota in the state of Illinois.

*First published at Final Draft. Can also be found in
Kenneth's book* This is not Black & White.

Fluid Shape of an Empty Womb

I am holy, Delphi murmurs to herself,
as she turns a rose quartz pebble over in her
hand,
recites an invented, non-linear rosary
where the crystal is all of the one hundred
and eight beads simultaneously.

She weighs the idea of soul
in her left hand and then her right
and measures a difference as stark
as the red-canvas tennis shoe
half buried in the river bank
when compared to the steady V of cranes
traversing the vernal sky.

Delphi mulls in her left mind
a theoretical diploid cell

with a simple count of neutrons, protons,
atomic mass of varying isotopes,
and in her right mind
the connected expanse of zygote
to the stone she sits upon,
to the river with its muddy banks,
to the old railroad bridge
with its rust and bird nests
where the swallows take insects back
to feed their young.

She holds her longing up to the sun,
examines it in both light and shadow,
fails to determine if it exists in her
as an emptiness or substantial mass,
but her longing weighs upon her eyes
and halts her nightly reading of constellations.

Claudio Parentela

I am holy, Delphi repeats to the budding tree
and fingers the branch that tangles her hair
when the breeze exerts just enough force
to bend the bough and brush her.

A soul stands outside of gravity's application,
speaks its own language,
points out the billowing clouds
as they slip under the bridge
on the deceptively calm face
of the merciless river, which,
by bits and wholes,
carries the dead down to the sea.

*First published in The Centrifugal Eye. Can also
be found in Kenneth's book* Fluid Shape of an
Empty Womb

Kenneth P. Gurney *lives in Albuquerque, NM, USA
with his beloved Dianne. His latest book is* This is
not Black & White. *To learn more visit: http://www.
kpgurney.me/Poet/Welcome.html*

ROBERT ARTHUR REEVES

The Other Truth

This agony in my lower back
is my trustiest memory of you.

It pounces on me about once a year,
stays maybe two-three days.

Wouldn't you know it today was the one
I'd scheduled to put clean sheets on the futon,

and I can't go immediately from standing to
squatting
so plotted out a system of gradated platforms

and did the tucking part scooting
my infinitesimal ass along the floor;
it'd probably take Sam Beckett
to describe it in further detail.

Three years ago when I threw the back out
I'd been changing abode for a week,

heavy boxes up and down stairs,
and now was helping you move too.

I started to step up into your Sidekick
and wham, and you could see it,

how fortuitous and how immense,
and your face went to panic,

and I was looking toward you, and saw
not the least flash of concern for me

but all the other truth instantly opened:
your chore day might have to be interrupted,

somebody might actually see us together,
this man in your life was an old man.

Previously published in The Closed Shrine.

two kids

he's one
& keeps saying his sister's name
over & over

she's three
& keeps answering "What!"
with more & more annoyance

she's learned
that names are beckonings

he's only learned
that names are bursts of praise

Previously published in the Rag and Reeves' book,
The Closed Shrine

Robert Arthur Reeves *was born in Urbana,
Illinois and grew up (so to speak) in the Boston
area. As a baby he sat on Carl Sandburg's lap.
Allen Ginsberg recommended his teenage poetry
to Gregory Corso. He lives in Albuquerque, New
Mexico where he has taught Philosophy, Religion
and Humanities at the University of New Mexico
and Central New Mexico Community College.
His poems have appeared in Fulcrum, Skidrow
Penthouse, The Blind Man's Rainbow, Arsenic
Lobster, The Homestead Review, Adobe Walls
and many other journals. He has published eleven
poetry collections and a chapbook,* Yossele: A Tale
in Poems, *with his partner Sari Krosinsky. Visit
them at* http://outerchildpoetry.com.

SARI KROSINSKI

Homesick in Truth or Consequences

In a courtyard where the trees twine
round awning posts like vines,
we nosh on New York bagels
with melting cream cheese—plus

lox & capers for Rachel. I'd wanted
to stay on the road straight to Albuquerque.
All the marketing advice Rachel gives
for our chapbook makes me more annoyed
I have to be grateful when I don't
wanna talk to anyone who isn't you.

We fall in with a poetry reading
stopping at the hip, used bookstore
(I assume there's just the one
in T or C, New Mexico). Jo and I
already vetoed the hot spring spas
adorning every corner. I hovered
near the front door, proving my readiness
to leave, but insensibly moved half step
by half step to the back room
where the poets circled. If you'd
been there, I'd've been home.

Complications

Toothbrush hitting the wrong nerve
at the back of my throat, I gag
and squirt into my sweats.

Ten years ago, the midwife's pool in the jungle
with the blue mist and the pink mist and the yellow mist
put my brother to sleep. I
couldn't speak to say, how silly.

When it was done, I wanted only to wash
and sleep. Palming the wall, swaying
before the empty shower, bleeding,
I said, "I'm waiting for energy
to get over the tub." "It won't come,"
the midwife's apprentice said. She was sure
two months later my depression was grief
over giving up Isaac. Wrong.

If I'd known then, I'd have chosen Prozac
over Isaac, stayed in New York, never loved you.

Later, I tucked cabbage leaves in my bra

to draw the milk from my aching breasts.
The midwife said I roared
like a lion, like an old birthing pro,
though it was my first and only.

Ten years later, all I have to show
are a delta of fading stretch marks
and a leaky bladder.

And a person.

*Sari Krosinsky writes about the mundane in
mythology and the sublime (and sublimely awful)
in the ordinary. Her first full-length book, "god-
chaser," is forthcoming from CW Books. She co-
authored a chapbook, "Yossele: a tale in poems,"
with Robert Arthur Reeves. She publishes Fickle
Muses, an online journal of mythic poetry and
fiction. Her poems appear regularly in literary
and genre magazines. She received a B.A. in
religious studies and M.A. in creative writing
from the University of New Mexico. She lives in
Albuquerque, N.M., with her partner and cat.*

DEE COHEN

My Husband Rescues a Plant

Oh crap, the thing is practically dead:
stunted branches hollowed out
and hardly a brown leaf left.
I haven't watered it in months,
not since November
when I shoved it onto the patio
between the rusty grill and the busted table,
and abandoned it,
tipped against the wrought iron rails
for winter to take a swing at,
do some real damage.
Then next spring, I'd drag it out
by the cuff of the pot,
wrap my hands around

its thin throated branches,
fling it in the dumpster, and listen
to the satisfying sound
of dry dirt hitting bottom.

But it's too late.
I watch him through the kitchen window.
He holds a plastic pitcher brimmed with water.
His lower is lip pushed out,
eyebrows locked with worry,
as he administers small sips
onto the parched soil.
How tenderly he moves his hands
over the limp body,
his fingers feeling the bark,
a blind search for buds of growth.
And now, he pushes his face
right into the last of the blighted leaves,
and I know, I just know,
he's murmuring something sweet.

Previously published in Fixed & Free Anthology,
Mercury Heartlink Press, 2011. P.33

Tiny Epics

When they realize they're being chased,
most people turn the stolen car towards home.
Not so different from Odysseus
who struggled to return to Ithaca for ten long years.
Even at 90 miles per hour, even in the dark,
even drunk or drugged, they try to loop around
until they reach familiar freeways
where they recognize the exit ramps of their past
and remember how to navigate the tangled streets.
Even when they're boxed in by police cars
and they somehow manage to roll out an open door,
and now on foot, they keep running through alleys,
jumping over walls as sirens wail,
into schoolyards and across scrubby lots,
lit up by the Cyclops of a searchlight.
Then down stairs, two at a time,
discarded Trojans on the steps,

into basements where they'd read comic books
and dreamed of being heroes as children,
until most of their friends were cannibalized
by poverty or hopelessness.
They'll push through the back doors of churches
where spirits still hover, calling their names.
Places they haven't been for years
but here they are, hearts thudding,
dogs howling in the distance,
running again through the old streets.
A tiny epic but an epic all the same.
Like Odysseus, filthy and torn up,
unrecognizable, dressed like a beggar.
Heading for home,
where everyone believes he is dead
or might as well be.

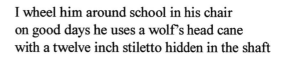

Mark Hartenbach

Previously published in Malpais Review

Dee Cohen *is a writer/photographer now living in Albuquerque. Her work has been recently published in various New Mexico journals. Her chapbook,* Lime Ave Evening, *was published by the Laguna Poets.*

MITCH RAYES

Friendship

I stick out my foot and a hemophiliac falls

I break his leg
and cement our friendship

we are in the third grade

his mom wants to beat up my mom in the
parking lot

for the next seven years
the rest of his life

I wheel him around school in his chair
on good days he uses a wolf's head cane
with a twelve inch stiletto hidden in the shaft

his baby brother
sometimes tries to steal attention by biting him
great green and purple bruises blossom
up and down his arms

he breaks his leg twice more in our time together
once on the just mopped floor of a supermarket
and once on his first and only attempt at riding a
bicycle
a birthday gift from his parents

we set fire
to faces torn from the pages of horror movie
magazines

we try to commune
with the spirits of the dead

sometimes I let him get me in a headlock

he knows
I won't try to fight my way out

The French Poet

Robert Desnos
stands in the rain at Auschwitz
reading cheery fortunes
into the palms of the other inmates

with such conviction
that for a moment
they forget where they are

the truth
can never do something like that

Mitch Rayes was born in Detroit. For years he worked as a professional outfitter in the jungles of Chiapas. During the '90s he was influential in the developing Albuquerque poetry scene as founder of the poetry non-profit Flaming Tongues, as publisher of the Tongue newsletter, and as producer of several Albuquerque Poetry Festivals. He recently converted part of his contractor's shop into an art space called The Projects.

JOHANNAH ORAND

Prayer

Lord, bless them that's soft in heart and let them be
soft in heart always. Let them that's hard be hard.
Them that's hard whose fate it is to rot to soft,
let them rot to soft. Like old fruit rots to soft.
Let them be mashed to pulp by the boots
of children in the orchard. Let them be born again
as light from which new hard fruit comes.

Lord, let our streams chuck up fish, glint-spined
in the sun, but let them that's hungry go hungry always.
Let our hands be blacked by the work
of seeking, the honest labor of longing—let us long
as long as the days are long, learn us that longing
is Your will as You have willed flowers to know
desire: how the stamen mimics the tongue.

Lord, let us rise to the difficult morning
with gratitude for all as it lies. Let them that's
disappointed be disappointed always & let them
die stale-breathed, stiff-eyed. But as for the rest,
Lord, let us bless each headache and bad dream,
mad dog, hard task, dead mother. Lord, let us be
consumed by gratitude, by longing for what is.

Women in Their Gardens

you're from the city so you learned to make poems
about dark rivers and women in their gardens,
though what beats in your wrist is the jagged syncopation
of dirty traffic, urban dusk—vulvar rose,
sullied chrome, the rouged-up,
dirty gold of headlights. in your room
above the interstate you are mistress of all
the wind-blown grit and glass-eyed trash you see

but go instead back and back to once in a pasture,
fireflies in slow hover like the hands
of that farmer's son. the dark river. women
in their gardens—you know this kind of poem,
the kind you make about what you don't believe,
when you're bruised up from bad sleep
and too sorry to sing of the sweet stink
of mouthwash and pissed drawers on the evening bus.

Johanna Orand is a proud native of Albuquerque, New Mexico. She recently graduated from the University of New Mexico's undergraduate creative writing program. She received the UNM Lena Todd award thrice and completed an undergraduate fiction thesis which received Magna Cum Laude honors. In addition to writing, she is also keenly interested in natural science, linguistics, and cultural studies.

LARRY GOODELL

Freedom Is

Freedom is an enigma that must be shared
by speaking what you will without amendment.
Freedom of speech can only be matched
by freedom to listen –
untrammeled, uncoerced, uninhibited,
an ideal thrown out and caught in reality
treasured as the only protection against
                              a police state
or a dictatorial trillionaire
or any power grown out of phase
        with the Earth & her residents . . .

Cry Baby

Life gets more stressful as time goes by
whatever happened to the pie in the sky
there's no pie, pie in the sky? don't be silly
how about that pot of gold at the end of the rainbow
pot of gold ha, no gold, there might be a rainbow, not now
I want it now! I refuse to be anything more
but a baby in a crib wanting out, unsatisfied with my rattle
face me, a baby with long legs, crying endlessly
take this rattle you gave me and shove it
I'll have you in the clink for incarcerating me
I want to complain I am complaining, every where I look
I can't get out, I'm stuck here with all my stress
my mountains of things to do suffocating me I can't move
unhappy pointless people like a vise in my community
babies worse than me already on crack or coke or meth
or weed or alkies wackos, incompetents, stunted humans
with no purpose or anything to do knocking at my door
get away! I'm sorry your truck conked out, your daughter
won't let you take your grandson, your son's been
thrown in jail or evicted or whatever and the baby kids
are all stressed out or the foodstamps got traded for junk
or you're sick from back injury and can't get disability
I'm sorry your brain's blown away from being smashed by a car

when you were dead drunk and stoned and now you've assaulted yourself
with risky blows to the brain, fights, accidents drugs endlessly
I just want to garden, devote myself to suffering fruit trees
love my wife of many years, cook, irrigate, weed-whack
organize things instead of having dump truck loads of paper work
household paraphernalia dumped on my head, so I can't move
I just want to take care of the dog and even the cats, pit cherries
grow moonflowers, clean irrigation ditches have friends over
for really good hand prepared food, I want peace and harmony
instead of chaotic deception, I want poets and artists to love each other
and publish and show each other instead of being at each other's
throats in endless ego agony, I want the creative spirit to move
everyone as it is and does if you let it if you open yourself up
to the dawn, the healing venture of nature, the tap dance of love
the simplicity of meditation untrammeled with bombardments of worry
and the avalanche of things to do enough, how about a trip
space travel no a trip to New York, Los Angeles San Francisco Oakland
Chicago, St Louis, New Orleans Roswell Denver Boulder anywhere
                    let alone Paris!
let me out of my crib for God's sake, let's go for a hike the only thing
we can do to get away dwarfed by trees spruce and aspens ponderosas, fir
and blessed by friendly cheery faces of little flowers a pastiche of surprises
and fresh air and colors of the sun slicing through towering trunks and the
lace of light falling around us like magic and lifting my tired feet into
the freedom they want to know, I want to know, I'm sick of wanting
I'm here to listen to everything made of stars.

on Ginsberg's birthday, June 3rd, 2012

Larry *is a poet, digital delver, poet-playwright, performer of "gringo-loco poetics". Born in Roswell, New Mexico in 1935 and living in Placitas since '63, He learned from USC in L.A., studied with Robert Creeley in NM, went to the Vancouver Poetry Conference of '63 to study with Olson, Ginsberg, Duncan, Whalen, went to the Berkeley Poetry Conference in '65, and married photographer/artist Lenore Goodell in '68. He founded Duende Press in '64, one poet per issue followed by Fervent Valley. In 1972 he toured the country doing poetry performances with Stephen Rodefer. He organized readings for Downtown Saturday Night, the Rio Grande Writers Association, the Central Torta Series, Albuquerque United Artists, and for many years the Living Batch Bookstore. More recently Silva's Saloon and the ongoing Duende Poetry Series.*

MERIMEE MOFFITT

open doors

wild honey runs in thick golden rivulets
down to where the trees give shade
where last summer tablecloths
flapped sails under tall
jars kissed with wax
like grandmother's
tree-lined lips

today the trees flap crying
what holocaust has fallen
what holocaust on the ground
where tablecloths held jars of honey

where now Hussein's wife lies bleeding
on three children's gathered limbs

the street runs thick with slivers of things
everyone slipping down to the shade
where last summer tablecloths
held jars of lemonade
where Danai and Omar
played with Arat's
baby goats they too
among the dead

Previously published in <u>Pemmican</u>

Three-Bucket Bath

a long sloping pasture to the river
across one ditch then down along the barb wire fence
the easiest way
galvanized buckets and a plastic jug—two people to tote
a 3-bucket bath
pour one-half into the washtub by the stove
another shower-like, squatting under your lover
who bends over pouring, dangling a hand-rolled cigarette
from his sweet lips
soak up, soap, splash
shampoo and pour slowly again
could be 30-below in bright-white light
the third bucket gives your skin a glow
half a minute of wet-skin NM morning bliss
the old cook stove heats the cabin
our clear plastic door inside the heavy keep-out-the-bear affair
welcomes the sun bouncing back across the valley
two tiny windows set into logs older than our grandparents
leak a little air, we didn't know to care
didn't think to re-chink mocha-colored adobe filling
Fermin came down that fall to let us know
about the winters how we'd need lots of wood
asked his curious, hat-crumpled questions

Geronimo brought a sheep and left us with half
packed in the blue trunk in the north-side snow
we had no idea how much we didn't know
all we could do was stoke the firebox
and keep each other company under
piles of quilts on your big iron bed from California
the week our son came into us it was 47 below
the beginning of just about everything
that winter in Vallecitos, 1971

Appeared in "The Sunday Poem," <u>Duke City Fix</u>

Merimée *arrived in El Rito, NM, in a shiny green Chrysler in 1970 with a carload of vets and their drug dealer. She brought her dog, her frying pan, cutting board, a few trinkets, books, and clothes. She fell in love with everything northern New Mexico, staying to raise her family and teach for 25 years in all levels of education; she also write poems and stories.*

LEVI ROMERO

Healing Hands

the warm wet washcloth
softens my three day stubble
she lathers my face evenly
her fingers swirl gently over my cheeks
and then under my neck

I imagine the cowboy in a barber's chair
of a late night black and white
Western television movie
and I think of my cousin whom I visited
in the hospital several months ago

and how the nurses in their cheerful gait
and sunbright inquiries to his well being
livened the drab room like a curtain
pulled open to let in the warmth and
light of the afternoon

"she has healing hands"
my wife and I would comment
when she was just a child
the feel of her infant hands
on a throbbing temple or across an aching joint
would ease the discomfort upon her touch

tonight my daughter shaves my face
for her high school internship
nursing program assignment

whose ache will she tend to
years from now
the warm buzz of her fingertips
the calm of her voice
the hope in her breath

Gavilan

en memoria de un gavilan:
Rudy "Sunny" Sanchez

aquí estoy sentado
en una silleta coja y desplumada
recordando aquellas amanecidas
cuando nos fuimos grandes y altos

en aquel tiempo que nos encontrabanos
sin pena ninguna
cuando la vida pa' nosotros
apenas comienzaba y la tarea
era larga y llena de curiosidades

entretenidos siempre con aquel oficio maldito
un traguito para celebrar
la vida
y otro para disponer
la muerte

ayer bajo las sombras
de los gavilanes
que vuelavan con sus alas
estiradas como crucitas negras
en contra del sol

pense en ti

tú que también fuites
gavilan pollero

con una locura verdadera
y aquella travesura sin fin
hoy como ayer
tus chistes relumbrosos
illuminando estas madrugadas solitarias
que a veces nos encuentran medios norteados
y con las alas caidas

tal como esos polleros
tirando el ojo por el cerrito de La Cuerda

así también seguiremos rodeando, carnal
carnal de mano y de palabra

amistad que nació
en aquel amanecer eterno

y si no nos topamos
en esta vuelta
pues entonces, compa
pueda que en la otra

Levi Romero, New Mexico Centennial Poet,
is the published author of two collections of
poetry. His photo documentary collaboration,
"Sagrado: A Photopoetics Across the Chicano
Homeland," is forthcoming from UNM Press.

RICHARD WOLFSON

Shaman's Allegiance
For Sandra Ingerman

Your seabreeze breath licks out another windowless
soul,
time parameters cannot dissuade injury,
magpie magic loosens your triangular tongue,
eyes bellow a song of grandmother caress.

Before Neptune' s slumber, time tiptoed carelessly,
liquid reason validated time stamp intuition
warm fingers knead life into shape and color,
the texture of individuation slithers from the Garden.

The insignificance of nothing, a pouting dove
that sits oe'r the shoulder of Atlas, Spiritus Mundi
weekly allotment reverberates in green round,
the orb of tomorrow holds secrets in abeyance

After time evaporated your tiny tune,
voices condensed as tangent to a total eclipse

Of Mice And Memory

Her dementia DNA firing like carnival cacophony,
the dead who bob endlessly below the Nile's hobo alley,
BB gun alter ego that fires at the ripples of mice,
fires at her own unwanted face,

slices open the entrails of a Sacred Heart,
ancient murmurs recoil, the Sphinx's itch
unrecorded in the small smile of the Pharaoh,
the history of dust, confabulation of time's tiny diary.

The antecedent of algebraic incantation,
the first sound of tongue of the wolf
ere dancing beneath the walls of Jericho,
a bestial balance between the flit of electron discharge,

when she released her grip on death's trigger,
her chromosomal memory jumped on the sandbox of joy.

*Richard Wolfson began writing after the death of his wife JoAnn ,a poet, in 2004.
Many of these poems come from dreams and shamanic journeys. He currently lives
in Albuquerque with his second wife Vicki Bolen, who is an artist who collaborates
with him on books, cards, and prints. Currently, he mixes comedy and poetry.*

Claudio Parentela

GEORGIA SANTA MARIA

Igor's (After Katrina)

Igor's is the World's coolest laundromat
Amber light and amber beer, a little neon,
Old dark wood, rococo chocolate ceiling tin
Pool tables crowd the dryers in the back
(A short stick enables those tricky shots)
Smells of soap and sizzling burgers,
The cook in a paper hat asks
"You want cheese with that?"
Cajun style, a little cayenne
"When's Ayala comin' in?" a regular asks.
"Now" the cook says, and the new bartender
Saunters in, break your heart beautiful,
Gives the regulars a gorgeous grin,
Shining eyes and coffee skin,

As she ties her apron behind her back,
Outside the trolly rolls down the track
"Ding, ding, clatter, clatter
Along its iron and live oak path.
Upstairs, the lady's room doors embrace
A long existential poem,
Some woman hung her heart out in here.
Above flood-line, along the stair
Frames of pictures, Igor's history, all the gang
Many no longer here. But a little mold
Won't ruin the memory of those good times.
Igor's is back, if not all of its customers.
I feel the cemetery, one block down
On Lafayette, the white tomb's dignity,

Mardi Gras beads along the graves,
Festivity, even in death.
The washers hum, the pool balls clack,
Up front, from the bar, a great big laugh
Light filters in from the Southern front,
Out on St. Charles, where the World goes past.
Clean clothes are the least of Igor's charms.
Bring $10, one for the wash, one for the dryer,
Two for a couple of racks, the rest
For that Cajun burger with fries
And a cold amber in good company,
Both the living and the dead.

Previously "The Sunday Poem", Duke City Fix.

Stereopticon Man

Somewhere tonight
Between here
on a loose
that stretches between
Nebraska was pink
by fifth grade
Now, a man alone
Who took the pictures
hoping to explain
of it all.
Stereopticons
and Railroad Barons'
Just how much dynamite
to reach New Mexico
So, you retrace with
in the trunk
Like an old ghost,
you might see something
It is half worn luggage,
Like a child,
What if it breaks?
with sleeping bag
and little else.
You said,

you're out on the road
and your mother
tightrope
your geographic memories
Missouri green
blackboard mappings.
like the traveler remembered
some time ago
about the unseen vastness
And those
on lacy tabletops
planning
would it take
from Minnesota.
That view-camera
of your car
just in case
Not too frightening,
half a pain.
requires baby-sitting.
and you,
and film
what, then?
"I ought to get a

little thirty-five,
Quick,
If I wanted."
the thunder of
could grab it
and you
Jump back in,
before
That tight-stretched
 leads you on
If you stop
means delay,
Will you wind up
to remember
Or, perhaps
it will fade
Half-forgot
There are ghosts
and scent
And those
Rising in the steam
Its surface winks back
The clouds are pink,
That was awhile ago,
And the surface
looks hard,
Too hard to drink.
being keenly aware
in the trunk of your car
to remember

just so I could,
Snap
As if for fear
a sudden rain
from your hand,
would race to
drive on,
You drown.
rope of highway
for dread.
to take a picture
for good or bad.
Wanting
This trip?
only hoping
into the others,
and also dreaded.
that shake your tent
your sleeping bag.
in the early dawn,
of your black cup.
at the sun's first rays.
like the skin of your first wife.
you think.
of the coffee
as hard as marble,
So you warm your hands,
of that awesome eye,
Waiting
This.

Previously published in The Harwood Review.

Georgia Santa Maria, MA, *has been an artist, photographer, and writer most of her life, and has been published in many anthologies. Most recently, her work may be found in Adobe Walls, Malpais Review, Mas Tequila Review, Bleed Me A River: A Domestic Violence Anthology, and on the web at Duke City Fix, Sunday Poem, and Duke City Dime Stories, archive of favorites. Work includes 2 self-published books, "Lichen Kisses" and "Miami Hippy Mommy Cookbook". She lives in Anton Chico, NM, in her Great-Grand-mother's antique adobe home, where her family has lived since the 1870's.*

SANTA FE POETRY
an Introduction by Jane Lipman

A CENTER FOR ALL THE ARTS, SANTA FE has a huge poetry community and holds poetry festivals, conferences and contests. Some are very inventive, such as those designed by Santa Fe's third Poet Laureate, **Joan Logghe**: a Haiku Road Sign Contest, and Odes and Offerings: a show, where Joan paired 36 artists with 36 poets; each artist, in a work of art, interpreted a poem, including words, a line, or the whole poem in the piece. Four art shows, two poetry readings, and a book, forthcoming from Sunstone Press, emerged from this project.

I could have chosen *thirty* fine Santa Fe poets as easily as ten. Those I selected range from a Poet Laureate to introverts who have written large bodies of beautiful work, published in poetry journals, but have yet to publish books

Joan Logghe, Santa Fe poet laureate from 2010-12, is a co-founder of Tres Chicas Books and co-winner of a New Mexico Book Award. As comfortable, wise, and entertaining on stage as off, Joan has taught all ages, and delights audiences with her poetry readings, workshops, and her beautiful hand-made pot holders with poems on them. I love how her poems bring the sacred into the every day. She notices the small, ordinary, touching, humorous details around her which make up this life and writes them into long poems or small sketches with amazing juxtapositions, verbal music, and observations. Her poems celebrate love for the people in her life, for the Espanola Valley, for Santa Fe, for the natural world—and for the quirky, wildly imaginative objects, pastimes, and communications of humankind.

Blair Cooper: From many of Blair Cooper's one-page poems, I have the sense of reading a novel—there's spaciousness, a Henry James sense of place, and she stretches out time, brings other eras into the present, weaving rich tapestries of narrative, quietness, imagery, feeling, description,

sensuousness, subtlety, and conversation. I feel I get to know the people and places, natural terrain, settings, objects, language, and complex relationships between and within people. Her poems (nature poems, too), flow from a deep wellspring and are deep, nourishing company. I love them. She lives very close to essence.

Elizabeth Raby: Elizabeth Raby and her husband, Jim, host a monthly open poetry reading at Lucky Bean Café in Santa Fe. A Board member of New Mexico Literary Arts, Elizabeth has been a poet in the schools, has taught from Vermont to Santa Fe to Romania, and given poetry readings in Chicago, Texas, and Eastern Europe. She has authored three marvelous volumes of poetry and three chapbooks. I love the way she navigates from science and outer space, to history and memoir, to the natural world out her window—to sorrowing over a dog abandoned in a snowstorm, or an item in the news, to understated yet shocking sexual capers—often mixing several of these elements in one poem evoking laughter, deep emotion, and startling ideas. Her compassion is vast, deep and unflinching as is her self-reflection. A truly humble person and spectacular poet.

Judith Toler: Judith Toler has a genius for creating deep emotion with spare, knock-out imagery, observation, fact, insight, irony, song, syntax, intimacy, grief, love and even the poem's lay out on the page. Masterful—as in "Bomblets".

"I Don't Think I'll Bother Dying..." shows another side of her, present in many poems— humor, feistiness, with a fierce passion to live and to defy the inevitable in the slyest, most delicious way! Judith wrote the sexiest, funniest flower poem I have ever read.

Another side of her poetry, not present in this selection, conveys profound, timeless, quiet love, supported by language in every detail, in every line and phrase. She is also a visual artist. Her first book will be published by Virtual Artists Collective soon.

Yves C. Lucero: For years, Yves Lucero,

a brilliant, outrageous, hilarious—politically, socially, and sexually astute performance poet, has been a phenomenon at Poetry at Paul White's, in Chupadero, drawing large audiences. He also writes a hell of a love poem. A classical and Flamenco guitarist, Yves plays Monday evenings at Casa Chimayó in Santa Fe. His book, subtitled *Collected Works 2010-1985*, "translating from the ineffable", is a 25 year retrospective of his process of creativity that includes poetry, songs, sheet music, drawings, handwritten drafts, and a CD. In his words: "It was a ride to experience all the versions of myself, and how I changed and didn't change!" Interviewed by poet Miriam Sagan, 5/16/2011, Yves said, "The [poetic] line can be a monofilament cast from my mental fly-rod into a river of words. What will I catch today? A shoe? A beer can? A worn tire? I'm actually trying to hook your ear!" "Writing is not what I do, it's who I am," he says, quoting Cristopher Hitchens.

Mary McGinnis, among other honors, won a NM Literary Arts Gratitude Award in 2009. Her poems weave conscious and subconscious in breathtaking leaps, the seen and unseen, experience and imagination—with power and playfulness, often in one of her favorite forms, the acrostic poem. The form brings surprising mnemonic information; combined with silence, sensuousness, humor, deep feeling, and word magic, Mary stuns and delights her writing groups and wider poetry audiences. Blind since birth, she writes color as though a sighted person, and as her book, *Listening to Cactus*, suggests, she listens and hears beyond ordinary range—with a sense of lunar otherness and poetic genius. She has published widely and works as a disability advocate and counselor at New Vistas in Santa Fe. She also conducts laughter workshops.

Gary Worth Moody: Raised on farms and ranches on the plains of New Mexico and South Texas, Gary Worth Moody uses the convention of long lines as a seductive horizon, drawing a reader to the edge of breath, thus closer to mortality. His subjects unveil the jubilance of human and animal survival in the harshest of landscapes. His work examines the brutality of humans toward nature, toward each other, and the brutal covenant between wild things that link predator to prey, and reveal the sentient mystery that renders us human. *Hazards of Grace*, his astonishing first book, is both a celebration and

Robert Branaman

threnody for the brutality, love, grief, praise, mortality, and terrible beauty of the *telling* of the hazards of grace.

Catherine Ferguson: Catherine Ferguson, winner of two NM Book Awards, one for her poetry and one for her art, lives in Galisteo, NM, where, in her garden, she writes and paints in quiet seclusion. Her connections with the natural world and with people alive, and not alive, are part of her spirit—her lover, mother, grandmother, neighbors, close friends. She communes with trees, animals, people, and shares them with us in images, both clear and surreal.

Catherine knows the veil between life and death is very thin. I love the companionable way she converses with her dead. To her, they're right here, visible, audible, in a dimension of wind in the landscape, "living precisely/ the moment a rainbow divides a rock." Memory, dream, reverie, and imagination flow into the here and now. "Night's Wife", to me, is one of the most beautiful of love poems. "The Gardeners", too——a gorgeous love poem.

Janet Eigner: Janet Eigner wrote a sheaf of poems as she mourned the loss of her daughter to a brain tumor. That ritual going down into, in order to come up out of, became a powerful, beautiful book, *What Lasts Is the Breath*, a courageous journey through grief, memory, remorse, and love—soon to be published by Black Swan Editions. With the comfort of nature, the love of her husband, son, grandsons, friends, and the warmth of an extended family, she searched, in her own and other religions and cultures, for a ritual that would bring some resolution and meaning to the tragedy, and reconnect her to life. She found it in Mimbres pottery (her daughter was a potter), in a Mimbres kill-bowl ceremony, and in a Hopi *knowing* taught to her by an elder. Her poems are beautifully crafted and musical, as in "Cliff Notes" and "Measures". Currently she is working on a manuscript of Grand Canyon poems. An activist and former dancer, she also writes dance reviews.

James McGrath: James McGrath fell in love with a magpie, stayed in his room college weekends to develop a relationship with it, and in time, with the magpie's extended family. He writes from his contacts with the world around him——feathered, human, leafy, or furred. When living in other cultures, he contacts the poetic spirit of the place and writes from that, whether in Ireland, Yemen, Hopi, the land around Santa Fe where he has lived for decades, or his childhood landscape of Western Washington. He lives, breathes, loves, *embodies* in his poems the creatures, plants, trees, and people in the natural world. In La Cieneguilla, Santa Fe, NM, James leads a poetic life in a home he built, with off-the-grid solar panels, animals, plants, and rock art around him. He paints, writes, opens his orchard for other poets to give readings. He teaches art and poetry at Ponce De Leon Retirement Center and on the Hopi Reservation. James was recently honored with a "Living Treasure of Santa Fe" Award. A biography of his life by Jonah Raskin has just been published… he laughs, "In my lifetime!"

GARY MOODY

Hawking In The Boneyard Of Stolen Cattle

Through Easter morning's starlit dark, I drive west toward the river,
     grateful for a week of wind and sun
that kilned the road to burnished clay so tight the jeep leaves no tracks
     despite last night's freeze and morning's thaw.
At the drainage divide, before gray shows in the east, I kill
     the engine, climb out, open the back,
take up canvas bag with spare jesses, styptic pencil
     for the bird's feet, should they slip
beneath an errant tooth of this morning's prey, washed beef-
     heart for the hawk.
I open the carrier. Kill starved, the hawk steps to my gloved left fist.
     From her anklets trail thin jesses.

Each I take between fore-finger and thumb, weave greased leather
        through my fingers to hold her tight against my goat-skinned hand
until wind sifts our scents downslope into barrancas that channel craved
        snowmelt toward the Rio Grande.
Pre-dawn violet creams toward cyan. Red shifts between
        sapphire and blood
orange. Sudden glare of sun sears my eyes. My boot heel rolls wrong off
        what I believe is stone.
Mistaken, I look down upon the bleached bone of a steer. A foreleg I think, then
        bleached pelvis still cradling
last week's dust. A scatter of bone emerges from the juniper's shade. Unsheltered,
        stripped and brittle ribs choir into this new day.
Above them, the dead steer's spine, naked of all flesh and hide, dangles
        in the lifting wind, unable to shake loose the frayed noose
that must have choked his animal keening beneath the butchery tree. What
        language, beast or human, echoed across this killing ground?
Did a swollen moon illuminate patient coyote eyes as honed steel severed tendon,
        flayed flesh from bone and bloodied hide?
How many days did fevered birds ride thermals in vigil before all that remained was
        white and scavenged bone?
How many rains before this stolen kill's blood melted into this same red earth?

Out of juniper's shelter I step into Easter light. The hawk unfurls her wings against
        a shift of air, talons tight as if my fist were prey.
Without warning she slips from the glove, wings beyond light, amber eyes
        sentient of any shadow that dares moving above this unspun earth.

From HAZARDS OF GRACE (Red Mountain Press, 2012)

Hazards Of Light

Through dust and shake of late desert night my sealed beams ride up
        the eyes of a coyote
stiff-legged under her prey's weight
        teats swollen blue

fur edged raw the color of burn of sun behind sand suspended in air

I can't help but wonder if she has seen me before
If she has watched invisible under ledge of sandstone from breaks
        of chamisa or sage

If her eyes are as blind in headlights as mine against sun

If this dry river of light is wide enough to let her pass
If her whelps are thirsty or hungry
　　　　in the dark
Like an offering she lets her wet kill
　　　　an antelope calf

slip from her teeth into heat crusted sand
She sniffs the air of the arroyo we share for scent
Familiar almost intimate she nudges the meat towards me
Patiently grinning across her tongue she stretches feathered
　　　　legs to lie down in the cinders

I kill the lights then the engine
As if silence and darkness bring memory
　　　　like a lover in dream she lifts herself from the earth
burning with moonlight
The shredded caul clings to the stillborn antelope's flank
　　　　shiny and blue passing me in the dark

From HAZARDS OF GRACE (Red Mountain Press, 2012)

Gary Worth Moody *is the author of* HAZARDS OF GRACE *(Red Mountain Press, 2012) and the forthcoming collection* OCCOQUAN *(Red Mountain Press, 2013). A falconer, Gary lives in Santa Fe, New Mexico with the artist and writer Oriana Rodman, three dogs and Red Rage, the red tailed hawk.*

JANET EIGNER

Measures

Consider excess — the river's summer breath on the bluff
where humidity's robe shelters a lush crop.
I leave my crowded desk for the path's deep shade.
Dew-grass and a small, white tea party sog my shoes —
wild hydrangea and aster, poison ivy berries among the pawpaw.

Unseeing, I face off and raze a web strung across the jeep road.
Will this spider mend her torn guy-wires precisely here
now that home is a ghost-mask adhering to my face?
To loose this fabric is to finger a texture
fingers barely feel, my digits less than deft.

Another moist radiance of back-lit thread hovers
well off the path. Its spokes anchor
just an outermost hub, a silvered circumferential.
At the precise center of this minimalist pinwheel,
the crusted Spider Grandmother rests.

She stirs my passion for design
a heat for novel sensation.
On the warmed way back
I feel a filament's gauze give out
like the goofy sensation when the doc bangs the knee.

By noon, the sun crests the bluff
spotlights another water-beaded net —
one side hooked to the butterfly bush
the other, to my cottage's limestone —
a vertical rectangle perfectly rigged.

And just inside one edge
she's twice dropped silk the web's length,
added between the parallel lines one zig-zag.
Will I never take her sparse advice —
to weave the dazzling minimum?

Cliff Notes

Up to the redwall sandstone,
past random springs and crimson snapdragon vines,
our tribe climbs the fourth day.

The guide knows unmapped paths,
leads us by sunset over a shrubbed ravine
to a cliff's mouth whose lips barely accept

our dozen sleep sacks set side by side.
Fetching the evening's water,
we squat on the ledge, and share out fuel and food,

then sink in our niche's darkness.
The black sky funnels stars through widening eyes.
Harmonicas shiver song.

Night hears tales pitched undertone,
lifts our tempered bodies,
swallows our limpid souls.

Published in New Mexico Poetry Review,
Spring 2011

***Janet Eigner**'s chapbook,* Cornstalk Mother *(Pudding
House Publications) precedes her forthcoming book,*
What Lasts is the Breath, *(Black Swan Editions).*
Her poems have appeared in Adobe Walls, Blue
Mesa Review, Earthships, Echoes, Hawaii Review,
Manzanita, Mudfish, Natural Bridge, NM Poetry
Review, Poets Against the War, Sagarin Review,
Santa Fe Literary Review, The Daily Bleed. "Isaac's
Blessing" appeared on Poetry Foundation website's
Am. Life in Poetry, and will appear in Hag Sameach
Anthology (Pleasure Boat Studio).

JOAN LOGGHE

Frida Kahlo's Daughter
for Norma

Yesterday, if I'm not mistaken, I fed
Frida Kahlo's daughter on our back porch.
I shook her hand, callused as any working woman's
And offered her rice and chicken, salad too.
Her voice almost sang when she spoke. Now
I have seen the blood spilled on the painting's sheets,
but I swear there are pregnancies of air, impossible
time lines and fame is a sort of a virus for miracles.
This young woman with the brownest of eyes and hair,
who's come to gather bees, spoke of "captivating a swarm."

I know there was a gene of Frida there, a wild molecule
borne from southern air, for I'd been to the old house,
a bunch of students led the young me there, in my saffron
gauze dress from India and my Hungarian half.
I have to admit that I also was bitten and am Frida's kin
Since the students nabbed me at the Anthropology Museum.
I'd never heard of her then and how we are born to sink
and to swim, so yesterday I was feeding myself and the Frida
Kahlo on my portal with her tea of Hyssop mint
and her salve of Bloodroot.

If anyone had to die or to live beyond her time
with her tooth of gold, and her many petticoats,
smelling of turpentine, with her mind entrancing
men, with her beckoning to bliss. It's the joy
brigade and the suffering's on hold.
She drove off in a yellow swarm, she left
a vibrant vacancy. One might call this admiring.
I call it feeding the stranger again, that is who
we always have to feed, with their hearts
of wandering and their tired feet, with their empty
gas tanks and their black and tied back hair.

Can you smell the honeysuckle and locust trees?
On another Saturday, on another porch there comes this other life
with no guarantees, to feast on happiness, a sipping
and flitting under the bird filled trees, a wing
like a hummingbird's you cannot see. It moves too fast
and we're caught in the solstice breeze.
The first day of summer already heading towards dark.
As the oil spill dominates, and chokes our seas.
I am offering myself to one day--a focus
On flowers and ease.

Previously published Malpais Review #2

In Praise of Drama

Praise drama that long opera of night
Turning daylight for giving the night birds to me
and my own white spider, part of a fear, by the white horse.

And drama, which writes in lipstick on the mirror
and since time passes but pain doesn't, edits
that lipstick smear. Drama, which places a sword
between the lovers, this never bodes for well.

Drama the femme fatale and drama the man in black.
Thank you, drama, for leaving my life alone
until I was ripe enough and could appreciate
your gift. You chose our hell and provided food
for the melt down night, liquids for the trysts.

Early morning walk and sacrifice, "Cut off the hydra head
and more grow back." This is what drama said.
And drama who loves the night, two people making claims,
staking out territory, watering the soil
because it never never rains.

Drama that Communist and drama the acrobat.
Entering my life with a taste of heaven
also at its wildest feast. A butterfly that died.
A galloping of hooves that beat past the kitchen window
where there were no horses, and beat and beat.

My peaceful life illuminated by grief, filigree
at the edges of the text. Days when nothing happens
will return, blessed as desert rain and winter heat.
Drama, thank you, for revealing the form within the life,
a body hunched in anger, dumb words spoken in code.

Huge queen with scepter and crown. The fat lady
endlessly sings. The curtain comes down, down, and down.

Joan Logghe is Santa Fe's third Poet Laureate, serving from 2010-2012. She has taught to all ages, from Santa Fe Community College to Zagreb, Croatia. Winner of an NEA in poetry and co-founder of Tres Chicas Books, her latest book is The Singing Bowl, *UNM Press and* Love & Death: Greatest Hits *with Miriam Sagan and Renée Gregorio, winner of a New Mexico Book Award.*

JUDITH TOLER

I Don't Think I'll Bother Dying . . .

it's way too much trouble—
all that commotion, the mess, the moaning,
not to mention tears, lamentations, recriminations,
    the pain of parting.

Why give my body over to this earth?
No, I won't be buried under all that weight,
won't let fierce fire burn me down to dust,
won't be caught floating belly up in some river,
    like a besotted Ophelia.

I've definitely decided
    not to open up a trust account.
So there's an end to it.
I'll stay right here just where I am—
no dark bed for me strewn with roses, calla lilies,
    thorns, worts, Venus flytraps,
no Jack preaching in my pulpit, if you please.

So don't practice any pretty speeches, no lies,
    no feasts of bread and wine.
Don't light a candle in the sanctum sanctorum,
because I'm staying here just where I am.
    Not moving
I'll trick death into thinking
I am made of stone.

Still as a statue, I'll stand right here
outside the garden, gazing down as people
pass me on the green—children chasing
butterflies, young lovers murmuring kisses,
old ones drowsing on benches in the fading light.

Still as a statue and as safe,
I'll watch the turning of the seasons,
stand impassive as chasms cleave and
radiant earth uproots herself again and again,
and Adam once again drunk on the smell of
    honeysuckle, the taste of apple, turns to Eve

while high above them, ravens swoop and wheel,
black wings outstretched, soaring white in sun—
Climbing climbing
    Caw   caw   cawing

Pulling down the light
high above me as I stand
still and safe as a statue
forever without dying.

Published in Adobe Walls: an Anthology of
New Mexico Poetry, vol 3

Bomblets

such a pretty little name
for these packets wrapped
in bright yellow
floating from the sun
on little white umbrellas

*each bomblet can splinter
into 300 little shards*

can of orange pop
no, but maybe crackers
maybe even toys
sing the little children
dancing in the dust
ring around the rosy
pocket full of

little bones fluttering
to the tops of broken trees
in Hilla, Babylon, Basra
and all those ruined villages
too small to remember

Published in Passager

*__Judith Toler__ has been an editor, an English
professor, and a faculty union organizer. Currently
retired, she now divides her time between painting
and writing poetry. Her poems have won a New
Mexico Discovery Award as well as awards from
Passager and the Santa Fe Reporter. Most recently
her work has appeared in Adobe Walls #4, Cha,
and the Lilliput Review. Her first book,* In the
Shine of Broken Things, *is currently in process.*

MARY MCGINNIS

Dream-Seeing

People want to know
the way my camera works;

(there are different cameras,
different ways of seeing —)

different ways of looking,
one where you strain

to see into shadows,
staring until confused,

and one where you appear not to be looking —
and the picture has a strange flower

outside the appropriate fence.
In dreams my body is my camera

I'm where I am, it's kinesthetic,
in the beginning the circles of confusion

are manageable
the way the child's world is supposed to be

   through a small aperture:
   the back steps, the anonymous square of bland lawn

   above the flood plane.

   But then I make my own colors
   bright and dark reds, blues and bluegreens.

   Whether they are like your colors,
   I don't know.

   And I bring in my own people:
   mother, father, therapist, lost lovers,

   the ex-husband of a therapist, whoever I
   didn't know I was thinking about before I fell asleep.

My Life As A Lover

I claim it with my fingertips;
tonight they are cold, my ears remembering rain,
I claim it with my voice,
husky, lower than it used to be.

I claim it with my arms,
with my elbows that can hold nothing,
with determination, with my Clark's sandals flapping through
rain, with my nose for intrigue.

It is my love of pears that keeps me in this life,
my love of flat stones from a beach in Cape
May, New Jersey; sand dollars, mesquite
chips, petrified wood abandoned on the window sill;

a friend's hair full of wind and sun,
a blue plate from a friend I rarely see--
it's a moment of comfort holding another poet's hand
as we leave a reading,

it's rain in air,
tiny bits of gravel that end up in my kitchen:
they keep me here
in my incarnation as a lover.

Mary McGinnis has been writing, working, living, eating, cooking and laughing in New Mexico since 1972. Her first full-length collection, Listening for Cactus, *was published by Sherman Asher Publishing in 1996. She has work forthcoming in* The Sow's Ear *and recent work in* Malpais Review. *She participates in three writing groups.*

BLAIR COOPER

In the Ice Cream Parlor

The daughter of the ice cream man
had pale blue eyes, straw hair, skirts
too short and of cotton even in December.
She lived behind the shop where we
bought ice cream after school,
alone there with her father since
her mother had died of a strange disease.
Sometimes she would come
through a door behind the counter
to stand near her father to stare at us,
safe from our making fun of her
because of her loping, lopsided running
or the way she never blew bubble gum
without getting it in her hair.
Her father silently took our dimes,
hard pale eyes, straight mouth
as he held our small change. When he
handed over the ice cream cones,
we would lick them, looking at her
while she looked at us.

Published in Sin Fronteras

Crickets in Hidden Places

I built a new house where the old one
crumbled down so I could watch doves
turn amber in the tamarisk tree
when the sun went down.

I built a new house from the ground up
using bricks made of mud and straw,
dried under the hot noon sky,
bricks laid one by one until walls

were eight feet tall and covered
with a roof of young aspen trees.
In my new house I killed spiders
before they made webs, chased away

crickets before they chirped,
tossed out old photos so I couldn't
stash them away. In my new house
no memories to trip me in the dark.

Published in Adobe Walls

*Blair Cooper lives in Santa Fe in the old
house where she grew up, but she spent
many years in Las Cruces where she wrote
poetry and taught in the English Department
of New Mexico State University. Following
her husband's retirement, they returned to
Santa Fe. They have often spent summers in
Vermont, where she has written in a different
environment. Her poems have appeared in
El Ojito, New Mexico Poetry Review, Adobe
Walls, and Sin Fronteras.*

ELIZABETH RABY

Aunt Millie

A woman on her own,
divorced
twice,
childless,
married a widower,
childless,
and moved to be with him,
but he died
and left her
to confront a stranger
in the sunshine
of Ventura, California,
July, three in the afternoon,
a strip mall
with a parking lot and a planter

into which she fell
when he shot her
for her credit cards
and the keys to her car
that he abandoned
one block from where she lay
a curiosity to the strangers
who gathered until an ambulance
carried her to a bed in which
she soon died
from one more
small hole
in her heart.

**Steve, on the First
Anniversary of his
Father's Death**

I'm going to leave now,
sit outside in the wild weather
in darkness like a crow's wing,
think about my father.

Clouds round and woolly,
backs of sheep
cover the moon—the moon
of infinite possibilities,
dark and light.

He brought both, lost both,
left me here, says
don't look for me again.

*Elizabeth Raby is the author of
three poetry collections:* The Year
the Pears Bloomed Twice, Ink on
Snow, *and most recently,* This
Woman, *all with Virtual Artists
Collective (vacpoetry.org). In
2010 her poem, "Bride-to-Be"
won the Kelton Poetry Contest,
Angelo State University.*

JAMES MCGRATH

My Winter Soldier

My brother played drums in his high school band.

He sang Bacharach songs to Fatima down the road.

He tickled my mother with a peacock feather.

He laughed at my 4th grade elephant jokes.

He teased Dad about his bright ties.

My brother came home last week from Iraq.

He wore a piece of shrapnel from his shoulder
    on a chain around his neck.

He had a prosthetic arm with five plastic fingers
    in a white glove.

He called Dad a motherfucker because he wore
    a tie.

He said he had shot elephants and peacocks
    in the Baghdad zoo for target practice
    with his buddies.

He said Fatima was just another stupid Hajji.

He sold his drums on e-bay.

Last night at dinner he told us how they poured
    gasoline on a library in Fallujah, shooting
    into the shadows until they ran red.

How the books burned, even Rumi couldn't escape
    the flames.

He cried in his room all night, tossed grenades
    of four-letter words into the dark.

This morning he never came down to breakfast.

Published in AGAINST AGAMEMNON, War Poetry
2009, *Waterwood Press, 2009.*
SIN FRONTERAS, Writers Without Borders, *2009.*

Dear Poem

Poem, I want you to be open
            with multiple meanings,
            like when I get up in the morning
            and the sun is shining.

Poem, I ask you to be mysterious
            and aloof, like how the wind teases
            leaves from October trees.

I really don't want you to hesitate,
            to leave hints how love can color
            snowbanks.

Oh, Poem, if you would, add moon-rising
            verbs to childhood loss. Add running
            watercolor adjectives to broken mirrors,
            remove gray hairs from that old man's
            shoulders who filled his pockets
            with stolen watches.

And Poem, if you speak of war
            without losing blood, write your words
            over again. Tell the truth.
            Tell us who you killed.

Poem,   you say there is no such thing
            as a broken pencil or a pen without ink.

Poem, I believe you.

I believe you.

James McGrath, in over 20 anthologies, is a Sunstone Press of Santa Fe poet with three collections: At The Edgelessness of Light *(2005);* Speaking With Magpies *(2007);* Dreaming Invisible Voices *(2009); his fourth collection,* Valentines and Forgeries, Mirrors and Dragons *is due out in 2012. He was designated a Santa Fe Living Treasure in 2009 and received the 2012 New Mexico Literary Arts award for his support and advancement of Literary Arts in NM.*

YVES C. LUCERO

Ruse

What trickery
that one man's children
should be a welfare check
disposed into his veined
and belted arm.

What subterfuge
that an orchid should invite
an itinerant bee into its nectared lair
only to be papoosed
with pollen.

What illusion
as the tongue of a mistress
glides upon her lover's shaft
bringing a primacy to his mind
only to be vanquished by cuckoldry.

What intrigue
that two men in an oval room
should play a game of political chess
for a debt to be paid
by the unborn.

What bluff
gone terribly wrong
as a Great White shark plays
dead in the jaws of an Orca,
never to be released.

What magic
that the universe should
create a theatre called mind
making it believe that there
is a God called man.

(July 9th, 2011)

From his latest self-published book,
Portmanteau...con carne.

Yves C. Lucero, *single Frenchicano male, 44
and proudly bald, seeks inspiration for long term
relationship. Hobbies include scribbling, musing,
teeth grinding and wiping beads of blood off
forehead after staring at blank page for extended
periods. If you are free spirited, fun-loving,
dangerous and neurotic, then you're probably
reading Rumi. No pictures. Surprise me!*

Raindog

CATHERINE FERGUSON

Night's Wife

When you arrived in the village, your name was on everyone's lips.
You noticed the smile on his face and didn't want to look away.
You noticed him like crossing the one lane bridge.
Still so new here, you held your breath.

He was the moon beaming into the crevices of arroyos.
You saw him hosing down the peach tree, wearing no shirt.
You saw him riding his black horse, wearing his rain slicker.

You lived a few houses down.
You were as pretty as a clear cut through the canyon.

It was summer. He asked you to go night riding.
He brought a second horse fully saddled to your door.
His eyes gleamed years of coyotes.
It was your idea to ride naked.

Shyly, you glanced.
His chest the color of pale crested wheat in moonlight.
His arms a rope of hills that surround the mesa.

Shyly, he glanced.
Your breasts broke the sky.
Your waist a cold and crushing winter coming to an end.

He wanted you to become that peach tree
That would unfold over his house.

When his father died you held him in your arms on top of the creston.
When his mother died you dragged him out to the ravine,
sat with him while he cursed and broke white rocks.

You said *marido*,
leaned into his clavicle,

woke to new startling
windows framing
the peach tree in bloom.

The Gardeners

What could be more holy than the edge of your
mesa jutting out, a fin of gold leaf at twilight?

You two joined.

    A handsome man
    and a tall handsome man.

    They got together over a car and night that lasted forever.

Let him save you, let him put his hands on your chest.

    They drive together to work, lawnmower riding in the truck bed.
    They shower with flower catalogues, photographs of the brain,
    geological tides.

    There was a man who laid his body down.
    There was a man who lifted his friend in his arms.

    In small cool rooms they sew, they lace, they bake pies.
    What could be more holy than tying ribbons to dolls,
    rattles, wigs, drums, leather beaded shirts?

Let him soothe you with the tales of a past, of a taco stand
in Mexico, of a wife and twin boys who loved their dad.

Of a wife and a little girl, because you knew she would be beautiful.

Let the shelves be strewn with owl pellets, tiny bird spines,
mice rosaries, the rib cages of doves.

You two in the water overlooking summer fields.
You two lying in April grass, undaunted by many daffodils.

*Catherine Ferguson is a poet and painter living in Galisteo, NM. Inspired by landscape,
animals, and the people of her village, she creates watercolors, oils, retablos and poems
that express her love of nature. She has written numerous chapbooks. She won two New
Mexico Book Awards: one for poetry as co-author of* The Sound a Raven Makes, *and
another for her retablo illustrations in* You Who Make the Sky Bend *by Lisa Sandlin.*

JANE LIPMAN

The Wind Takes a Long Time to Say It

Indigo darkness.

Pitched against
shivering, slicing,
brutal wind,
waiting—
clutching coat and hood tighter,
at the edge of endurance, wondering
if I have the stamina to stay—

a pale cloud
emerges—
snow geese
asleep
in the temple of the pond,
new moon risen in their hearts
incubating flight.

The only thing moving is this wind.

In an instant, like a Mayan meeting
everyone talks at once—
cranes in their rattling song
outvoiced by thousands of snow geese.
Rising light and sound.

Dimly I make out distant geese
flying across the sky
toward the brooding fold.
The world fills with bird cries.
The geese lift as one being,
join the incoming throng.

Suddenly the dense, clamoring cloud of birds
in wild, ecstatic
emergence
whirls overhead.
Intoxicating dance—

a moving revelation from different directions.
Currents of wind and water made visible.

Raucous epiphany.
Festival of souls soaring.

Cranes stand in the water, long necks
entwined,
others hunched, like us, against freezing wind,
feathers riffling. One on long skinny legs
steadfastly flaps its wings,
practices the gesture of flying. Another
with open beak, over and over, makes its call.

A few mallards and shorebirds arrive,
an ibis. Sighted overhead in a bird cloud,
the yellow wing-shape of a harrier.
A mingle of blackbirds.

They co-exist in such harmony
interwoven in water and air.
In oneness with them,
myself, my species—
breathing and being—
interbeing—invisible energies
exchanged between livingkind.

All wandering is from the holy to the holy.

Triumphant light and song.
Jubilation of human flocks witnessing
bird flocks witnessing….

The wind takes a long time to say it.

(Bosque del Apache, NM 2007)

Previously published in the book, On the Back
Porch of the Moon, *2012*

Lightning from the Ground

1

Surprise, in the way love hides in flakes of darkness
in the luminous dusk, in how the rose gives away
everything—its perfume, leaf and petals, its arrows.

Surprise of a bird touching Blake's mouth—
he said, *I'm taking dictation*; of Duende speaking
into Lorca's ear: dark spirit, death, daimon.

In a junkyard, surprise as a dirty, nearly toothless man
approaches a well-dressed couple, asks if they like music.
They say yes. From his pocket he pulls
a miniature, inch-long harmonica and plays…
a Brandenburg concerto.

Once there was a time when camels and crowns
had antlers.

Surprise—thunder lives in mushrooms—
in the ground as well as the sky.

2

In occupied Iraq, a U.S. platoon
stalks main street, guns drawn.
Armed Iraqis from every home.
The sergeant shouts,
Kneel! The men kneel,
place the butts of their guns on the ground.
The Iraqis return to their homes.

3

To understand black energy,
scientists measure echoes of sound waves
that—surprise—go back to the Big Bang.

At first light, pine warbler wakes us
with his brilliant cry: *Awaken, to the day,
to the song of existence, to a strange voice
in the wing beats. Listen
to what's become increasingly silent.*

Published in On the Back Porch of the Moon,
Jane Lipman, Black Swan Editions, 2012

Jane Lipman's *chapbooks,* The Rapture
of Tulips *and* White Crow's Secret Life,
*from Pudding House Publications, were
finalists for New Mexico Book Awards in
Poetry in 2009 and 2010, respectively. Her
first full-length collection,* On the Back
Porch of the Moon, *is hot off the press
from Black Swan Editions, 2012. Her poems
have appeared in Runes, Santa Fe Literary
Review, New Mexico Poetry Review, Sin
Fronteras, Adobe Walls, Malpais Review,
Echoes, and elsewhere.*

THE POETRY I

After the Tsunami

cleared the shore like dollhouse toys, the photos
looked as if the coast had been ravaged

by extraterrestrials, some nuclear holocaust:
boots, chunks of concrete, mud, twisted bodies,

boards, boats, broken glass, grim in black and white,
silence palpable, hard as a beaten drum.

We looked in safety, a long world away
where washed sunlight stripped day open

to color and where spring would soon provoke
the cherry trees, an aching beauty unrevoked.

The world is like this now and it has been
this way before, its beauty and its rage

waiting for us as we go out a door,
deflected by whatever view we choose.

   Aaron Poller

Originally published in Indigo Rising, March, 2011

Aaron Poller is an advanced nurse psychotherapist who has been writing and publishing his poetry since the nineteen sixties. He lives quietly in a very small house in Winston-Salem, N.C. with his wife, four dogs and three cats.

[why he hangs]

   -for claude neal (lynched in jackson country, florida 1934)

     a   horsehair   rope

tore bark   from   limb

       where he hung

                south   winds   touched

                            what   was   left   worn   piñata

            she   kissed   his   long neck

before   its dislocation

                                    the tongue cut   swallowed

            found in   entraila   that lay   in   grass

        along with   scrotum   fingers

            i am sorry for

            bringing him in

            locking him up

            tightening   the rope around

            his neck   but

            there was nothing

            i could do

            we all know

            how it is in this town

            o   how his mother suffers

            i'll make sure

            tomorrow i   buy her

            a case   of apples

                        the deep red ones

Adam Walsh

My poetry is of projective verse as noted by the second generation American Modernist Charles Olson. Its form visually is as important verbally. The double spaced lines are intentional as with all elided words (elision). I earned a BA from the University of Montana and a MFA from Eastern Washington University under the tutelage of Christopher Howell. My poetry will appear in The Journal by Ohio State University, Edge Piece, Crab Creek Review, FeatherTale, and Ascent Aspirations in 2012.

Mountains

Poem for John Thomas (1930 – 2002)

he once wrote:

'year after year, the mountains
are ground down, blown away'

another mountain fell
a mountain of poetry

where it stood
a new landscape is left

in it's wake
after its passing
rocks of words
stand strong
tough but beautiful in
their carving

Adrian Manning

*Originally published in a 2 poem broadside
by Feel Free Press, UK*

Adrian Manning *hails from Leicester,
England and has had poems, broadsides
and chapbooks published around the
world. Find out more at http://www.
concretemeatpress.co.uk/ and http://www.
adrianmanningpoetryandart.blogspot.co.uk/*

OLD JOE

He sleeps in doorways
Or on park benches
Doesn't want to go
To a shelter
Not even when prodded

With the heavy weight
Of the beat cop's nightstick

Under threat of jail
He curls up in a fetal position
And closes his eyes
Trying to shut out memories of Vietnam
Nightmares that whirl inside his head
Like helicopter blades

The alcohol the drugs
The Failed years gather like locusts
Inside the cranial guitar of his mind
Playing all night rhapsodies inside
His head

Warrior troubadour of Pharaoh origins
Pale spokesman of lost tribes
Masked as a homeless transient
Poet Prophet of beauty
And all its imperfections
Ravished by the streets
Kissed by angels
Left tired withered
Like an unattended Kansas
Grain field

A.D. Winans

*Previously published in Spare Change
Magazine*

A.D. Winans *is an award winning San
Francisco poet who has published 54 books
and chapbooks of poetry and prose. He edited/
published Second Coming Press for 17 years.
He won a PEN National Josephines Miles
Award in 2006 and in 2009 PEN Oakland
awarded him a Lifetime Achievement Award.
In 2002 a song poem of his was performed at
Alice Tully Hall in NYC.*

Uptown Gunners

They were the guys everyone
warned you against: part feral
street creatures, part hard core
psychos. All of them brought
up in packs with names like
Uptown Gunners since the age
of nine, working as delivery boys
or lookouts, paid in dime bags
and bumpies, gradually working
their way through the ranks to enforcer,
then to full-fledged dealers,
earning blood stripes and tattoos
along the way, mouths to feed,
and an attitude only people in
the trade could truly understand.
None of them can read or write,
have a license to drive or a wage
earning job, and, never will, pay
cash for everything, even buying
wheels, Jaguars and Benzs in
the driveway next to falling down,
firetrap safe house they crash in.

All of them barely out of their
teens, communicating by cell
phones and tapped lines, using
hand signs and drive by signals
to let clients know when the product
has arrived. None of them wonder
why an elder of their tribe is maybe
twenty-five, parents, if they have
them, much older but living elsewhere
as guests of the state for life; the ones
still on the street, dead men walking
digging shallow graves with one hand
drawing cards against a busted flush
with the other.

Alan Catlin

*Alan Catlin has been publishing widely since
the middle 70's. He has well over sixty published
chapbooks and full length books of poetry and
prose. His most recent full length poetry book is
"Alien Nation" from March Street Press.*

Punt E Mes

Ecru tan in color
with that bitterness
spilled entirely
and christening me
over broken swivel chair:
another wheel snapping off,
another battered seat,
another ceiling looking down at me,
another breath in context,
another year spinning,
the spackled ceiling
looking down at me.

I've learned a point
and a half lesson.

My blood alcohol level has risen
about a point and a half.

All my books of knowledge
sit heavy
and the aftertaste of vermouth
is the maraschino
in my arteriosclerosis:
an arm over glutinous chest,
other arm underneath the bed,
one hand softly rubs
cobwebs of a brown recluse,
the other clutches jaundiced
secrets long buried there.

Now elbows prop up the carcass
of the man with nine and a half toes.
He needs to enjoy the next breath
in context; if not enjoy then
experience and survive,
swallow the fortified wine
and savor the affair,
even while he fails at savoir faire.

Angel Uriel Perales

*Angel Uriel Perales is a poet and
journalist currently residing in Valley
Village, CA. Please visit his poetry
website at www.rumrazor.com.*

Contact

Shall we live without hope?
Wendell Berry

Walking home this June day from big, garish
Amoeba Music with Callas, Philip Glass,
and Vivaldi in a big, garish paper bag, along
DeLongpre Ave., my own street of dreams, just
under Sunset Boulevard, *the* Sunset Boulevard,
passed the courtyard of our first living space
with its standard downtown-Hollywood-
apartment-sized pool, toward the park where
we first conceived, a tall man, black, taller than
me, in jeans, striped shirt, gray wool-type cap,
strode out the diagonal wrought iron gateway
to the park. We saw each other as people do,
walking passed each other. He looked up and
around with a quizzing expression, then at me,
seeing what? Tall white woman, not as tall
as he? In jeans, *Giants* t-shirt, carrying a big
garish paper bag? He pointed to his wrist. I
said 3:15. He nodded and turned the corner. I
felt sure and solid in those seconds of almost
wordless communication, grateful, almost
gleeful, imbuing them with more significance
than deserved as if they heralded the human
will to collective acknowledgment, here, under
Sunset Boulevard, *the* Sunset Boulevard, at the
entrance to a small urban green, staking out the
commons.

Angela C. Mankiewicz

*Angela C. Mankiewicz has 4 chapbooks out,
including* AN EYE, *published by Pecan Grove
Press and* AS IF, *from Little Red Books. Recent
publications include: Full of Crow, Long
Poem Magazine (UK), PRESA, PoetsArtists,,
Istanbul Literary Review, Arsenic Lobster,
JerseyWorks. Last May, her chamber opera,*
ONE DAY LESS, *music by D. Javelosa, was
performed at the Broad Stage - 2nd Space in
Santa Monica, CA.*

MOM, THE ORIGINAL METAPHOR

here, she says—
this is life
and you can
have it,
      then seduces us
right away
with warmth and sugar
—before we
catch on

Anne MacNaughton

*Anne MacNaughton is adjunct professor of
English and Communication & Journalism
at the University of New Mexico-Taos, and
past-director of the long-running Taos
Poetry Circus. Her work has been published
in numerous journals and anthologies,
including The Best Poetry of 1989 (Scribners),
Robert Bly's The Rag and Bone Shop of the
Heart (HarperCollins), and In Company: an
Anthology of New Mexico Poets after 1960
(UNM Press). She and her partner Peter
Rabbit received the New Mexico Literary
Association's first Appreciation Award, as
well as The Eternal Flame Award at the 2009
Verse/Converse Festival where the youth
event trophy, named after her, is given in her
honor each year. A founding member of The
Luminous Animal, a jazz-poetry performance
ensemble, she is also a visual artist and
organic farmer.*

Mark Hartenbach

Salvation

Could you put a gun to my head and pull the trigger,
if I told you it was for love,

after you've looked upon picture perfect darkness
with the clippings of your own eyes,
the distort of soul   sliced into smoky segments?

But you who've
loved too much are no longer here (goodbye)—

you've driven past the pretense of salvation

so elegantly   where it would merge
with the apex of forgiveness   on a Sunday   any day,

and then eternity.

Ariana Den Bleyker

Apology to a Love Poem

Your secrets
are always yours
kid.

And yes I miss you.

And yes
I really liked
having coffee
the other night –
any night.

And yes,
I had to look
at the streetlights
to catch my breath
too.

So we're even kid.

Don't be mad –
it's just a poem,
maybe it caught
a moment,
only a moment.

Sometimes
we can't help it
they arrive
unexplained,
unexpected –
those moments

and we think
they're not
supposed to –
not to me,
I'm different,
immune.

But they do happen
and you get lost

in a kiss
and you don't want
anyone
to know.

No one will.
I like your secrets
and will keep them
forever...

Don't be mad.

Bill Gainer

__Bill Gainer__, the legendary Northern California poet, has contributed to the literary scene as a writer, editor, promoter, publicist and poet. He currently edits for the Pen Award winning R.L. Crow Publications and hosts Poetry With Legs in Sacramento. His latest book is A Note in the Window. *Visit him at* billgainer.com.

SHE BECAME SO BEAUTIFUL I HAD TO TURN AWAY

we finished my 6-pack of Black Snake
& she produced a bottle of port
we drank that too
I had couple joints as well
she's given up grass
makes her doubt herself
become paranoid
etc

doubt can be a useful tool
"I have no fixed idea about anything" I said
she seemed very surprised
"hey wait a minute
no one can say that
we all want to be there
but nobody is..."
her face kept flashing from one aspect
of her nature to another
(madonna slut tigress dove muse amazon goddess)
good nights are like that
drunken flirtatious gazes
flames of conversation
seductive images
everything is new
you haven't been to bed yet
it may never go that far
but you sit very drunk & stoned
listening watching wondering what
her flower will feel like
with my stem
pulsating
inside
her

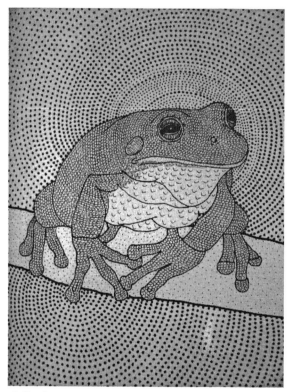

Billy Jones

I love drinking with
women I'm just
beginning
to know

Bill Jones

*The late **Billy Jones** died in July 2012. His poetry has appeared in hundreds of journals worldwide. He is the author of 8 books including CRAZY BONE, Poems and Drawings (LUMMOX Press, 2012)...his first American book. The rest were published in Australia.*

NIGERIAN POETRY

NIGERIAN POETRY TAKES BOTH THE traditional and contemporary. Traditional in the beautiful poetry that is rendered sometimes as panegyrics from a mother to a husband or child, at private gatherings, to the king of a town. These are more like the griots of Senegal in tracing the oral history of a family. It is beautiful. The Nigerian is a natural poet in the way he uses idiomatic expressions to state his observation of things around. Or in dirges. The Contemporary Poetry is a different kettle of fish and Nigerian Poets from the Nobel Laureate Wole Soyinka to John Pepper Clarke have given us insights to a uniquely Nigerian style poetry that we have emulated from professors to the simple English student doing Literature homework and trying his hand at Poetry. It has been an experience that has taken on a spiritual nuance for me.

It is thus my pleasure to bring to the table some Nigerian poets. Not necessarily the best nor the worst but definitely the honest writers dedicated to practicing their craft and willing to explore avenues that will afford them opportunities of improvement, for life itself teaches us daily. A poet is a dreamer who sees in every emotion, nature and lessons and pointers to a dream he endlessly changes and has no idea what he might get at the end of his journey.

Please meet my Nigerian poets

Biola Olatunde

KAYODE ARIYO

The Land Of My Birth

The land of my birth, Nigeria
The giant that dwarfs peers
The blackish nine hearted cat
Dreaded trigger of the black world

The land of my birth, Nigeria
Abused by adventurous strangers
Raped by despotic men in khaki
Pauperized by men elected by the ballots

The land of my birth, Nigeria
Mineral resources sources of rivalries
Black gold black goals black means
Your vultures devour the doves

The land of my birth, Nigeria
Much hated but much loved
Much despised but much adored
Your once rich land now bare, empty

The land of my birth, Nigeria
Though devoid of internal peace
Yet filled with endless possibilities
You remain a land of limitless hopes

Friendly Fires

When friends fire friends
What strange friends they be
When fires triggered by trusted friends
Burn so painfully as from hated foes
What sort of terrible fires they be
When fires enkindled by detested foes
Burn as deep as from lovely friends
Then fires know no friends nor enemies
Fires tell tales of pains, agonies, deaths
End joy, kill dreams, shatter hopes
A foe's fire smiles not but destroys
A friend's fire laughs not but shatters
What then is friendly in a friendly fire?
For from a friend or foe fire is fire

Kayode Samuel Ariyo *hails from Ilogbo-Ekiti in Ekiti State of Nigeria. He is currently a lecturer in the Department of General Studies, Rufus Giwa Polytechnic, Owo, Ondo State. Kayode is married to Wumi Ariyo (nee Akindele) and they are blessed with children. His writing has appeared in numerous anthologies including A* Basket of Beauty; Sounds from our Hearts*; and Verses from the Sun. His most recent collection, co-written with S. I. Adewumi was Sounds from our Hearts (Somerest Ventures - 2009).*

DANIEL OBASOOTO

The Scorched Earth

Life and death
Pain and suffering
Joy and sorrow
All points to them
And reconciled in them
The 'Me first' generation
Notable consequence of our economic mismanagement
We yearn desperately for the novelty of their insanities
In our festoons of eyesores
The white castles they built were painted red
    by the spatter of their blood
Some try to daub them white
But paint them black in obeisance to greed
Tilting our treasury to the ranting of their deep pockets
Within our pride they become the worst of role models
Enslaving in the clutches of the expired guerillas
Setting a snare for the masses
Who bear all and gain none
To our pains I tout no prescription
The poor man's pains passes unnoticed
But when the rich man farts, it makes cover
The antiquity of their knowledge we need not
In their antiquated knowledge
Ignoring the lone voices in the wilderness
Scorched by the sun
And buffeted by the rain
To be devoured by the antiquated beast
Lurking in the wilderness for so long
Perfecting its mission on the masses
To be clutched in mire privation and squalor
The bountifulness of the land is of no significance
The storm seems unabating
The gun salute of the day
The distant sound of war
The war songs of angry men
Nicknamed with many names by our antiquated brains
Who despair the advise of the wise
Choose imperviously his antiquated knowledge
All points to the state of the people
Who require economic emancipation

From the public accentuation
To saturate the economic accumulation
Rather than the commuting of common
    wealth to private wealth
When the masses will be deprived

PLANT TO PLUNDER

More than just a spell of melancholic blues
Afflicted with pain, anguish and deep sorrow
Life suddenly darkened by a cloud of hopelessness
Our hope swallowed up by the plunderer
Living our wealth
To the lazy life of a sloth
In our land full of wealth
We live by the riverside
Yet wash our hands with spittle
Like the sloth, we die of starvation
With a stomach full with food
Poverty sings the song we dance
Sound a discordant note
The rhythms of the day
We all dance the good footstep
To the tone they play
Who well to act our woe?
As it is of disconsolate and pain
Beating by the plunderer
Who dance their way to fortune
Depleting the country to the fullest
Depleting our common wealth
Victim of their own desire
In the deadly grip of thirst
The motley plunderer
A fair cruel lord
Daring not the morrow's dawn
They are known discreet men
We are fortified against any denial
Yet we take delight in such barren rascals
Who do nothing than repel

Raindog

Mercury endue them with lying
What they can't do no more they talk about
Dancing and dicing dawn and dusk
To eat and drink far more than they can hold
To barren the land where water will not dwell
Bringing overture of pains
As we lead these graces to the grave
As we cry wolf our pains
Singing the anthem of war
Against the plunderer
The more merriment of wealth they make
Till we be rotted down in straw and dung
That's how we get to be
Till we be rotten as never ripe
Our will always catching on the nail
Hoping as long as the world will pipe

NOTE: *Mercury was said to be the
god of liars*

Daniel Obasooto *hails from Owo in Ondo
State of Nigeria. He is a Postgraduate
student of the Obafemi Awolowo University.
He is a young prolific writer whose writing
cuts across all the literary genres and is a
member of Association of Nigerian Authors
(ANA). He is a man of great disposition,
serious-minded, determined, enterprising
and focused.*

SOLA OWONIBI

Dialogue With Silence

Gazing at the blinking
Eyes of the sky
My soul danced to
The music of silence

On Idanre mountain top
I resigned as the day
Closes its shutters

I accompanied tonmon-hoko*
To his golden nest and
My soul reciprocates
The smiles of the sleepy sunlight

A conspiracy with the cloud
Not a finger of light
From the moon

Like withering banana
Leaf tendrils with brittle skins
The young and the aged shiver
To the hostile damp of dusk

As I listen to the
Whisper of silence
In a self excavation

*Tonmon-hoko is a deceptive African
sun at sunset that lures people to work
till nightfall in the farm.*

Idanre Hills

Stealthily I tiptoed
To the basement of your heart
I retired
Mermaid of Idanre Hills
Your smile, the softness of the sun
That disarms
Terrorists on oath
Your bosom, the coolness
Of a midnight moon
Your appealing eyeballs
Send fingers of stars
To illuminate my heart
Your favour regulates
The cyclical rhythm of the earth
Your kisses wear
The silvery-velvet of a setting sun
The mystery of your existence
A wonder for all ages
Together we shall traverse
A serpentine footpath
Visible to great hunters
A path to the land of bliss
A template you are
In the mirror of heart
My Queen baby of Idanre.

Sola Owonibi (PhD) is a Nigerian poet and a playwright. Chairman of Association of Nigerian Authors, Ondo State chapter, Sola Owonibi is the author of 'Homeless not Hopeless' a poem in the 2011-2015 Literature in English syllabus of West Africa Examination Council (WAEC). Dr Owonibi teaches, among others, Creative Writing in the Department of English Studies, Adekunle Ajasin University, Akungba Akoko, Nigeria.

JOE OPEYEMI OLANIHUN

Infinte Fury

tired hope, jaded from waiting
dying dreams, famished and fainting
consulted the Fates,
they denied complicity!

who is there to tell me
why our common destiny
treats us with drear disdain?

Or how do we explain
this unusual longevity
of harsh penury,
this dearth droughty
of a respite flimsy,
a morrow dark and frightening
who can really dree?

maybe, just maybe
these messengers of fire
- who depart daily -
will care to mouth our woes
to souls yonder,

and whether somehow
they will let us know
if those silenced souls fare any better?

for yesterday,
a courier went his way.

he was a graduate
he hanged himself
he said because his whole days
were toils and much pain
that he felt his young age
was lenghtier

Each Day

each day
tragic recurs

women expiring
after much labour...

veteran tort-feasors
before the stern judge
always are first-timers
as gibbet beckons.

the future is entwined
in overwhelming malaise

poverty seem the perfect excuse for every disgrace.

Joe Opeyemi is still student at Obafemi Awolowo University in Ile Ife and when not in class uses his phone to send poems to some writing sites one which is "Poets without borders". He is what you might call one of the angry young men of our society.

than Methuselah's,
when he was mere
twenty and nine!

Yet, if my faith be right
as the writ prescribed such a flight
our man is bound for
brimstone and fire
and a wrath eternal
for taking his own borrowed life!

EBIOWEI PERETU

The traveling man

Standing at the ships bridge
 Crew side by side we watch the casket sail away
 Today we bury one more at sea
 In death he earned his own ship
 Sail away far away
 Where none has returned to share tale
 Where grief and sorrow will never find
 Where eternity makes nest and ever after is true to its words
 No unpredictable waves only gentle ones
 That cradles you as the oceans coral sings you a lullaby
 Hat to chest we give last respect
 Finding solace in memories shared
 From stormy nights In the heart of sea to gentle current at the wake of land
 Our journey through life made us kin
 Now we part still to meet again
 On that day singing will be heard far out at eternal sea
 And tears will flow for joy as it Shedds its skin of sorrow
 Travel light travel free

You owe the world nothing now
All debts paid in full
History will forever hold that you were here
Forgetting remains an uphill task
But in celebration not mourning

Exposition

The night is loud with the sound of silence
 As everything seems brighter in the glow of darkness
 During this hours the body remains alert with slumber

Gently life's hand rubs of the truths of today in preparation for tomorrow
 Today's failure hopefully will be forgotten in tomorrow's victory

The curtains close to the end of another scene
 God the play write takes one last look through his script
 Its actors prepare, some unaware of their next role
 yet tomorrow they awake into character
 adorned in makeup and costume as need be

Every play has its end
 While it lasts, some will awe the world and others terrify it
 Maybe leave the world in stitches others in their wake will leave behind mourning

Roles sometimes inter mingle yet no two shall ever be a perfect parallel
 The world and all around, our stage and props

You may not have written this play
 Yet the choice is yours
 Stick to the script or add a pinch of innovation
 Become a beacon of light or a cloak of darkness

The key to interpreting each role will always be choice
 Molded in love or hate, each key will open a lifetime of scenes

Some from the onset prepare for the final bow
Some sit around waiting for the stage lights to go off
Others find the end short of a few scenes

But a cheering crowd was never promised
A standing ovation may be asking too much

Sometimes the silence from the gallery is worth far more than a thousand words
For the strongest emotions find no words for kin and the best stories never understood.

Ebiowei is an architect who lives in Abuja. He says Poetry has always been a pull he has never been able to resist. He belongs to some writing communities and has some of his poems on Poets without Border.

BIOLA OLATUNDE

An Agonized Prayer

Here in the street,
we call it democracy
some say it's only transition
I think it is attrition
No need for truth

Their necks have grown
from the former hungry state
to layers of drunken folds
I step away from their waste

Pregnant at sixteen,
her hopes dead at fourteen
her lover is fifty
he made promises to ease her poverty
but she only picks at the garbage
from the buses.
his promises foreclosed
by the senator's lusting greed

They loot his hopes
and dump his future
within the thighs of
today's political whores!

This is the street
where we make politics with death
AIDS stalks his dreams
his past forgotten
his future denied
they make dollars from his hopes

Garbed in obscene wealth
The politicians tell him
He should wait for a dead tomorrow
As they put the jobs under the bridges
Dad's four month wage
Has disappeared down
The councilors throat
my sister has gone to Italy

With money she got
dancing naked for the representative of filth
the chairman has built
new bridges across his lawn.

What shall we collect from the
degenerated thieves
who took my mandate
and gave me hate
If only I had a bullet for every wrong
I will send them to kingdom come!

Ritual

She wore red
midriff across her breast
she took the path
that led to her nest

The crickets sang
a melody to the breeze
Jasmine scented night
Moonlit kissed sky

They stood hidden
amongst the brambles
machetes gleaming

She sang along the path

thoughts of loved faces quickened her steps
they moved one pace closer too
the owl screamed a warning
lady you are led
to a fiery slaughter
by the field of your dreams

The moon dipped
they jumped out
incantations galore
faces smeared with terror
one pinched scream
then a whimpered silence
the march to the grove
of the ancestral spirits

Now her red is spattered
with the red of her blood
it is the ritual of ignorance
danced by dead and living
In the eerie market square.

*Biola Olatunde is a poet and author. She
is also a TV and Radio producer. She has
published some six volumes of poetry. 3 of the
books are listed on amazon.com. Biola belongs
to some writing communities online, runs a
blog and website where she has introduced a
forum to encourage Nigerian poets and writers
to exchange ideas.*

THE POETRY II

Remembering It Like
Yesterday

sun's set
in southern
chile
across the
rio cautin
in meadows
oxen and
mules silent
maniceros
in the plaza
shutting down
hawkin what
few bags of
peanuts are left
orsono and

villarica sleep
scent of
rain lingers
   up north
in vina
stunning
rosa
her long red hair
waiting the counter
at her father's
deli   haunting
smile and those
eyes
thoughts
pensamientos de

america
carried like a
worn journal
kept
always.

Brent Leake

Brent Leake lives in Salt Lake City, Utah. He works for the County of Salt Lake trying like hell to keep folks out of jail and out of the criminal justice system. When that's not going well, he's hooked on graphic novels.

---

jon's eyes

jon is my lover. we have lived together for over 20 years.
sometimes when i look in his eyes, i am startled by
the intensity that i see there. jon is a complicated
guy. he's smart. he knows a lot of stuff and he
understands a lot of things.
sometimes when i look in his eyes, there is
this kind of pulsing little fire i see there. calm,
quiet, strong, restful, but there's this fire
that burns and glows and hungers
and worries me. and sometimes i'm
just on the verge of wanting to say to him
that i see how involved it is in there, how
complex the whole business is in there,
how full of thoughts and dreams
and emotions he is.
but i don't say it, i just go on talking, listening to
what he answers back, looking in his eyes,

then away, then back again,
i feel eager and
humble and
dumb.

Carl Miller Daniels

Previously published in RIOT ACT (2010); Nerve Cowboy #16 (2003)

Carl Miller Daniels just hit the magical wonderful age of 60 fuckin' years old. His first full-length book, Gorilla Architecture, *was recently published by Interior Noise Press. Daniels loves ginseng & catnip -- well, the concepts, anyway.*

Late afternoon.
Pale blue sky
White clouds lined with gray
Not silver.
I set aside my game of solitaire
And will the sun to move,
To color the sky and clouds
With coral twilight.
At sunset I pour a glass of Chardonnay
Arrange a small plate
Of brie and savory crackers
And settle on the sofa,
Peacefully awaiting the presence in my living room
Of the man I see more than any other –
Brian Williams, NBC News.

Catherine Dain

Catherine Dain *has a degree in theater from UCLA, studied at Neighborhood Playhouse in New York, and got her SAG card doing a biker flick in 1968. After five years as a television newswoman, she returned to graduate school and came out a writer of mystery novels. Her Freddie O'Neal series was twice nominated for a Shamus Award by the Private Eye Writers of America. The novels are now out of print. In the last ten years she performed often at Ojai Art Center Theater. When she moved to Ventura a few months ago, she started writing again … this time poetry. And she is happy to be back in print.*

M.C. and friends in Eygalieres

I noticed the other day
how our photograph was fading.
Like the days,
the photograph seemed to reflect
time itself slowly fading away.
Pascale sunning, you holding a tiny Darjeeling,
me with a piece of embroidery,
Gerard behind the camera.

All together,
we were captured in that one moment of time
to remind us forever of summer, our friendship
and Eygalieres.

Celia S. Lustgarten

Celia S. Lustgarten *was born in New York lived on the West Coast for many years and recently returned to her roots.   Her short stories and poetry have been published in the U.S.A., Canada, England and New Zealand.*

Mark Hartenbach

Raindog

Persimmon

Bursting within
        Your cracking skins
Is your eager heart
A heart full of
Even more eager tongues

No, I am not eating you
But embracing your heart
        Inside out

A sweet, penetrating kiss

Changming Yuan

*Changming Yuan, 4-time Pushcart nominee
and author of* Chansons of a Chinaman, *grew
up in rural China and published several
monographs before moving to Canada. With
a PhD in English, Yuan currently teaches in
Vancouver and has had poetry appearing in
nearly 550 literary publications worldwide,
including Asia Literary Review, Best Canadian
Poetry, BestNewPoemsOnline, Exquisite
Corpse, London Magazine, Paris/Atlantic,
Poetry Kanto, SAND and Taj Mahal Review.*

On The Retirement Of Gerald Locklin From Cal State University, Long Beach

Coffee without beans
Coke without fizz
Shortcake without strawberries
Chili cheese nachos without cholesterol

Boys without dirt
Kids without noise
Kindergarten without kids
A priest, a minister, and a rabbi without a joke

Cars without engines
Halloween without haunts
Texas without guns
Father and Son without the Holy Ghost

Baseball without summer
Summer without vacation
Watermelon without sweet
Heaven without Mom and Dad

Football without cheerleaders
Sex without sexy
Basketball without dunks
TV without *The Simpsons* and *Tonight*

Croesus without cash
Attila without Huns
Elvis without hips
Rock without roll

Einstein without brains
Shakespeare without Hamlet
Hamlet without doubt
Romeo without You-Know-Who

Trees without leaves
Cliffs without high
Dogs without fetch
Cats without to-hell-with-you

Men without women
Art without passion
Books without reading
Laughs without fun.

Clouds without water
Rain without clouds
Rivers without rain
Beaches without sand

Sea without shore
Wind without air
Sail without wind
Skiff without oars

Ship without rudder
Ship without floating
Ship without port
Ship without friend

Charles Webb

Charles Harper Webb's latest book is Shadow Ball: New & Selected Poems, *published by the University of Pittsburgh Press. What Things Are Made Of, also from Pitt, is forthcoming in 2013. Webb teaches Creative Writing at California State University, Long Beach.*

Family Tradition

He was scarred as a child you know
    Weaned at his drunken father's teat
        Splintered sobs, his lullaby
Delicate five year-old ears
    Overhearing brutal sex
        Forever shattering childhood dreams
He can't help it
    Still just a lonely child waiting for love
        He needs my love
It's ok really
    He didn't mean it
        Just lost control
He promised
    it won't happen again
        He won't carry on
            the family tradition

Charolette McDonald

I lived a lot, wrote some from the heart, some from the gut, but always a word miser. I am just me and happy with that.

THE DEATH OF BILLIE HOLIDAY

They found a packet of heroin
in her Harlem hospital room,
$750 strapped to her leg,
70 cents in her bank account.

The policemen buzzing over her bed
moved on to another call. A nurse
lowered the window
against traffic horns,

the scratch of July street-clang.
Outside, men in bowler hats
wiped the slow, rough heat
from their necks.

Christine DeSimone

Originally appeared in Poet Lore; also placed second runner-up in the 2004 New Letters Literary Awards, judged by Cornelius Eady.

Christine DeSimone *was born in Los Angeles, a fourth-generation Californian. She received a J.D. from the University of California, Hastings, and practices law in San Francisco. Her poems have appeared in over 30 journals, including Alaska Quarterly Review, Cream City Review, Pearl, Zyzzyva, and Verse Daily.*

Van Nuys

I bought a car today
my old on
the one that has carried me through brokenness and depression
and attempted suicide
for years
complaining - but faithful as a stinking old dog -
finally sprung a heavy oil leak
to go with the struts and the master cylinder and the radiator
that needed immediate attention eighteen months ago

And the smell of gasoline was making my passenger choke
at every stop light
and
my newest wife decreed that she would never ride in the beast again

So we stopped In Van Nuys at a used car lot
and I found a shiny three-year red old
(I always buy red whenever possible)
and
said good-bye to my old pal flipping her keys to the used car guy and
he watched me as I put my hand on her trunk and patted her one last time
"So-long old car," I said. You saved my ass over and over and never quit on me"

Through the showroom window I saw her smiling - approving - this new wife - my happy co-signer

It was then that I grasped in immutable truth -
wives come and go
but a good used car is a
treasure

Dan Fante

Previously published in "A Gin-pissing Raw Meat Dual Carburetor V8 Son of A Bitch From Los Angeles"

Dan Fante is the author of twelve books including poetry, plays, short fiction, and novels, and the upcoming Detective/Thriller POINT DOOM, *Harper Perennial April 2012. He teaches Creative Writing at UCLA. He is married to Ayrin Leigh Fante and they have a son, eight year old Michelangelo Giovanni Fante.*

Slipping Away

It's the insipid religious beliefs
and it's the insipid pronouncements
from insipid politicians
(yes, I'm using the word 'insipid' three times in a row) …

It's the incredible ignorance of deficits and debt –
combined with an insanely inadequate
understanding of taxation (yes, I said taxation)
as a necessary public policy instrument …

It's our irrational treatment of the environment –
it's more than just a "free good"
in the never-ending production process
but we act like we really don't want to know this …

It's the insidious way we still treat each other
all over the planet
after all we've supposedly learned
about human rights, civil rights and something we call democracy …

The twenty-first century is already slipping away –
not in calendar years, one could claim,
but in every other way …

I'd say that we are sleeping while it does –
in reality, it's much worse: we're being
recklessly and willfully blind …

I'd also say I'm holding out hope
for the twenty-second century
but I won't be there …

> *D.A. Pratt*

D.A. (David) Pratt lives in Regina. Saskatchewan, Canada. He maintained a "common reader" interest in real reading while working far too long in the field of taxation policy for the Government of Saskatchewan.

friday night in the drunk tank

floating over drunk tank hum
a voice
at the back of the holding cell
demands a phone call

warm blood
begins to move
through numb hands
from cuffs—too tight

tiny shards of glass
from a beer-bottle bar fight
embedded in my
blood-matted hair

crystal ringing
in my brain
like a beautiful
girl's name

left eye swollen closed
thirteen dollars
stashed in the soles
of my old dingos

not enough for bail—
another friday night
in the city jail
for trying to make something

out of the emptiness
that crawls along
this boulevard
of half-remembered things

DB Cox

*DB Cox is a blues musician/writer from
South Carolina. His poems and short stories
have been published extensively in the
small press, in the US, and abroad. He has
published five books of poetry:* "Passing For
Blue," "Lowdown," "Ordinary Sorrows,"
"Nightwatch," *and* "Empty Frames." *STUDIO
BOOKS recently published his Ebook,*
"Unaccustomed Mercy," *a collection of short
stories—available online at Amazon Kindle
Store. He has been nominated three times for
the Pushcart Prize.*

Claudio Parentela

STATE O' POETRY

by Don Kingfisher Campbell

HERE IN PASADENA, LIKE MOST WORLD-wide cities I'm sure, poets write either in isolation (at home or a coffee shop) or in a local workshop (a library or whatever), then head out to poetry readings to share, or don't go, if not inclined. The most seriously involved are adventurous enough to venture to a far away city to check out another enclave, with the hope of being asked to feature there. Thanks to email and Facebook, arrangements can be made well in advance to participate and feature.

Now, the poetry, that's another story. Post-traditional. Post-modern. Post-beat. Post-stand-up. Post-spoken word. Post-MFA. There's almost as many styles as there are poets.

Individuality is prized, as long as you can deliver vivid visceral images, produce never-before seen/heard metaphors, and be able to make declarative statements with conviction. Publishing? Practically required…and the more prestigious the publications you are published in, the more prestigious the crowd you'll be a part of. But poets are venerated at every level, whether you're wowing 'em at a neighborhood read, or being paid at a charging venue.

The only real problem, other than distance between scenes, seems to be getting other poets to purchase your chapbooks, books, CD's, broadsides, etc. If they really dig your stuff a lot, ca-ching…otherwise, you're experiencing negative cash flow. Poets gotta support poets, I mean, who else will? (Of course, if you're reading this, you are doing just that, thank you.)

The poets I've selected to be included in this issue of LUMMOX are each individually brilliant at creating their own brand of poetry. These ten poets have crossed my poetic path and moved me enough to want to push them into the spotlight.

The poet who sometimes travels the farthest to my Saturday Afternoon Poetry series in Pasadena is **Jim Babwe**. He's a wickedly funny and intelligent poet from Encinitas. His poems in this anthology are "Taking photographs of Barbie on fire" (and that's just one quoted line).

CaLokie is (and has been for years) Pasadena's unofficial poet laureate. He's a transplant from Oklahoma student-preacher who became a Los Angeles history teacher challenging fundamentalists with lines like "if your creator said in 4004 b.c. / let earth and sky be / his universe is much too small".

Joseph Gardner lives in not too far away Long Beach, and regularly attends the San Gabriel Valley Poetry Quarterly publication readings where he devastates listeners with chronicles of his own life with a "head like cotton / concern past and forgotten".

Jeffry Jensen is notorious for showing up midway through the aforementioned SGVPQ reading, guess he comes over straight from work in Altadena. He's an award-winning master of idea combination experimentations which actually make quite a lot of gorgeous poetic sense: "A hero for the ages, for the seas clogged in the pipes of pregnant fishes."

Lalo Kikiriki, a somewhat local East Los Angeleno, member of the Zzyzx poetry group, humorously serves up not-so-reverent nostalgia for her hippie past in broken sentences that flat out confrontate, like: "We who cannot remember hunger, only diets stand by helplessly as banks and tax collectors take our neighbor's houses."

Lately, I've been pursuing an MFA in Poetry at Antioch University in Culver City. There, I've met two amazing poets who visit and compose powerful poetry that rivals any diary. **Julie LeMay** (from Palmer, Alaska): "His gray mother perches on a swivel stool / like a dumbed parrot, studies / the flesh colored linoleum with confetti / pattern of yellow, red, green – all shades / of bodily fluids." and **Janice Luo** (Burbank resident): "where sad girls danced against the steel stalks of their dreams to dead-ends."

Radomir Vojtech Luza, a North Hollywood

renaissance man from the east, first came to a west coast poetry reading in Pasadena, happy to find company with fellow poets. This people person is an actor, comedian, politician, and now host of the Unbuckled: NoHo Poetry reading series. His two tribute poems published here offer sensational metaphor, internal rhyme and alliteration mixes like "Over there on the intersection of asphalt and pain the city stops making sense / It is a brown flamingo, a flying submarine, an undiscovered leper colony".

Lisa Marie Sandoval first wowed me some years ago when she performed her poetry with balletic movement and gestures, that don't detract, but add to the enjoyment of her poems. You'll just have to come to the Lummox publication reading at Beyond Baroque to see what I'm talking about. Check out this sample from her poem "Marriage on a March Morning": "The perfect bed for budding red breasts / and a romantic roll through the tree branches."

Finally, **Mary Torregrossa**, one of the core poets of the San Gabriel Valley scene (her home is centrally located in Baldwin Park) creates stanzas with deeply perceptive eyes and mind: "a grimy Super Tech filter / sits on a countertop / polished to a worn patina / by the push and push back / of commerce". She rarely publishes her work, so having her poetry here is a very special sign that this is a quality publication.

Oh, and me, the Alhambra cosmic joker, publisher of the San Gabriel Valley Poetry Quarterly and host of Saturday Afternoon Poetry in Pasadena (both my self-serving vehicles to get me opportunities to commune with more and more poets). I've put forth two of my personal best for your approval (isn't that why we publish in the first place, for the encouragement), a sestina, "Green Bell Apples vs. Dreadful Toenail Assholes" and "Planet of the Oreos", which has been previously published in Poetry Midwest.

Hope you enjoy reading these as much as I enjoyed selecting them.

JIM BABWE

Sneakers

I don't remember
the whole list
you handed to me
but I do remember
how weird it was to read
your opinions about
the top ten
cutest things you do.

Taking photographs of Barbie on fire.

Pouring salt on snails.

Calling your old boyfriend's mother
and telling her you're the cop
who needs to speak with her son.

Using a familiar laxative
as an ingredient in brownies.

Some people wouldn't think
any of those are cute
or funny.

You asked me
whether I'd noticed
any changes in your dimples
and when I told you
No
I don't see any changes
you said
The psychiatrist agrees
that I should file for divorce
but he didn't suggest
that I return the turquoise sneakers
I stole
from the Goodwill store.

You asked me
whether I've always

liked girls who are not afraid
to steal.

You said

After all
I'm not a kleptomaniac.

Not until they catch me
but they won't
because I'm too cute.

Tell me I'm cute.

*Jim Babwe is a native Southern Californian living in Cardiff-by-the-Sea
where he creates art in the form of writing, photography, and a variety
of other multimedia experiments.*

CALOKIE

mini-gods

if your god can only be contacted
through your guru's cell phone
he's too small

if your creator said in 4004 b.c.
let earth and sky be
his universe is much too small

if the top one percent feast from
your heavenly father's banquet table
while the rest scramble for the scraps
and crumbs trickling down to them
his providence is much too small

if your divinity is offended by clerks
who wish customers happy holidays
instead of merry christmas
good lord
does he ever need
to lighten up

if your heavenly ceo is too busy
to return your call
you may be the one
who's too small

if your man upstairs can't be a she
then he's not only too small
he could also be a male calvinist

if your director of the celestial intelligence agency
likes to hire avengers to take care of the ungodly
i swear to god you ain't never gonna get that old boy
small enough

*Calokie is a retired LAUSD teacher. He was born
during the depression in Oklahoma and came to
California in 1959 and has lived here ever since.
His pen name was inspired by the Joads' struggle
for survival in The Grapes of Wrath and the songs
and life of Woody Gutherie...His poems have been
published in Blue Collar Review, Pearl, Prism and
also in the anthologies,* AN EYE FOR AN EYE
MAKES THE WHOLE WORLD BLIND *and* In the
Arms of Words: Poems for Tsunami Relief.

DON "KINGFISHER" CAMPBELL

Green Bell Apples vs. Dreadful Toenail Assholes

I want to write a poem about clipping one's toenails
That's my idea: to start with something dreadful
But then I think of what is even worse: assholes
And realize I need a pleasant counterbalance, like apples
A universally loved fruit, historically important, red or green
This contrasts wonderfully, causes my brain to ring like a bell

I decide I'll try to get every word to sound like a bell
For example, I dig the noise made by each clip of toenails
It's good to cut them, it's like eating something green
Which results in fine digestion, a subject considerably dreadful
To some, until you remind them that it is grown apples
Chewed and swallowed that help to unplug stopped assholes

You definitely want to keep doctors away from assholes
When they get a hold of you, you reverberate inside like a bell
Thus a diet of the good stuff is essential, like mature apples
And bananas and oatmeal and gelatin for your toenails
I hear it comes from animal fat--how nauseatingly dreadful
To contemplate--I've got to shift theme: a tree is green

That's better, our world is mostly filled with glorious green
Trees and bushes and grasses and hopefully not just assholes
That would be unpleasant, right? Another notion dreadful
Like oil slicks and car exhaust and stock traders clanging a bell
To signal the start of trading--there's a concept without visible toenails
How do we get back to nature in this concrete land of few apples

By focusing some time on what gives us a quality of living like apples
And take an afternoon off to walk in a park or wilderness that's green
A place where one can remove one's shoes, expose them toenails
Maybe even find a lonely spot to excrete onto dirt from assholes
Like design intended, remember we discovered how to cast a bell
Forge furnaces, direct sewage through corrugated pipes so dreadful

And what about us, the modernized people who've become dreadful
With our loud stereos, air conditioning, paper waste, prepackaged apples
Filling landfills and stopping up rivers--we need a real warning bell
To toll in our heads to call us to ponder again the value of green

Instead we drive and fly our cyberspaced opinions like assholes
Everybody's got a justification, but what about freeing those toenails

Yes, it's all down to toenails freedom or leather shoes dreadful
When it's the assholes that rule, we diminish the number of apples
So go for the green life and make your own cause a cleansing bell

*Don Kingfisher Campbell, listed in Poets and Writers, is the
founder of POETRY people youth writing workshops, publisher
of the San Gabriel Valley Poetry Quarterly, leader of the
Emerging Urban Poets writing and Deep Critique workshops,
and host of the Saturday Afternoon Poetry reading series in
Pasadena, California. Don is currently studying for an MFA
in Creative Writing at Antioch University, Los Angeles. He
has taught Creative Writing in the Upward Bound program
at Occidental College and been a Guest Teacher for the Los
Angeles Unified School District for 28 years.*

JOSEPH GARDNER

2.5 Grams of Hash

head like cotton
concern past and forgotten
I'm not even here I'm not even human
I don't exist;
lost in a different
brand new unexplored dimension
number 7 of the 10
string theory like an acoustic guitar
like ancient Hindu texts that read like German physicists
does anyone know the name of the cat in Schrodinger's damned box

lost
in the forest of my mind
contemplative head wandering in thoughts
what new wonders will I find

to leave me
like leaves from trees
drifting in breeze

twisting syllables
into tales
that tell parallels
of the loose perils
that we all face everyday
twisting syllables
into tales
that tell parallels
of the beautiful trials
we all face everyday

*Joe Gardner was born in June of '74, in San Bernadino, CA. At the age of two he moved to
Modesto, CA. At 13 he moved to L.A. County, to East Lakewood, CA. There he graduated from
Artesia High School in '92. From '93 to '96 he was a paratrooper in the United States Army.
From '96 to present he has walked the blue collar roads of America. Joe has previously been
published in Modern Drunkard Magazine and The San Gabriel Valley Poetry Quarterly.*

Norman J. Olson

JEFFRY JENSEN

Clogging Up Tradition

A hero for the ages, for the seas clogged
in the pipes of pregnant fishes.
Brooding inside the skull of Darwinism
ditched on Route 66 before cell phones
could find us in the wilderness with our
tongues up the ying or a mother's yang.
Enough space for a parable to fester
a compound eye to view the gravity
of little bodies to buttonhole a future
communal wrists flow with pronouncements
that blood is the footstool of tomorrow.
Eyebrows for eveningwear, shoelaces
for fact checkers who cannot spell
any Latin roots in public places.
Amateurs are bold with imaginative
answers to the physics of our fathers.
Average oxygen and Einstein
passes gas in the street of public opinion.
Repair the circuits with tapeworms
of trouble toil away on telescopes
too long vertical for their own good.
Comets chill the hands of children
delayed by ancestors of rural life.
Slippery to the touch, eternity itches
all the way back to a black hole of a beginning.

*Jerry Jensen is a native of Southern California, who is currently employed as
an adjunct reference / instruction librarian at Glendale Community College,
an instructor of Library Science 101 at Los Angeles Valley College, and a part-
time reference librarian with the Los Angeles Public Library. Over the last forty
years, his poetry has been included in various anthologies and journals. He is
the author of two nonfiction books and has written hundreds of scholarly articles
and books reviews for various reference publications.*

LALO KIKIRIKI

The Musician's Wife's Tale

Who says April is the cruelest month? – try August.
Parched, I go to the fridge
to score a Seagram's cooler
(I relish those sweet red drinks they call
strawberry
margaritas
though they're neither)
and there's not even one left!
You've drunk them all or served them to your
derelict musician friends and,
in their place,
(as if I wouldn't notice)
have stocked
a bitter dark ale
or something equally vile.
At first I'm pissed,
then I remember
my secret stash
in the downstairs icebox,
behind the drywall and the plywood sheets
you never managed to turn into a studio,
and that reminds me to get pissed again.
But I move aside the building materials,
open the icebox door, and DAMN!
you've got to those drinks, too,

and replaced them
with a rancid goat's head
you've been saving
from the last cabrita feast
for your album cover.
I head for the knife drawer…
Then I hear your Harley
roar into the drive…
"Hey, babe come see what I gotcha!"
and there's that ruby glint
at the top of the stairs.
I grab the fourpack, thinking,
"you just saved your life,"
"Hi boys" I smile,
as the rest of the band
files by.

*The illusive tejano poet **Lalo Kikiriki**, originally from Houston, arrived in Los Angeles in 1979, after publishing the dual chapbook* Old Movies/Other Visions *with Pamela Lynn Palmer. Previously host of KPFT's (Houston) Mandy in the Morning radio show, lalo has performed at venues all over Southern California and holds BA and MA degrees from California State Dominguez Hills.*

JULIE LEMAY

Emergency Room, Wednesday 4pm

He is patient 26 Hall,
as if an addict couldn't earn
an actual examination room in the E.R.
Sprawled in a hallway chair next to the nurses
station, black jeans and hooded
sweatshirt hang on his too-thin frame, two
sizes too big, an overage teen leaning
into a ruined adulthood.

Black ski goggles hang around his neck,
when he puts them on
he looks like a giant fly.
His gray mother perches on a swivel stool
like a dumbed parrot, studies
the flesh colored linoleum with confetti
pattern of yellow, red, green – all shades
of bodily fluids.

It's a two hour wait for the doctor who arrives
like a light breeze in his untouchable
hospital whites, erect from his polished
brown loafers to his perfect
blond haircut. He throws back his head
and laughs when 26 Hall says he doesn't know
whether to O.D.
or put a bullet in his head.

Two hours more and he limps
like a black beetle
to the end of the fluorescent-lit hall
where they have him check into detox
for a three-day hold.

Julie Hungiville LeMay *was born in*
Buffalo, New York and moved to Alaska's
MatanuskaValley where she has lived since
1978. Her work has been published in a number
of journals including Pilgrimage, Bluestem,
Sugar Mule, and The Mindfulness Bell.

JANICE LUO

In the Korean bathhouse

Someone else's mother
Is scrubbing down
Every inch of my body
From clavicle to toe
With a single piece of cloth
Coarser than sea salt
Shedding gray layers
Once invisible to the eye.

She wears the standard issue
Uniform of black lace
Bra and underwear.
So close, her cold belly
Sometimes slaps
Against my bare wet skin
A vague scent of kimchee
Emitting from hers.

Earlier, the question always asked,
"You Chinese or Japanese?"
And when she makes
The international gesture
For flipping over
Then gently pats my leg
I turn over obediently
Both of us giggling
When I start to slip
And slide uncontrollably
From side to side
On the beige gurney
Bolted to the ground.

A few hours later
I emerge from the heaven
Of perpetual steam
Into the dry asphalt heat
Of Koreatown, LA
All along Western Avenue
Rainbow-signed restaurants
Displaying photos

Of raw meat
No English translation needed
Just the giant letters "BBQ"

Cross Wilshire Boulevard
A dessert café
Specializing in fruit
With red beans and ice cream
On top of shaved ice.
Through its large window
I see myself glistening
A mermaid in sunlight
Smelling sweet as a soufflé
Now lighter than air.

*Janice Ko Luo is a writer and lawyer
based in Los Angeles. She practices
immigration law and is finishing up her
MFA in Creative Writing at Antioch
University. Currently, she is the Poetry
Editor for the University's literary
journal* Lunch Ticket.

Robert Branaman

RADOMIR LUZA

Cleveland

The Starbucks on West 6th matters tonight
It slices through the poetry critic in my head like
The birth of death

Over there on the intersection of asphalt and pain the city stops making sense
It is a brown flamingo a flying submarine an undiscovered leper colony

Girls walk down Superior thumb prints in caffeine jungle nonfat milk not included
Boys sashay Lake Erie buttons bend below cuff
Water runs through levee of lips

Fish lying still
Finding me away from me
Raping the riverbed of retreat

The love we share
The backs I break
Cleveland free me
Squeeze me
Believe me

The easy way is getting harder
The numbness of instinct
The intrusion of genius
The arrogance of confidence

Your warehouses and flats
Buy words my sweaters take
My angels fake
My sister makes
Your rivers snake and shake through castrated causeways and bulletproof heartaches

At the parking lot across from the steak house I park my ulcer red Pontiac rent-a-car
And give Sam the attendant four dollars. I give the homeless guy down the block 35
Cents. After buying a Plain Dealer newspaper from a bilge box across the street I admit it
To myself: it is your people Cleveland your black, your red, your white, your green
Your baritone meadows and your rustic rattlesnakes
You close earlier than death my Midwestern mohawk
You open later than life Ohio ovary
Over there by the chophouse children lean on charred chandeliers and press tomatoes
Born while they ruled the universe in naked pinstripes
Cleveland you are my father
Guarding borders with sunflowers

Radomir Vojtech Luza owes his love of poetry and art to his father Radomir Sr. and mother Libuse. Radomir Sr. was a resistance fighter during WWII and Libuse studied at the Czech National Dramatic Conservatory before Adolf Hitler closed it down. They then both escaped Communism in their beloved Czechoslovakia in 1948. Luza has published over 20 collections of poetry and has been published by over 40 literary journals, anthologies and websites. Luza has featured 70+ times across the country and organized a dozen readings including UNBUCKLED: NOHO POETRY at T.U. Studios and ALLITERATION ALLEY at Republic of Pie, both in North Hollywood, CA where Luza lives.

LISA MARIE SANDOVAL

Name on the Wall

77,000 names of exterminated Jews
paint the walls of Pinkasova Sýnagóga, Prague

Your letters stretch across stone
living sideways twelve feet
high and floating. Your syllables
in graved silence sing. Your wife's memories
mold to the drone of the cantor's moan,
as he intones the sound of you.

Sheathed in black, she mutters pearls of prayer,
while white tendrils bow at her temple.
She sweeps them away
with no word. Her lips linger
pressing a kiss
over the chilly, white-washed rock.
Like David's Bathsheba
she wraps herself in the mention of you
while the sound of her soul
disintegrates through
shudders and weeps.

In decades past, before the wall,
your own voice used to wisp and
curl by menorah light on those sweet Sabbath nights.
Flames draped the sweet scent of your woman,
this woman, veiled in the shadows. Now
the old man from next door still
watches and desires her, as he used to do so long ago.

Lisa Marie Sandoval is a nationally published performance artist and two-time City of L.A. Artist-in-Residence, best known for The Yowling & Other Sounds from Highland Park: *a poetry collection (tcCreativePress), one-woman show, and congressionally awarded urban youth project. Her work has been published in* The Southern California Anthology, The Christian Century, Texas Poetry Review, *among others. She recently launched YowlingCreator.com, an interactive blog to help people birth their passion, also a how-to book recently picked up by an agent. She presently teaches for the University of La Verne and Azusa Pacific University. For more info: YowlingCreator.com and TheYowling.com.*

MARY TORREGROSSA

At Mack's

At Mack's Auto Parts & Repair
the great wind turbine
affixed to the ceiling
has only one slow rotation speed

After twelve thousand miles
of freeways and turnpikes,
a blackened Super Tech filter
sits on a countertop
polished to a worn patina
by the push and push back
of commerce.

I wait my turn as pistons
slide across the surface -
battery, tail light, serpentine belt,
oil pump, camshaft, caliper.
My starter won't turn over.
My ignition has lost its spark.
I need a new wheel stud.

The parts guy only looks up
to confirm the order,
a heavy gold cross
hangs from a chain
under his open-collar blue shirt.

I sense the customer behind me,
catch a whiff of his cologne
mixed with sweat.

A woman straddles a Harley
in a poster selling bolts.

It occurs to me, sure
as the price of gas
rises in the morning
no one in this shop
uses a condom.

Mary Torregrossa is originally from Rhode Island and now lives in Southern California where she teachers ESL at the El Monte Adult School. She has been a member of the Emerging Urban Poets in Pasadena, Poets Conspiracy, Poets in Distress, and the Pack Rat Poets. Her poems have appeared in several writing group anthologies, as well as RI Roads Travel Magazine, poetic diversity, suddenprovidence, Inscape, Poetry and Cookies, and the SGV Quarterly. Mary has taught poetry workshops to children, youth and adults. She is a community activist working on issues such as anti-racism, immigration and life- long learning.

THE POETRY III

Zoot Sims Crying

softly

through the gruesome
plaster walls

There were bloody
screams earlier
of fuck you ,asshole!
and I'll kill you, bitch!

And something horrid
like screaming death pounding
again and again

on the unyielding linoleum floor

But now there is only jagged
laughter, the clanging of glasses

and Zoot Sims his sax
crying Autumn Leaves

softly

through the gruesome
plaster walls

so softly

    it breaks my heart

again

    Doug Draime

First appeared in Gargoyle.

Doug Draime *emerged as a presence in
the small press and 'underground' literary
movement in Los Angeles in the late 1960's.
Forthcoming full-length collection,* More
Than The Alley, *from Interior Noise Press in
2012. Always on the outlook for prospective
publishers for both new and older work.
Nominated for several Pushcart Prizes in last
few years. He lives in the foothills of Oregon
with his wife and family.*

THE BOSTON POETRY SCENE

by Doug Holder

IN A CITY WITH OVER 100 COLLEGES and universities in the immediate vicinity, a poet outside of the academy could feel lost, a fish out of water, a veritable barbarian at the gate. So what I have been doing is working in the grassroots— forming a community of writers independent of the tweed people who hand out foundation grants, and the like. The poets I have decided to present on these pages are part of the community of poets I am part of, and poets that I admire. All of them are accomplished—a lot of them collect pay stubs from a variety of jobs that keep them afloat.

About a decade ago, a good friend of mine Harris Gardner (Founder of Tapestry of Voices in Boston) and I formed an informal literary group in Harvard Square, outside the ivied gates of Harvard Yard. Now this group called the *Bagel Bards*, (that later relocated to Somerville, Mass at a local Au Bon Pain Café) has about 80 members, with a core of 25 people that meet every Saturday morning rain or shine. From this group come a yearly anthology, and online magazine *Wilderness House Literary Review*, and a great place for poets and writers all stripes to congregate.

There are a number of literary camps in the Boston area. The slam poets strut their stuff and attitude at the *Cantab* Lounge in Cambridge; there is a saucy mix of jazz and poetry at the Lizard Lounge in Cambridge hosted by Jeff Robinson; there are the *Stone Soup Poets*, directed by Chad Parenteau, who meet at the Out of the Blue Gallery in Cambridge, Harris Garner and Gloria Mindock run *The First and Last Word Series* in Somerville, and the list goes on.

All these venues are fed by the rich mother-lode of artists, poets, etc… that resides in the area. At times these groups clash, as writers tend to be passionate, and mercurial—especially around their work—and of course there are many fragile egos to be nursed.

On these fertile literary grounds we have any number of magazines, both university affiliated like *AGNI, SALMANDER, PLOUGHSHARES,* but also many small presses that print books and journals. Offhand I can name the *Off the Grid Press, The Cervena Barva Press, Pressed Wafer, Inman Journal, South Boston Literary Review, Ibbetson Street, Loom Press,* and *Upstreet.*

I guess what I am saying is the Boston area is a great place to be a poet. Whatever your sensibility, your school, you can find your match here. And like the *Mimeograph Revolution* in the 60's in New York City there is a plethora of small presses sprouting up to give you an opportunity to get your work out there. I don't think there is a night without some event happening—somewhere.

The poets on these pages are small press poets, publishers, social workers, drug counselors, art teachers, artists, editors, adjunct instructors, literary activists, and yes even a professor or two. The group is a microcosm of what's out there. But I do think they offer a flavor of the *Paris of New England* that I call our special neck of the woods.

Doug Holder
Somerville, Mass. July, 2012.

DAN SKLAR

A TIME OF HORSES

I want to live
in a time of horses,
a time of horses.
The country went to hell
when the horses went away.
You had to ride a horse to get
to Appomattox when horses
were still the principal means
of transportation. I mean,
what is more dramatic
than Robert E. Lee riding
his horse, Traveler,
to surrender

the southern troops
to Ulysses S. Grant
and the northern troops?
You cannot tell me
that Lee did not know
this day was coming.
Walt Whitman
had a horse named Nina
when he started
The Long Islander
before he wrote poetry.
He said the first time
he knew he wanted
to be a writer was when
he saw a sailboat
on the water
and wanted to describe it.
I imagine he had a horse
named Prospero when
he wrote Leaves of Grass.
I think it is important that
people ride horses
to get to the places
they need to go.
Instead of a horse,
I ride a bicycle.
There is no hurry
on a horse,
unless it is
the Pony Express
or you are Butch Cassidy
or someone like that,
and there is no hurry
on a bicycle.
The only hurry is when
you are going to see
the ones you love.

Dan Sklar *teaches writing at Endicott College. Recent publications include Harvard Review, New York Quarterly, Ibbetson Street Press, and The Art of the One Act. His play, "Lycanthropy" was performed at the Boston Theater Marathon in May.*

ZVI A. SESLING

Blame

How easy when they are gone
to blame the dead
Our faults reflected in their
weaknesses
Adultery or theft
Power hungry or corruption
Failure or drunk driver
We rely on ourselves
in our cage
the eggs we lay rotten
our inner snake swallowing
truth
Pattern develop, exist, repeat
like a journal of unsworn
entries
Reality a forged document

Zvi A. Sesling has published poetry widely in numerous magazines including Ibbetson St., Poetica, Voices Israel, Asphodel, Haz Mat Review, Istanbul Literary Review, Chiron Review and Main Street Rag. In 2008 he was selected to read his poetry at New England/Pen "Discovery" by Boston Poet Laureate Sam Cornish. He is a regular reviewer for the Boston Small Press and Poetry Scene and is Editor of the Muddy River Poetry Review. He is author of King of the Jungle, *(Ibbetson St., 2010); a chapbook,* Across Stones of Bad Dream *(Cervana Barva, 2011) and a second full length poetry book,* Fire Tongue *to be published by Cervena Barva Press in 2012. He lives in Brookline MA with his wife Susan Dechter.*

TIMOTHY GAGER

walking out of the woods

there's a condom and ten suboxone
in the inside jacket pocket
but I won't use

either

it's been awhile
or there's a tree
standing in the forest,
gracefully not falling
not seen, except
through the branches,
there is brilliant blue,
look up,
god.
look up.

Timothy Gager is the author of nine books of poetry and fiction. He lives on www.timothygager.com

Raindog

DEBORAH FINKELSTEIN

Self-Portrait

I am a child of photographs and language.
Commuters mistake me for a student
but bartenders have stopped carding me.
I am a child of Chernobyl and the Challenger,
born after Kennedy and Watergate.
Watched The Secret of NIMH and E.T.,
learned not to trust the government,
like the vets outside my window
blocked by my sheers.
I am sheltered in a world of purple
where Pavarotti sings Christmas music,
I pretend he's still alive
as blossoms dance off my tree,
a feast for my eyes
enemies of my nose,
they do cartwheels over tree roots
spinning around the porch.
Is there enough haiku in the world
to capture all these moments?
I grew up with Polaroids
expensive film meant
this moment was worth capturing.
That camera is long gone,
now I whisper about my day
as I lie next to you
in the light of the gas station
that we pretend is the moon.
Sometimes we create our own beauty.

Deborah Finkelstein has an MFA in Creative Writing from Goddard College. Her poetry has been published in anthologies, newspapers, and literary magazines in 7 countries as well as online. She has also published plays, and short stories. She teaches Creative Writing at Endicott College.

ROBERT K. JOHNSON

Two Portraits

The moment I met her,
    for me

the sadness in her voice,
so quiet and so complete,

was a forest cabin
I, hurt and lost,

was sure I could
find comfort in

--learning later
her sadness

had no room
    for other people.

Robert K. Johnson is a retired Professor of English who taught for many years at Suffolk University in Boston. He was also the Poetry Editor for Ibbetson Street magazine for several years. His poems have appeared in a variety of magazines. His newest collection of poems is Choir Of Day/New and Selected Poems.

HARRIS GARDNER

Bombs Away

Say kisses A-bomb the wobbly world.
Masses dance in the fallout of falling petals.
Nuclear warheads have a falling-out; can't agree
on a plan to counter-attack. They unfurl a white flag
that boasts a pair of pursed lips.
Uncoupled missiles touch head to head.
They lack the power of a deluge of flowers.

Throngs crown the silos with wreathes and roses.
The bombs stand mute in disarray.
Their pink slips are en route to the ticker tape parade.
The blast of one billion blossoms defuses brute strength.

Touch is tops, tangos in streets.
Creative ways to compete:
"My smooches are softer than yours," some say.
"Our sugar is sweeter," others reply.
Saccharine songs muscle along.
"Just one tender…, so much bliss."
 Molasses oozing grip.

Interlocking linguae intoxicate.
Corks cannonade; frothy bubbles flood avenues.
Wine-stained mouths march to rapturous hymns.
"All we are saying is give love a chance."

A sudden roar, and all eyes leap skyward.
Fleets of missiles flout their escape
from an unfamiliar earth.
"We're going to the moon," they shout.
Luna is for lovers, voices trumpet.
"Not when we get there," the grim bombs sneer.-
A new mantle of fear.

Harris Gardner is founder of the literary outreach program Tapestry of Voices in Boston. Gardner is also the founder of the Boston National Poetry Festival held each April at the main branch of the Boston Public Library. His work has appeared in Ibbetson Street, Harvard Review, Jewish Advocate, Endicott Review, Fulcrum and many others.

GLORIA MINDOCK

Skin

120 chemicals are on my face today to
keep it youthful, pretty, something you
will want to look at.
Eyeliner, how many in that?
Eye shadow, lipstick, moisturizer, mascara,
the number rises, and oh, to take it off!
To think men only use 80 on their skin.

Day after day, what I do will cause damage,
vanity for Cancer or some other disease.
To die at an earlier rate for that perfect smile,
that face with no crows feet.
If I kiss you, will our chemicals combine and
reach 200, combust into some sort of monster,
with a plastic face or will our faces melt into
each others and form one big glob?
No wrinkles there-
Where is the nose? I think that's an eye.

Either way you look at it, the chemicals are
changing the skin.
Now instead of that fresh glow,
you get a fresh growth.
Lumps here and there and brown spots so
you add more chemicals to stop that.
Now we're up to probably 20-40 more chemicals and
if you are alive after this, good!
If not, time for embalming fluid, more chemicals.
Either way, you are doomed.
Give up. Enjoy your wrinkles.
Float a boat in them.

Robert Branaman

Gloria Mindock *is the author of* La Porţile Raiului *(Ars Longa Press, 2010, Romania) translated
into the Romanian by Flavia Cosma,* Nothing Divine Here *(U Šoku Štampa, 2010, Montenegro),
and* Blood Soaked Dresses *(Ibbetson, 2007). She is editor of Červená Barva Press and the
Istanbul Literary Review. Gloria's poetry has been translated into Romanian, Serbian, Spanish,
and French. Widely published in the USA and abroad, her poetry recently appeared in Levure
Littéraire (France), Vatra Veche (Romania) and in the anthology Hildagards Daughters
(Belgium). Gloria's flash fiction can be found in the new issue of Thrice.*

DOUG HOLDER

Eating Grief at Bickford's
(From Allen Ginsberg's "Kaddish")

There are no places anymore
Where I can sit at a threadbare table
Pick at the crumbs on my plate
And wipe
The white dust
From my pitch
Black shirt.
The old men
Who used to spout
Marxist
Rants from
The cracked porcelain of their cups
Are gone
The boiling water
Ketchup soup
The mustard sandwich
They use to relish
All that so lean
Cuisine.
Oh, Hunchback
In the corner
Your lonely reflection
In the glass of water—
And Tennessee Williams' Blanche
Eyes me through her grilled cheese
"Pass the sugar, sugar"
She teases.
Maynard
The queer
Late night
Security guard.
His policeman's hat
Draped on his head
Looking like a
Sacrilegious rake
This countless
Renditions
Of defending his honor
In the amorous, crazed embraces

Of muscular young men
How he protests…
Too much…too much.
The discarded men
Blue blazers
Shedding their threads
Outcasts with newspapers
Stains of baked beans
On their lapels
Fingering a piece
Of passionless Cod
Lolled by their
own murmur.
Winter is outside the large, long window
Pushing pedestrians
With its cold, snapping whip
The cracks in the pavement
Are filled
With flakes of melting,
Dying, snow.

Doug Holder *is the founder of the Ibbetson Street Press. Holder's work has appeared in the LUMMOX Journal, Poesy, Rattle, The Boston Globe, Endicott Review, and many other magazines, etc… He teaches writing at Endicott College in Beverly, Mass. and Bunker Hill Community College in Boston.*

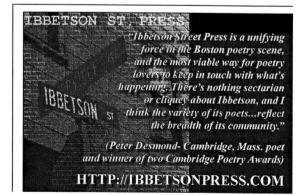

DENNIS DALY

Dead Horse Beach

After the pipe had burst,
The crew from public works
At the scene dug the trench
The horses evident,

Drawn into the dig's wall
Like stone-age artifacts
Or an artist's drawing
From antiquity's face.

The dour Puritans dropped
Their dead horses, ditched them
Here, flung them off wagons
On this remote, wild beach.

Later the name caught on,
Lost meaning. Old photos
Of wooden barrels stacked
On this same spot; a new

Century celebrates
Liberty. A bonfire
Flames, a pyre of cheers
Over crumbling bones.

Dennis Daly is the author of the poetry collection The Custom House *(Ibbetson Street Press). His work has appeared in the* Muddy River Review, Dark Horse, Soundings East, Istanbul Literary Review, *and many others.*

IRENE KORONAS

maybe its simple

maybe its as simple
as that. she just wanted
to live her life

yes there would always
be thorns, thistle picked
the wrong way

walking the tracks

slipping out

skirting town

chewing her nails

she didn't give in to him
all the many many hims
tramping through the back yard

sure the sticky burrs caught onto
his pant legs. everyone knew where
the burr patch was. did him have to
take it all. did him have to widen the path
between fences

when the roses were in full bloom
yellow, white, red, pink and orange,
rental gladiola, chickens in the garage.
did him have to cut off the heads

maybe its as simple as picking roses

holding the stem in the right place

she didn't think about chickens,
all the hims. he wasn't the first to kill

hell. this is all she talked about.
count on that and there was no escape

herself in a vase

Irene Koronas is the poetry editor for Wilderness House Literary Review.. Her poetry has appeared in many publications, on line journals and anthologies. With two full length books, 'Self Portrait Drawn From Many,' Ibbetson Street Press, 2007, 'Pentakomo Cyprus' Cervena Barva Press' 2009. Her most recent chapbooks, 'Zero Boundaries', Cervena Barva Press, 2008 and 'Emily Dickinson," Propaganda Press, 2010. She is also a member of Bagel with the Bards, which meets Saturday mornings. Bagel Bards is a community of writers who exchange literary information.

SAM CORNISH

Old Men in the Check-out Line

The old men   you see them
In the check-out line

Waiting with their peas
String beans and Wonderbread

The steak and hot dogs
For the grill

White men   creases in their red
Back year necks   old

Men grandfathers sons
Brothers   waiting

For the cashier   in their bright
Shirts   black string ties

On Sunday   the spit-
Polished shoes

The serious Sunday suit
They don't talk

Much
These men of the Great

War

*Since 2008, **Sam Cornish** has been the Poet Laureate of Boston. He is the author of seven books of poetry, the most recent of which is* Dead Beats *(Ibbetson Street Press, 2011. He is currently teaching poetry workshops at the Boston Public Library at Copley Square. In February 2012, a theatre presentation of his book* An Apron Full of Beans *was presented at the Boston Latin Academy, Roxbury Community College and the Boston Public Library. He is the recipient of an NEA Award, the St. Botolph Society Foundation Award and the Somerville Arts/Ibbetson Press Lifetime Achievement Award as well as a nominee for an ALA Notable Book Award and a ForeWord Magazine Finalist, 2008.*

THE POETRY IV

I went to a poetry reading, and all I got was this lousy poem

Traveling down a long dark road
Through the hills
Many miles
To see a poet who traveled many more miles
Than me
I walked up the stairs to the second floor bar

I ordered a beer
And sat at a table, alone-

Mark Hartenbach

I waited
For the reading to start

I ordered another beer

The young poets were drinking, chatting, laughing,
signing up to read after the feature poet finished.
They wore no wrinkles
The men were prettier than the women

I ordered another beer

The people next to me talked poetry and politics
And knew little about both

I ordered another beer

The feature poet was in the back of the room
Alone, reading to himself

A football game was on TV
I would rather talk football than poetry, but I was the only one watching the game
It was time to leave

I walked down the stairs and to my car
Traveled back down the long dark road
Through hills
Many miles
To my neighborhood bar
Where people wore wrinkles
The women were prettier than the men
And nobody talked poetry

Edward Jamieson Jr.

*My name is **Edward Jamieson, Jr.** I've been writing poetry for
many years but not as often as I once did. At one time I was poetry
editor for LUMMOX Journal, so many years ago. Now, I'm busy
driving to work and driving back home.*

POTENTIAL ENERGY IN POETRY

by Ed Nudelman

WE SPEAK OF POETRY, FINE POETRY, AS having movement or cadence. A great poem goes somewhere, and the greatest poets, with their words, lead the reader someplace they haven't been before. This quality or distinction can be thought of as a kind of stored energy, or more properly, potential energy. A large rock on the ground has little potential energy, but if you place it on the top of a large hill, it has the ability to unleash energy on its downward roll. Great poetry that illuminates and changes hearts and minds often accomplishes this with an explosive force. But you don't have to be knocked over in your chair. It can happen in an instant, the first couple of words or in the very last line, in reflecting on a feeling or in strikingly simple, yet evocative, phraseology: "The woods are lovely, dark and deep," is an image with energy because it unleashes the poet's ambivalence and wonder, achieved only through his mastery of preceding lines.

When I look for good poetry, I look for energy, not obsessively, but intuitively. Has the poem earned the right to move me? Has it laid a groundwork of tension or drawn me into a problem, a bewildering decision, a picture of unrest or tension? Is there something compelling to resolve. Not all great poems achieve this, but many do.

In **Patricia Fargnoli**'s poems, I'm never left unmoved, and I've read many. Her poetry seems to effortlessly glide down the page, and somewhere along the way you realize you've been transported from one room to another, from one vantage point to a much higher view. In *Hunger*, the lift is almost imperceptible, but the view from the trees is as provocative as unsettling:

> *It is the gnawing within the silence*
> *of the deep body which is like*
> *the pool a waterfall replenishes*
> *but can never fill.*

In the poem, through beautiful word choice and imagery, the difficulty of need and the strain of wanting is brought steadily forward, until the poem turns on the poet's own reflection. The reader is drawn back to familiar ground, to emblems of shared experience, "the rain which comes in to my house through the untidy gardens..." "Summer is dying and I grow closer to the shadow moving toward me..." "And the wind stirs, rattles the panels singing its own water song." A lovely, if not haunting poem.

I am drawn to these kinds of poems that swell with passion and color, but do so unpretentiously, hidden in the craft and dexterity of a poet's meandering eye. **Grace Cavalieri**'s poetry emits this kind of *heat*, which is easily seen in a poem with one of the best titles I've seen in a long time: *Here is a Poem You Can Hide In*. This poem packs its potential energy at the very outset: "When you come to wherever failed hopes go, turn here instead..." And the aforementioned *here* is superbly brought out and expanded as you move down the poem with the senses, through a child's voice, through snow, and then inwardly, looking at success and failure, aloneness, solitude. Finally, the energy is released at the end, almost literally, "under the same sun and same moon,"

> *above darkness,*
> *right here, the source of prayer,*
> *right here in my hand.*

Sam Rasnake's poetry, riffing off idioms or immediate experience, often displays this kind of energy in his artful appeal to the senses. In *A Day in the Life*, I'm piqued by both visual and audio imagery, not unlike flying down the road in an XKE, switching songs and living the life of each one. The energy in the poem presented lies in its ability to tap into the reader's personal identification. Rasnake freely exchanges from sense to idea, song to song, reflection to excitement, to achieve a powerful and witty surrealistic poem.

I've loved the work of **Pris Campbell** for years, a poet who draws heavily on her own experience, transposing her ideas into beautiful, if not tempestuous, flowing streams. Her poems are often tinged with a bit of sorrow, and the energy from the burst of telling seems to go on, well after the poem is read. *Moonlight Rider* is such a poem; it keeps on burning with its lament and its almost irretrievable plaintive cry. She masters the art, here, of peeling away layers of pain and loss, beyond the physicality of succumbing to a wasting disease ("It wasn't so much/ that she minded her hair loss, hiding the thick black locks…") extending into a sorrowful image of apparent futility and the foggy world of irreconcilable differences.

> *…be Bess all over again, breastbone shattered into a thousand irretrievable memories, trying to save what could never be saved from the get-go.*

Reading a **Tara Birch** poem is often an exercise in patience. You see the long lines and stanzas below, and you begin to read too fast, trying to get to the bottom of the waterfall. When you finally get there, you can take a breath and then go back up and read it again with more clarity (my method). The energy in her poems is often cascading, pouring downhill, and in the flow, you're filled with manifold sensual data. The poem presented here puts you unilaterally into the scene (i.e. written forcefully, in the second person). You're already going down the chute whether you want to or not. I like that quality, and a good deal of authorial self-assurance comes through. In, *The red motel*, though particulars of separation and alienation are not made clear, what ultimately impresses, and provides tension release, is the speaker's

triumphant exultation of action and resolve.

An interesting and provocative way **Aaron Belz** tells us about his world is through humor. An accomplished poet and noted standup comic, he delivers his wit in discrete bundles, not all at once, but often throughout the whole poem, interspersed and well-placed. I love the sardonic voice in *Thomas Hardy the Tank Engine*, where he lets us know right off the bat (and from here on): "my poetry shall be like Thomas Hardy's…" However, we're immediately dispatched into a wild and whacky sketch of all there is that is *not to be liked* in Thomas Hardy's poetry. Which is what I love about the poem, its topsy-turvy structure, its devilishly honest tone and phrasing. And it doesn't hurt to know a little about Belz, who really doesn't write much at all about 'dying trees' and the "sadness that creeps into love." And what of potential energy? Well, read the last line!

April Ossmann is a poet with a great heart and a broad mind, and one to look for in your bookstore wanderings. Her poetry is always tightly written with impeccable word choice and powerful, compelling imagery. *Infidelity* delivers a wallop, this taut poem of couplets with its deceptively gentle tone. But the energy forms here early, in the subtlety of the context, and in the intimacy shared in a direct way (in the first person). I especially like the way she uses language itself, as if a disinterested party,

Norman J. Olson

to draw us almost sideways into the central argument ("its syllables tumbling so readily/ off the tongue, the tongue slapping lightly, repeatedly…"). The gut is soured by a bad taste before anything is eaten: the ease by which a sorrow can take root. The imagery in this poem is so palpable and appropriate; no words are used that don't perfectly bring home the poet's intent. And there is one word in this poem that brings a lump into my throat and leaves it there; and that word is "solo."

I wish I had more time and space to talk more about these poets and all the poems presented here, just a sampling, and a small one at that. But, I hope you'll find what I've seen and admired in these artists, a willingness to share their lives and experiences in a meaningful way through their words. Each and every poem here is charged with the hidden powder of explosive feeling, purpose and energy.

Ed Nudelman

AARON BELZ

Thomas Hardy the Tank Engine

From now on my poetry
shall be like Thomas Hardy's—
I shall write about ponds
and about dying trees

and of the sadness that creeps
into love, over time—
and that life is absurd
and death sublime.

And I shall be like Hardy
in the way that I think,
no longer contemplating
my kitchen sink,

its bottle of Dawn
and unwashed dishes—
instead, haphazardness
and lovelorn wishes.

But I shall not grow
a broad mustache
and wax it each day
into a flamboyant swash

or wear a starchy shirt
with its collar sticking up
or drink expensive tea
from an overly tiny cup

to emphasize how big
the head of an author
tends to be,
nor shall I bother

to refer to myself
as the tank engine.
People already know
I'm a tank engine.

*Originally published in
Court Green 6 (2009)*

Tilling Charles Reznikoff's Back

Tilling Charles Reznikoff's back yard
Brought up a dozen lions and several patches
Of wildebeest hearts.

The home itself sat lively in endless shadow,
Its picture windows gazing half-wittedly
In five directions.

Inside, a phone sang triumphantly,
The sole technological hormone driving
Countless blushing shutters.

But my errand had to do with grass,
So I sat and thought alone in endless shadow,
Speaking to myself

On the bed of wild violet that formed a border
Between Charles Reznikoff's back yard
And my own,

Making no sound. Making no sound.
Making no sound. As I stood to look around,
Verbs fell everywhere.

His awkward roof repelled them blankly,
Staring wakefully over the wild, half-witted yard
That formed its bed.

Downfall morphed into downpour, and of a
sudden
Cartoon-like animals emerged from thickets,
Surrounding that home,

And I must have looked like a startled duck,
Trees above my head whipping madly,
A car pulling up.

Such a schedule had been in my mind,
Such a tedious map, that could not even hear
The writer at work.

Originally published in Drunken Boat 9 (2007)

Aaron Belz is the author of The Bird Hoverer
(BlazeVOX, 2007) and Lovely, Raspberry *(Persea,
2010). His poetry has appeared in Boston Review,
Gulf Coast, Painted Bride Quarterly, Exquisite
Corpse, Mudfish, Jacket, Fine Madness, Fence
and many other poetry journals. Recently, Aaron
has appeared in comedy venues such as the
Tomorrow Show (Steve Allen Theater), Comedy
Meltdown, the New Orleans Comedy Arts Festival,
and Comedy on Parade.*

APRIL OSSMANN

Infidelity

I never stopped to consider
its less illicit pleasures:

its syllables tumbling so readily
off the tongue, the tongue

slapping lightly, repeatedly,
the roof of the mouth, the mouth

left open, as if with expectation,
or in surprise, or song—this solo

which leaves you alone,
holding the final note.

(first published in *The Spoon River Poetry
Review*)

How Like a Dog

Because he likes cats,
he doesn't realize how like a dog

he pets her—with the patience
bordering on impatience

one allots a too affectionate dog;
petting and worrying

she might do something distasteful
or inappropriate—lick his legs,

drool, or show an unwelcome interest
in his crotch, when all he wants

is to leave with his conscience clear:
she wants affection; he grants it.

She, like any dog, knows the rules
of *this* game: gratitude

for any stick thrown,
however feebly.

(first published in *Prairie Schooner*)

April Ossmann is the author of Anxious
Music *(Four Way Books, 2007). She is a
publishing, writing and editing consultant
(www.aprilossmann.com), and teaches
poetry at The Writer's Center in White River
Junction, VT. She is among the inaugural
faculty for the low-residency MFA in
Creative Writing Program at Sierra Nevada
College at Lake Tahoe; and was executive
director of Alice James Books from 2000 -
2008. She lives in Post Mills, VT.*

PATRICIA FARGNOLI

Hunger

It is the gnawing within the silence
of the deep body which is like
the pool a waterfall replenishes
but can never fill.
The watery room of the body
and its voices who call and call
wanting something more, always more.

Once in a dream, the trees in a peach orchard
called out saying: Here, this bright fruit,
hold its roundness in your palm,
and I held one, wanting
the others I could not hold,
as the light fell through the trees,
one cascade after another.

Now, the wind, from the hurricane,
that veered out to sea,
and the hard rain, blow through the space
where yesterday men felled the spruce,
its height and beauty, for no good reason.
Where it was, only emptiness remains,
and the stump, level with the ground.

The wind finds its own place
and waits there holding its breath
for a moment, calling to no one,
surprising us by its stillness,
surprising even the rain which comes in
to my house through the untidy gardens
where it has been sending its life breath
over the dying mint and blood red daylilies.

Summer is dying and I grow closer
to the shadow moving toward me
like the small spiders
that inhabit and hunt in the corners.
And the wind stirs, rattles the panels
singing its own hunger, its own water song.

(first published in *Harvard Review*)

Prepositions Toward a Definition of God

Beneath of course the sky,
in the sky itself,
over there among the beach plum hedges,

over the rain and the beyond and
beyond the beyond of,

under the suitcases of the heart,
from the back burners of the universe.

Here inside at the table, there outside the circus,
within the halls of absence,
across the hanging gardens of the wind,

between the marshland sedges, around the edges
of tall buildings going up
and short buildings coming down.

Of energy and intelligence,
of energy-- and if not intelligence then what?

Ahead of the storm and the river, behind the storm and the river.
Prior to the beginning of dust, unto the end of fire.

Above the wheelbarrows and the chickens.
Underneath the fast heart of the sparrow,
on top of the slow heart of the ocean--

against the framework of all the holy books.
Despite the dogmas that rain down on the centuries.
Concerning the invisible, and unnamable power,
in spite of the terror

considering the spirit,
because of something in the body that wants to be lifted.

Because if not God, then what in place of

near the firebombed willow,
beneath the quilt that tosses the dead to the sky,

beside the still waters and the loud waters
and among the walking among?

(first published in *Massachusetts Review*; published
in *Then, Something*, Tupelo Press, copyright 2009
Patricia Fargnoli. Used with permission).

Patricia Fargnoli, the NH Poet Laureate, 2006-
2009, has published three award-winning books of
poetry and 3 chapbooks. She's received an honorary
BFA from the NH Institute of Art and a MacDowell
fellowship. Her poems have been published widely
in such journals as: Poetry, Ploughshares, Harvard
Review, Rattle, Poetry International and in
translation in China and Turkey.

GRACE CAVALIERI

Here Is A Poem You Can Hide In

When you come to wherever
failed hopes go, turn
here instead,
where my child's voice is heard
in the night, still damp from dreams.

Talk of sweet surrender against the
February snow, and then turn inward,
where silver trims the bitter limbs.

I'm not afraid to mention
precious aspirations, and
all we know went wrong,

I'm here with you,
under the same sun and same moon,
above darkness,
right here, the source of prayer,
right here in my hand.

(first published in *Sounds Like Some-*
thing I Would Say, (Casa Menendez)

HIV

The Chelsea Hotel was the most
exciting place I'd ever been –
where artists in the grand
tradition had always lived and worked,
high arched ceilings, marble mantels,
I, anxious to meet my friend, called,
"Take me, Taxi,"…"to the Chelsea."
This was it. New York City. So
Greg had finally made it,
Visiting was like our casual talks
in Houston; he'd made an apple pie,
unwrapped my book, inscribed to him,
touched and kissed the cover. 1984.
Downstairs is where his lover lived, a
slim and gentle Japanese, critics called
a genius, the loveliest man
you'll ever meet, moving like an angel
across the room to point to paintings
standing free, large as his entire
wall, canvasses of angles, pale pure
yellow spheres barely there, creamy lemon
moving through a distant light, transparence
stirred with breath so slight
the drifting images melted through me,
and then within the month it takes for
oil paint to dry, they were all gone.

(first published in *Sit Down Says Love*
(Argonne House)

Grace Cavalieri *celebrates 35 years on air*
with her series "The Poet and the Poem,"
now produced at the Library of Congress
for public radio. She has 16 books and
chapbooks of poetry published and several
plays produced on American stages: "Anna
Nicole:Blonde Glory" was in NYC 2011,
"Quilting the Sun" in S.C., 2011.

SAM RASNAKE

A Day in the Life

Someone left the cake out in the rain –
Mayflies and Pachelbel, then Boo Radley.
A hot summer's night, the world drifting on
without them. They slip unnoticed between
waking and silence, commit their lives to
the moment's softest cords.

It's Jean Vigo,
his one film out of reach – or Ivan Denisovich,
no food and a hard winter crowding every wall –
the faceless smear, the searchlights' sweep
in a Juan Genovés' painting – It's young Tom
Beddows, never finding his beach, a simple,
wasted death for the war machine
and England.

The news, rather sad. A broken
vase, mistaken note, determined windows. It's
Leopold, brewing his morning tea. The one day
that carries its dread with sure hands – Ask Anna
Karina, ask Renée Falconetti. Woke up, fell out
of bed, you would say. We should just live
in silence, I would say. The rest puddles

Raindog

at our feet, each step closer –

And here,
words thin to empty page, leaving the reader
a stone for story, narrowed alley for theme,
building rubble for form.

Someone left
the cake out – so I turn off the radio, while
the road's dark hum disappears into
Möbius belts of a starless sky.

(first published in *kill author*)

*Sam Rasnake's works, receiving five
nominations for the Pushcart Prize, have
appeared in* The Southern Poetry Anthology,
Best of the Web 2009, Wigleaf, OCHO, Big
Muddy, Literal Latté, BOXCAR Poetry Review
Anthology 2, *and* Dogzplot Flash Fiction 2011.
His latest poetry collections are Lessons in
Morphology *(GOSS183) and* Inside a Broken
Clock *(Finishing Line Press).*

PRIS CAMPBELL

Precipice

Under the hammocked bend
of a shrinking sky,
the latticework of moaning
trees poking into lost illusions,
you and I walk a path
littered with missing friends
and once bright-eyed lovers.
Older now, we no longer
put up our peaches for winter.

We are swept aside
as the buffalo streak past,
plunging over the edge
of the approaching precipice.
You hold me until the dust settles,
then pick flowers, weave them
into a pink & blue halo for my hair.

(first published in *The Outlaw
Poetry Network*

Moonlight Rider

It wasn't so much
that she minded her hair loss,
hiding the thick black locks,
piece by piece in her dresser.
Like a bride storing her trousseau.
Like waiting for a bridegroom to charge
down that old Highwayman's
street of dreams and carry her away.
Away from sad sanitized masks and the whoosh
of chemicals hostaging her bloodstream.

No, it was hoping that this time
he wouldn't be shot like a dog
in the moonlight and that she wouldn't
be Bess all over again, breastbone
shattered into a thousand irretrievable
memories, trying to save what could never
be saved from the get-go.

(first published in *Chiron Review*

The poems of **Pris Campbell** *have
been widely published in journals and
anthologies, earning her three Pushcart
nominations and other honors. She has
six collections of poems out through the
small press with a collaboration due in
the fall of 2012 from Clemson University
Press with Scott Owens.*

TARA BIRCH

The red motel

The red motel's parking lot was full of blob cars
of many colors, the color being the only distinguishing feature
in most cases. Toyotas, Fords, Kias, so many alike,
  and through the walls comes
the sound of a baby crying in the evening as the sun descends.
You had forgotten the noises a baby makes when hungry
or in pain, or in need of a change of her diaper, or simply
 when she is tired, so very tired of all the sights and sounds
  and smells,
hungering for the heartbeat of her mother
 that one pulse to tell her she is safe, she is one
re-joined to her creator again.

The instant oatmeal was tasty, its artificial flavors of maple syrup
mixed with real brown sugar,
   dry and old, it is true, but it still melted
when you poured the hot water from the tap
over it in your plastic disposable bowl.
   You were so pleased as you ate it
with a white plastic spoon, even though it was slippery
 and kept falling off as you ate, falling on your chin
and throat, warm and wet and sweet.

   The light through the ragged green curtains has bathed the room
in a curious shade of teal, an unexpected blessing. You sit,
naked on the bed, wet from your shower, towel wrapped on your head,
   the sheet pulled up to your neck, the damp air
and the light and the baby's cries lulling you into a trance,
a waking trance, and you wonder, if it ended now, would you die happy?
Is this what happiness means
 to have run away from home, from the husband
waiting by the phone, waiting for your call, perhaps calling you,
not knowing you turned your phone off, and now lie on cheap cotton sheets,
but clean sheets
   not caring that he is alone.

For you are still marveling at the teal light from the curtains and the setting sun,
the color of the sea by the Cayman Islands,
  an intimate, friendly light, full of charisma, full of the voices of
an unknown future. That light comes through the branches

of a dying willow tree, over the top edge of the red motel's sign
  straight through those curtains and thus changed,
 it has changed you. *Yes*, you say, *yes, I am happy!*

The baby still cries. Whimpers. Falls asleep, just as the stars come out,
so few, so very few, Venus and those that form Orion and his belt
  and the dippers, big and small, Ursas major and minor.
That is how the sea light leaves you -- to the stars
and the sign wrapped in red neon standing on a metal pole
by the motel office door, and street lights that buzz like insects,
  like small bees.
  You remove the towel, pull your fresh yellow t-shirt, extra long,
that you had washed that morning over your head, slip into your jeans,
and walk out the door.
  There is a lake nearby, and a path along its shore, waiting.
It calls, and you hear the words *happy! happy! happy!*
  and you know it must be so.

Tara Birch, *disabled 55 year-old former attorney, has published numerous
poems over the last ten years. She is currently working on her first novel.*

James McGrath

EDWARD NUDELMAN

Like Clockwork

I must have gotten up every ten minutes
checking carbon monoxide levels.
Sometimes it seems nothing happens
until everything happens; a sudden storm,
unrelated events that turn out to be related.
Friends and loved-ones remember how pale
she looked, how strange he acted near the end.
Mere acquaintances huddle to remember
heralding signs and debate what went wrong.
I found her on the couch with the dog.
But the tree never fell through our bedroom roof,
the cancer never appeared in the x-ray
and the furnace, though spewing something noxious,
never registered even one part per million
of a toxic, odorless gas. Still, morning
found us both feeling dizzy and disoriented
while the alarm buzzed all through breakfast.

Poets and Artists, What Looks Like
an Elephant (Lummox Press, 2011)

Another List of Intangibles

The best team won, but nobody knows how.
Studying the film, you begin to see
chinks and cracks, fault-lines
invariably leading to earthquakes—
but we're told the gravity of stars
is defined by the weakest of forces.
What looks like an elephant
is a cloud on an updraft.
What sounds like a freight train
is only rain. Ultimately,
what holds anything together—
sub-atomic muons or bubble gum?
Bubble gum, with my luck.
Sometimes I scare myself into thinking
I understand how it all works:
what peace in not having to wonder

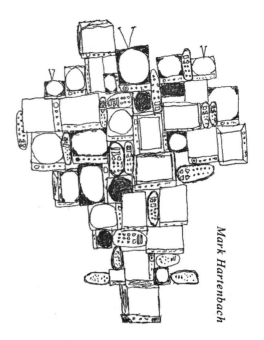

Mark Hartenbach

or worry about wondering,
back on the couch
with a beer, watching my team
go down for the thirteenth time in a row.
And this is all you can offer me?
Will? Heart? Desire?
Intestinal fortitude? Or lack thereof?
A shrew crosses a field at night.
Galaxies of neurons explode in an owl's eye.
Give me a break.

Chiron Review, What Looks Like
an Elephant (Lummox Press, 2011)

Edward Nudelman's latest book, What
Looks Like an Elephant, *published in 2011 by*
LUMMOX Press, was runner-up for Indie Lit
Review Poetry Book of the Year. His poems
have recently appeared in Cortland Review,
Valparaiso Review, Chiron Review, Evergreen
Review, OCHO, Poets and Artists, Ampersand,
Syntax, The Atlanta Review, Plainsongs, Tears
in the Fence, Floating Bridge Press, and The
Penwood Review. Nudelman lives with his wife
in North Seattle where he manages Nudelman
Rare Books, which he founded in 1980.

THE POETRY v

Ashes

He's been to this Starbucks before
Someone at a nearby table says
he rotates to avoid arrest
A mountain man or maybe Santa Claus look
Except skinny as a stage-four Jesus
Guitar on top of his grocery cart
over piles of clothes and a bag of cat food
Cat food for Christ's sake, when there's no cat
Twenty-six degrees last night and damp

Yesterday it was a moth beating against
the outside glass
A feverish fight for survival
that I instantly knew I'd assist
But my mental clock ticks slower now
In considerations about connecting
to a man without roots
One who could become a daily complication

Minutes pass that prefer moths
before the man leaves his cart
and heads for the alley
An image of dumpster food replaces denial
of my Montana heritage that decrees humane as religion

Mountain Man returns from the direction
of the Mobile station with a pack of Camels
Rips off the plastic and lights one up
Burning with it the sandwich I was about to buy him
and the conscience that forbade my vanilla bean scone
When I walk to the car
his head and back bend over guitar scratches
that no one would ever pay to hear

At home I sweep up the ashes
Moths that chose flames
Salem cigarettes and Valium prescriptions
smoldering somewhere in the past
The day has disappeared in smoke

Ellaraine Lockie

Previously published in Heavy Bear

Ellaraine Lockie is a widely published and awarded poet, nonfiction book author and essayist. Her seventh chapbook, Stroking David's Leg, *was awarded Best Individual Collection for 2010 from Purple Patch magazine in England, and her eighth chapbook,* Red for the Funeral, *won the 2010 San Gabriel Poetry Festival Chapbook Contest. Her chapbook,* Wild as in Familiar, *was a finalist in Finishing Line Press 2011 contest and has recently been released there. Ellaraine teaches poetry workshops and serves as Poetry Editor for the lifestyles magazine,* **Lilipoh**.

Commiseration

This poem is for those who have whispered
in desperate urgency:

"Let me get away with it this time."

Perhaps finished this invocation
with a promise to change:

"Lord," you may have called upon
a power greater than your own,

"Don't let anybody find out."

"Let it all be okay."

"Let me slide."

"Just this once."

I have offered to the universe my wobbly fate.
To whatever power casts the lots
I have pled my case, appealed and begged
not just for forgiveness,

(All day long I relived my stupidity,
my lapse, my bad judgment, the mistake.)

but to let it slide – to let this blunder go
unnoticed, like:
the tipsy driver who makes it home safe,
the thief who gets the goods,
the user who has this one last time,

a shame that's never exposed to light.

Maybe you're in a car,
on an airplane,
or behind the dark of your own closed eyes,
and you implore, with all the mindfulness of a mantra:
"Please, please,
please let me get away with it this time.
I'll never ask again."

"I am a screw up," you admit,
own it, call yourself out,

"but, please,
please let it turn out okay
in the end,
this one time."

For the burnout in the stall copping the buzz,
the mother who leaves her kids alone for just fifteen minutes,
the big talker who's got the score to settle all scores,
and that girl who books without so much as a call,

for knowing it's bad and doing it anyway.

For anyone on their knees
supplicant and ashamed, guilty,
this poem is for you.

Not that it matters,
not that a poem is what you need,
but because it's the only way
I have to reach across this page
to let you know,
it is not be easy to find your way back,
but try.
Try.

And if you can't, this poem is still for you.
I'll never take it back,
because it might be all that you've got.

Someone wrote a poem for you once.

Ellen Wade Beals

*Trained as a journalist, **Ellen Wade Beals** writes poetry
and prose. Her work has appeared in literary magazines, in
anthologies and on the web. She is the editor and publisher of
Solace in So Many Words (Weighed Words LLC, an imprint of
Hourglass Books), and she has been working on a novel for what
seems like forever. Her website is: www.solaceinabook.com*

DO YOU FEAR ME

Do you fear me cause I wear
a purple friendship bracelet?
Do you fear having me as a friend?
Are you afraid to introduce me
to your grandparents?
The only perfect thing about me
is my perfect lack of confidence.
Does that freak you out?
I'm fat.
How does that sit with you?
I wear political pins.
Does that bother you?
I'm a bookworm.
Does that depress you?
Are you terrified cause I've been bas mitzvahed?
Are you scared cause I think spiders are sacred?
I'm left handed. ooooooooooooo No comment.
Do you worry about me cause I'm a virgin?
Cause I'm loud and sometimes embarrassing,
are you wary of spending time with me?
I know where the feminist bookstores are
in a whole bunch of states.
Does that make you tremble?
People think I'm younger
and older than I am.
Does that reflect badly on you somehow?
I don't always comb my hair.
Can you hear it coming?
Is it my ugliness or beauty that
frightens you the most?
Are you afraid of me cause I'm human?

*Previously published in The Cowardice of Amnesia
(2.13.62 Publications)*

Ellyn Maybe

*Ellyn Maybe is the author of many books, has toured
nationally and internationally, both individually and with
The Ellyn Maybe Band. Her work has garnered high praise
from such luminaries as Greil Marcus, Henry Rollins and
Jackson Browne. www.ellynmaybe.com*

gestures: the russian riot act

i am an old man
been around more than a few blocks
i know what gestures are worth
gestures of all sizes like
scattering someone's ashes
attending a wedding
blowing out birthday candles

clinking glasses in friendship
standing holding your cap over your heart
clapping in an audience

a simple handshake
an apology
a tip of the hat
opening a door
ten bucks in a card
another round for the table
defending an unworthy home team
a phone call to a friend for no reason
crying over a black & white movie

an angry middle finger
an up thrust fist for victory
or defiance

the evil eye

the list goes on &
every gesture has a meaning &
has a worth to it
that counts for something

i know that even
an over the top protest by
occupying & rocking out
in someone's church in mother russia
is worth something

but no
not two years
a far cry from the gulag
of past gestures

but no
not two years

Evan Myquest

*Evan Myquest is Sacramento CA based
where he lives in retirement with his wife
Eva in Rancho Murieta. He has been
published and featured in the Sacramento
News & Review, Blue Fur, Primal Urge,
Poems-For-All, and WTF. He has a poem
in the upcoming decennial* Sacramento
Anthology of Poetry 2012. *He is a 1974 alum
of the Clarion Science Fiction and Fantasy
writers workshop.*

*Editor's note: this poem is about the
sentence given the Russian protest punk
band, PussyRiot, for occupying an Orthodox
Church and defying Vladimir Putin.*

Einstein

I make in a year what some people make in a month.
How do they do it? It doesn't make any sense.

She edged out of her pants.

My question hung,
like drapes in a room without a breeze.

I watched her.

She took off her underwear and stood in front of me.
I looked at her thighs.

They make in a day
what you make in a lifetime because
you're a loser, she said. Do you want to fuck?

Father Luke

*Father Luke contributes to quality publications
when he can find them. You can find him on
the web at FatherLuke.com*

All Those Dying Daisies
On All The Mantles
Of The World

every single
cigarette
that I crushed
into those lonely
yellow glass
hotel ashtrays
of the world,

& every single
beer that I
guzzled,
smashed,
& tossed

while making
a last minute
buzzer sound,

was a love poem
to you.

Frank Reardon

*Frank Reardon was born in
Boston, Ma., but has lived all over
the world the last 10 years. His
first book,* Interstate Chokehold,
*was released via Neo Poiesis Press
in 2009. His second book, 'The
Nirvana Haymaker,' also from Neo
Poiesis Press, is due out this fall.
He's currently working on a 3rd
collection for Punk Hostage Press
titled ' Blood Music'.Frank has
been published in various print &
online magazines.*

Raindog

Her Room

It's been three o'clock for days
walls are lilac
windows plum-trimmed
no curtains
no open blinds
potted flowers on every sill
violets match her garden eyes
rumors of green
plucked away
The bed has no pillows and is never made
dresser drawers lined with pink and
scented paper
white underwear without secrets
glass bowl with matches by the door
ashtrays always shimmer clear
Four clocks
all pale porcelain
all chipped
all read three o'clock
permanent afternoon
while darkness slips all about the place
there are no mirrors in her room
it is her world
without green

Frances LeMoine

Her Room originally appeared in
13th Warrior Review

Frances LeMoine *lives and writes in
New Hampshire.*

Nothing In Blue Gap

There is nothing in Blue Gap.
The air moves through the creosote and sage.
The plain slopes upward
toward a range of ridges miles away.

Joey's shack is off the road,
reached by a rutted driveway

where a ceremonial circle of stumps
guard a fire wood pile.

In the distance a hundred sheep graze.
They know to come back at night
to the old sheep pen of quartered logs,
grayed and cracked with age.

A mile up a dirt road
are the remnants of winter camp,
where the wind blows the grasses clear
of ice and drifting snow,

where his mother as a child
stood guard against the coyotes,
and slept with the sheep
through the long cold nights.

She left for California,
a quest that became an exile
the anchors of children and chains of money
and an old weaving loom in her living room.

At night she dreams
of the sunset light,
the gap between the ridges,
blue gray in the distance,

and the emptiness that Joey left
when he headed East,
past Flagstaff to a place
that pulled at his bones.

As the sun slants low, the wind
is the only sound that moves across the mesa,
at this place, Blue Gap, that makes no claim
on the map of Arizona.

Frank Kearns

Frank Kearns *was brought up in New England. He
lived above Beyond Baroque when it was on West
Washington Blvd. and now resides in Downey. He
was a steelworker in the Bethlehem Steel Plant in
Maywood, and now works in the aerospace industry.*

Where I Come From

I come from a Victorian house
   with a gravel driveway.
Winter afternoons under a grey sky
   rushing into blue-black twilight
   snow shovel heaving
Anticipating the heat inside
   on my toes as I removed boots
   and socks and socks.
Or, just as often, the driveway free of snow,
   now freed from my chore,
I would run through, fall in, love the snow
   I had so hated only moments before.

I come from a trimmed suburban lawn
   descending into a swamp.
I come from the challenge
   of exploring that swamp in the winter,
   testing the strength of the ice,
always coming home with my boots
   full of slushy water.
I come from the tedium
   of mowing that lawn
   for summer pocket change
(I think it was a buck fifty for the front lawn,
   three bucks for the back),
eyes ever vigilant for the gravel left
   from last winter's shoveling.

I come from walking tree-lined streets
   to school, to the store,
   to wherever my young legs might take me,
But always home by 5:30, the magic moment
   when the carpool would drop my father off,
   and he would walk up the driveway
   to my mother's kiss and dinner always ready.
Then, free again, back out into the neighborhood's
   games and wonders, tag, kick-the-can,
or just exploring under the streetlights,
   or, even better, in the shadows they created.

I come from the space between
   the streetlight and the shadow,
   the lawn and the swamp,
   the gravel and the blade.

G. Murray Thomas

*Previously published in My Kidney
Just Arrived (Tebot Bach, 2011)*

G. Murray Thomas *has been an active
part of the SoCal poetry scene for over 20
years. He has performed throughout the
L.A. area and beyond. He was the editor
and publisher of Next... Magazine, a poetry
calendar/news magazine for Southern
California.* News Clips & Ego Trips, *a
collection of articles from Next..., was just
published by Write Bloody Press. His most
recent book of poetry is* My Kidney Just
Arrived, *published by Tebot Bach in 2011.*

Ones and Zeros

The movie starts late because
the projectionist is bleeding,
lost inside we follow
The heart hesitates and the forehead is leading,
mistaken, taking more than it can swallow

Distended birds cannot fly,
helpless beneath our unwashed feet,
lost inside we follow
Abused by the sky,
it's ourselves that we eat
in others, to fill the hollow

Smashing all the childish eggs,
coma struck in the summer of our head,
lost inside we follow

Breaking our soft boiled legs
to make us small and alone in bed,
precisely numb and callow

Pull off my tail
it will grow again,
lost inside we follow
When I succeed I also fail,
the lonely part of the reptile chain,
my indulgence sick and sallow

If I shout, come back at me
We were made to be this wall,
lost inside we follow
Its always better to disagree
than not to speak at all,
Raise us from the shallow
and
all that
ones and zeros and ones and zeros allow;
only
lost inside we follow

Gary Jacobelly

*uplink-lock filename garyajacobelly:format
begin: //#36873configure:bio mode:* **Gary
Jacobelly** *is stored in the basement of a
windowless office building in the south bay.
He is quite beautiful:/awaiting new protocol
Perseverance furthers*

Second-Hand

In the second hand record store I sift
through row after row of dusty LPs,
pausing from time to time to consider
a name scrawled lazily in blue ink,
a coffee cup stain, a trace of ancient
lipstick smeared across a dog-eared
copy of Fleetwood Mac's Greatest Hits.
It is in these places we discover the
true history of the world, of ourselves,
the way things were and in some fashion

will always be, though the discs
of plastic have turned to metal,
and the people with whom we shared
these songs are vanished or
changed, our emotional landscape often
untended, like scratched vinyl, hissy
and unlistenable, as we ride
the endless turntable on its circular orbit
into all our dusty tomorrows.

Glenn Cooper

*Glenn W. Cooper lives and sometimes writes
in Tamworth. Australia. He hasn't written a
poem in nine weeks; he wonders if it's all over.*

Chimeric Corpus 61.

winds drop
a note on shutters;
deafness unfurls.
along shoreline
wet legs of gulls
skim wide reflections
under carpet of sand
looking for the
right meal.
shadows clutter their forms;
the wind flutters,
& up a pathway
tracks stretch out
holding a box car waiting for goods.

Guy R. Beining

*6 poetry books & 25 chapbooks published
over the years. Have appeared in 7 different
anthologies. Appear in the Contemporary
Authors Autobiography series V. 30 (1998
Gale Research) & in the Dictionary of
Avant Gardes, 2nd edition (2000). Have been
published in Chain, Ep;phany, Perspektive
(Germany), the New Orleans Review & the
New Review of Literature.*

Moore's Ford Lynching, 7.26.1946

There aren't a lot of prayers rising
I ain't sung before, at least sincere,
Hang me in a meadow for my soul
To dry, katydids and sparrows shout
Over the wheatgrass and river oats,
Pass me over to the laurel
And hemlock so I can watch
The Appalachee flow all green to brown,
Coneflowers and aster pave
The red dirt banks,
Scratch my nails on the rocks
Here so I can follow my way
Back home again,
A low sun breaths out
Last shadows left for me to see,
Nothing is as dark eyed
As this stupid lonely dusk,
Curtains draw out on the horizon
And the Southern stories
Of Cormac McCarthy line up
Like Walton County pines
Waiting for the ax to fall,

Smell of smoke,
Remington crack and wet rope,
All I saw before the light died out
Was this beautiful Southern land,
Four dead, and an unborn killed,
Dared argue with a neighbor,
Now just a road marker,
A pastoral song more alive
By Moore's Ford Road, shot or hung,
Where trickle meets a stream
And at last I've run out,
Years before JFK and Johnson
Rose to clear the way,
There's never a good lynching,
Tick, tick, tick…..
First it was race and now it's wages,
The winds snap and fade.

H. L. Thomas

Executive Chef, cookbook author, poet (over 200 poems published) living in Athens, GA sometimes wishing I was back in Mendocino, CA.

Death Is Tailgating
(for Winston, written Feb 2009)
RIP- April 14, 2009

I have watched Death tail gate my friend.
His sharp turns, sudden taps on the brakes
or grand prix skills cannot out maneuver
Death's fixation on his fate.
Crystal Methology is my friend's psychology
and she's in the passenger
seat with the window down
smiling wanting to paint
the whole town red before he's dead.
My friend's hands are gripped on the
steering wheel tight and zombie like.
The smell of death
flows through tail pipes and flashing reds
of motel signs and street lights
control his nights.
As air blows through Crystal's hair
Highway patrolmen pass and stare

while his skeletal reflection
in their mirrored shades
is a detection that Death is near.
I am just a jay walker
rushing to avoid a deadly collision
as days and nights of bad decisions
pop his veins.
No bull's eye on my breasts
or daggers through my chest.
I may flirt with the mysteries
of the night but I do not, will not flirt with
Death.

Jackie Joice

Jackie Joice's writing is influenced by travel, her blood type, and watching thrillers on television in 3rd grade. She has one published novel entitled Kanika's Burdens.

FIVE IMPORTANT SOUTHERN CALIFORNIA POETS: HELL YES!

THE TITLE MAY BE SOMEWHAT geographically incorrect because one of the poets (Hannah Wehr) actually relocated to Northern California. That said, I chose these poets because they are vital and unique voices in a scene that more and more leans towards two extremes: either the overly dry and form obssesed worlds of MFA straightjackets, or the whirling dervishishes of the slam world. Both do have their plusses and minuses, but it's nice when you find a poet that skirts these two norms to bring you something a little more experimental and refreshing.

In some way you can make a valid argument that ANY voice is important, to some extent. But to me, who, admittedly, has become jaded by 17 years of lackluster open readings, assigning the title of "important" is a little more involved. There are actually a plethora of really wonderful and talented Southern California poets, so it was not just a matter of talent when it came to start the process of choosing. I finally was able to whittle it down to ten possible poets. This was eventually whittled down to four representatives.

In terms of styles there is very little in common but the connecting thread is that, yes, I believe these poets are vital and important. Not just important because of their poems, but also because of what they do to inspire others. The poets I chose, (the aforementioned) **Hanna Wehr, Chris Davidson, Jennifer Donnell**, and **Raundi K. Moore Kondo** certainly fit this bill.

Hannah's poems mix a deft blend of melting clocks, heartbreak and wit. She is an important poet because, in poetry the surreal is often presented without a beating heart. Hannah is not afraid to look a few Rhinos in the eyes but she is always careful to tie it in to the human experience, sometimes adding a knowing little wink and a sly little smile. Hannah also teaches poetry to troubled kids in the prison system despite her assertion that "I have never been the caring type, at least not with children" and that a friend of hers once described her as "Most Likely to Eat Her Young" Google her and you will find some VERY entertaining blogs...

Chris, on the other hand, looks like he could have fit right in with The Beats. Often wearing a soul patch and a laconic easy smile, Chris is one of the most genial and charming of hosts. (he, along with a rotating line-up, has hosted poetry events for the Casa Romantica Reading Series bringing in top notch talent like Jeffrey McDaniel and Patty Seyburn) He also teaches, is in a band (The Santiago Steps) and has written for Rumpus. Chris's work presents itself as a humble narrator: someone immediately relatable and comforting, even as the subtle pinch of sinister undertones suggest that something might not be quite right with the big picture. In a scene where grace has become an endangered species, Davidson is both, refreshing and very much appreciated.

Jennifer is a very beautiful girl. This has

Raindog

presented some obstacles and backlash from certain entities in terms of acknowledging and respecting her work. Jennifer has persevered where others might have given up, has hosted many of So Cal's top talent like Ellyn Maybe and Rachel Kann, and is one of the most prolific writers in the scene. Jennifer's poems, much like herself, are intoxicating little mischievous souls. They are not shy, a bit exhibitionist, and are not averse to a little controversy. They are not so much flashy or extravagant. They don't shout or scream at you. They tackle sex and politics with the same matter of fact mouth. Jennifer is the kind of poet needed to bridge the extremes of Southern California poetry. She is neither, wallflower, nor howler, but a far more rare combination of the lyrical and the sassy.

Then there is Raundi. If So Cal poetry has a Wonder Woman. It is Raundi. Her efforts to bring poetry to the masses are extraordinary. Better yet, she often hosts events who's proceeds go to charitable causes like The Red Cross and Cancer Recovery Centers. She also runs a monthly workshop, often bringing in iconic poets like Daniel McGinn to be guest instructors. She is also in a band!

If that wasn't enough she is instilling the same kind of fervent love of literature in her kids, (especially her daughter, who is quickly becoming a poet to watch out for) In fact, There are so many hats that Raundi wears (and wears expertly) that she could open up a very fine millinery shop. Anytime someone groans about the dying art of story telling, I simply point them in the direction of Raundi's work: varied, witty and with a true sense of detail. The reader is invited-never pushed-into her sweet and sour narratives. She is both charming reporter, and the trusted friend who shares her most ribald, wild and entertaining adventures with you. Even if, most likely, none of it actually happened.

So, to paraphrase Rod Serling and his great Twilight Zone monologues; submitted for your approval, four poets. Each with their own unique shine, but each equally important to the vital landscape that is Southern California poetry.

Jaimes Palacio

HANNAH WEHR

A Life Done Wrong

At the age of 88, my heart will attack me 82: all you really need are large handled jugs of chardonnay and cat food

I am 71. I tell my husband that I understand. Sometimes the only thing we can control in life is how we kiss it good-bye. I sleep beside his body for two days before I call anyone

In my 62nd year I learn that mercy imposes no conditions

At the age of 58, my husband sleeps with a woman who is not me. I wring my heart out like a sock

I am 52. I bury my son

56: I make casseroles for the homeless, read to underprivileged children, start a neighborhood recycling program. I wonder when I will feel something

In my 49th year, I become far too interested in the lives of celebrities. I buy a Crock-Pot. I make too much food and my family looks at this weird abundance in silence

At the age of 47, my life does not suit my shoes or my cigarettes. I go out to get canned pineapple and I come home with two cocker spaniels and a homeless man

41: my son tries to tell me something. I ask him to wait. And he waits for years

I am 34. I realize that I love anyone who reads to me

In my 31st year, I wonder if I care for anything. I wonder if I am hungry out of habit

At the age of 30 I have a son. I am afraid to touch him. I leave him in the bathtub for long periods of time

27: I marry because that is what is next in the natural progression of things. I will spend the rest of my life feeling like I am living in someone else's clothes

I am 22. I believe in God because I refuse to accept that seahorses are an accident When I am 17, I make the choice to look like the type of trouble certain men choose to get into 12: I learn that these are only words and we never mean them 9: I am punished for bringing home a stray cat. I learn that it is a liability to love 7: I believe in snowmen. I hope for more 5: I learn to be quiet 4: I believe that my mother's red car will be a fire truck when it grows up

1: I learn how to say no. Two decades later, I will forgot how

And at the point when I first meet myself, I already know that my ghost bones are engraved with directions.

JENNIFER DONNELL

My Last Oat

My wild oats have become romantic suicide bombers,
adrenaline junkies on a mission to *do* or *die*.
My last oat heads to a club to occupy the dance floor.
There, she skips ship and barricades herself
in the hemline of the pants on a gentleman next to me.
She makes her way up his trousers and into his *boxers* or *briefs*?
Boxers. I shoo her hand out as fast as I can and give my Oat a serious
talking to- *You weren't born in the sixties Oat!*
There's no such thing as free love, love is heavy,
costly, dangerous.
Oat assures me that love was the last thing on her mind,
but the whole time she's talking, she's got a public hair stuck between her teeth.
I remove it with barely willing fingertips and shudder a little.
I wish she hadn't worn a skirt,
I should have said something, should have known
what she was after.

Oat says I don't live in the moment enough,
that her voyage to the underworld of a stranger's nether regions
isn't half as ugly as the places I've gone, under the guise of love-
singing happily, as the soundtrack to all love affairs is a nursery rhyme.
 My hair braided like the little girl I'm not anymore,
my eyes so full of stars she got queasy from their light.

*When **Jennifer Donnell** was small, she read* Harriet the Spy *six times and decided she was a writer. She also realized that, if Harriet was right, writing was a dangerous job. In addition to being published in an assortment of journals and anthologies, Jennifer's recent/upcoming work appears in* The Scrambler, Bohemia Journal, Tin Foil Dresses, Marco Polo, Borderline, "Slut", *and* A Few Lines Magazine.

CHRIS DAVIDSON

Doppler Effect

I'm driving at night with the radio
on broken into by another voice:
an ambulance through traffic slides,
and the traffic parts before it
in an anticipatory wake, that lingers.

People comply without complaint.
Will a fire truck follow? What else
can we do? The ambulance goes by,
and a physics lesson drifts into view
like a once-forgotten face—a word

for why in passing the siren's tone
moves from shrill to sad, why the red light
on its roof flashes into a beating heart,
why retreads on the shoulder should
appear as crouched, cowering dogs.

***Chris Davidson**'s poetry and criticism have appeared in* Alaska Quarterly Review, Burnside Review, Zocalo Public Square, The Rumpus, *and elsewhere. He lives with his wife and two sons in Southern California.*

RAUNDI K MOORE KONDO

Only One Of These Things Is True

I was conceived in a right-front, shirt pocket,
in the middle of the summer of love. The baby boomers'
biggest bang. In utero I developed an extra exclamation point.
All of the side effects are still being misunderstood.

Six months early, on a grassy knoll, I was born--a bullet
from the barrel of a man with an unsteady hand,
whose aim was a lie. He'd never met anyone named
Allison. He never wanted to, so he never would.

My first tooth tasted like a lemon drop. Sweet and sour
became hard to separate A year later I was weaned
off of milky ways and learned to heat up and manipulate formulas
of women who could reach the cookies, white rabbits, and me.

I military crawled my way through red, hot
colic. My first steps were taken along the edges
of a million year old meteor crater. I've never felt
more steady. I am half asbestos, half Snow White Dwarf.

As a direct descendent of St. Valentine I naturally grew up
to be the back seat of a '75 dodge dart, every prom dates' wet,
back-alley, dream-come true. Yet fulfillment never arrived.
So I married an axe-salesman. We both love trees,

long rides through nuclear power plants, and the windexed
aftertaste taste of each other's corneas. We sometimes
fight over "who gets to eat the pupils". When I miss being
a bullet he tucks me safely in the right front pocket of his shirt.

Raundi is convinced the zombie apocalypse is just another metaphor for poetry-
-which explains her compulsion to want to infect everyone she meets. Alas, she
founded For The Love of Words, offering creative writing and poetry workshops
for writers of all ages. She is published in Don't Blame the Ugly Mug *on Tebot
Bach,* Aim For the Head *on Write Bloody Press, and recently in the blog My
Poem Rocks. Most recently she was the Poet of the Month for Moon Tide Press
and the winner of The Lightbulbmouth Literary Adventure Part V. Her first
poetry collection,* Let the Ends Spill Over Your Lips*, will be available in Fall of
2012. https://www.facebook.com/TheLoveOfWords*

JAIMES PALACIO

I SAID, I AM

I am big mouth screaming obscenity.
I wonder, wonder who torched the book of LOVE.
I hear the wounded music of a far off train forgetting it's place.
I see history breaking bread like war's old bones.
I want silence at my breakfast table.
I need a fast car and a slow kiss girl.

I pretend she loved me once.
I feel the corrupted engines in my blood.
I touch the gasoline of memory.
I worry the guests at high tea.
I cry like a lost rocket.
I know the earthquake heart.

I understand the whispers in dark closets.
I say nothing in your forever nightmares.
I dream like a big, brutal, carnival.
I try to see the light from the top of the Ferris wheel.
I hope falling doesn't hurt.
I am not rock, paper, scissors. I am not island. I am big mouth.
I am
obscenity.

08/10/12

Jaimes *has done lots of stuff. Some very detrimental to his health. He has been
published in a number of places. He dares you to Google him. It will be an adventure.*

EIGHT POETS

SETH ELKINS

Seth is a poet I came across many years ago on my program [Jane Crown's Poetry Radio]. He represents the depth of youth for me. His work is the sheer force of breathing, sometimes this being difficult to procure and other times the fluidity of the lung rising and falling seems to move with ease. His work is powerfully presented, intellectively approached and his formation of the language used and manipulated gives me chills.

1-

SITO

winter always arrives
with such a fierce
abruptness.
we can never be prepared

for the wind-
it's brisk un-comforting;
the icy grip,
an ever clandestine

friend of all foes
(the winter in my heart, is warmer).

offering very little
to calm a shivering spine
this is only a fistful of words;
a handful of memories.

the chattering of tooth
and nail,
only amplified
by the presence of a shadow

careful to be heard
(in the aftermath of a wake).

2-

IT'S BEEN A DECADE,
IF IT'S BEEN T(W/O)O.

the years (r/a)ge(d)
    without reason,
            concern
    (and/or) the (w/h)ands of a clock.

they've become...
the whole-
    to have
        and to hold,

folding reason
into little prayers
    -pieces of paper-
twisted into kindling
and carried by the fistful
to be washed,
        buried
        and later, exhumed

        in every attempt
        to attack forfeiture
        of memory,
        limb, and hunger.

the directions
to follow the ghosts
            home,
        have blurred.

Seth Elkin is a Midwestern poet moving towards the wilds of the North East and loving it. He is due out with two books in 2012/13. Both been published in print and online. He continues to write and meditate as often as the law allows.

JASON MASHAK

Jason's work is precision personified. Few words, languid language and an ever -longing play of words that express the need to enjoy the life we are given. His counterpoint of wit and undeniable cheeky sensuality encapsulates his work for me.

SUITE: LOVE NOTES

"Celestial Premonition of Pathetic Heartbreak"

—Joseph Heller (Closing Time)

*

The inertia of sitting still
in daylight

and another of your kind
spins you

without even trying she
breaks you

and all she does is study
her notes

*

Oh, Goth Girl, with your black nail polish,
You move me, like a sale on tonic.
I would give you three fingers
for your collection, maintaining long enough
my devoted insurrection.

*

We're never at a loss
for small talk, as our bodies
try so well not to touch

*

All day long I wanted to fall
asleep
between your breasts

*

Thunder down under
Flower power in the shower
Hello, Happy Highway Head
Funny money for bunny honey?

*

Let's bleed the cock to delay the dawn.

Raindog

*

Uncongenial unicorn
with discordant cognitive
congenital conundrums

*

Lovemaking today
makes a mockery of psychology

*

Damn the hours I've spent staring
at the ceiling to see your face

*

Souvenirs are just reminders
that we pay for everything

*

A woman will save a man
from death by natural causes.

*

I wrote all my love songs to drugs

Jason Mashak (b.1973) *is a Michigan native who also lived in Georgia, Tennessee, and Oregon, before returning in 2006 to his family roots in Central Europe. His first book,* Salty as a Lip, *was published in 2010 by Haggard and Halloo (Texas) and was listed among Black Heart Magazine's six "Most Kick-Ass Books of 2010." He currently lives in Prague, Czech Republic, where he plays with his daughters, writes for his day gig, and occasionally makes music that can be heard here: www.reverbnation.com/jasonmashak*

JANE CROWN

1 -

secret kissing
Grabs your hand form underneath and curls my knuckles pale into yours weaving the duchess delicate slip ..so silent and so unseen into your grip.

2 -

the rose

Oh, that fragrant mentor to my heart as it beats in triumph my body, too, just clings like a stem with watery need you make me bend, i am weak as i grow into you.

Jane Crown is an American Archivist. Her program Jane Crown's Poetry Radio beat out NPR in the Library of Congress' "Favorite External links " (2010) and has been running for seven years. She has had guest hosts sit in for her since late 2011. She recently retired from the weekly Sunday presentation and focuses now on her journal, Heavy Bear, and her free-lance works. She is the author of "A Love Letter to Darwin" (Lummox Press, 2010) and "Her Delicate Shoe" (Polymer Grove, 2009). She was also fortunate enough to have been a judge for the Bay Area Poet's Coalition in 2011. More information can be found here: janecrown.com

DIANE KLAMMER

Diane is a multitudinous representation for me. Her works long for affection and understanding at the suffering of the living. She gives me the sense she knows some secret out in the Universe and I am dying to get to its source in her poems. Her work inspires me to be a better person, writer and Humanist.

1-

These Are the Rules

"What matters most is how well you walk through the fire."

The whole world may be burning
around you,
but you have knowingly
chosen this.

You must confront the blizzard
with a tattered umbrella.
These are the rules.
You must stop the gaping

head wound
with only a tiny circular band aid.
You do not have more
and you cannot do less.

This is the choice you make:
to wash it with your tears,
wring it out,
and begin again.

Eventually it may stick.
The role you take
is only as a guide.
Your patient is the one

who struggles each day
through the snow and the wind
but for the band aid,
naked.

2-

A Hundred Words for Sorrow

Thousands of dolphins are slaughtered in Taiji.
How can sunrise be peppered with such death?

Too much wailing happens before midday.
Before the murdering, a mother cradles her young.

Children do not understand levels of mercury rising.
Waves leave blood prints on stones at morning.

Can any ray of light reach this kind of suffering?
A harvest moon brightens when she honors a newborn.

Dolphins recognize their reflections in a mirror.
White birds flee from darkness where innocents die.

Blossoms fall from bridges into a helpless ocean.
These lines contain a hundred words for sorrow.

Diane Klammer feels she has lived many lives as a Biology Teacher, Counseling Psychologist for several populations, musician, wife and mother, and writer, not necessarily in that order. Her poetry is in many print and online journals magazines and a couple of anthologies. She now serves Boulder County Parks and Open Space as a naturalist, sings for seniors and is a Registered Psychotherapist in Colorado. She tries to write or read at least two hours a day. She has contemplated throwing out her TV, but hasn't done it yet.

JOHN BENNETT

"Juan" as he is affectionately called is a poet I can always count on for the masterful swell of a nagging world displayed and ripped open to view. Viscerally unhinged; just as it is. His writing, publishing and sheer force of personality keep me constantly in wonder. He is a humble and talented individual to whom I am forever grateful to have shared my first live reading with in 09'. He is a comrade, a mentor and a damn fine old rough-neck. I would not have him any other way.

1-

All in How You Look At It

There is no
empty space.

From where
we stand a
quark is the
loneliest
thing in the
universe,
passing thru
planets without
making contact
with anything,
but in
other registers
of awareness
a quark is a
clumsy giant
caged in a
claustrophobic
nightmare with
no room
to breathe.

2-

A Mother's Advice

The hardest
thing for
me to
accept is
diminished energy.

Maybe it's
time to
open the
envelope my
mother
gave me
when I
was eight.

John Bennett, alias Jabony Welter, Achilles Jones, Jacob Black…Born 1938, Brooklyn, New York, stint in the army, bouncer in New Orleans, window washer in Washington, black sheep in Berkeley, surrounded at the moment thru circumstances beyond my control by Japanese students, milling about with vacant eyes, as if the aftermath of Hiroshima is still shimmering down through the generations…http://www. hcolompress.com/Books.html

CHARLES RAMMELKAMP

Charles poems are filled with both gaiety for living and the common man standing bare ass naked in the middle of his life entirely perplexed. His work is poignantly simple, strives to tell his own uncanny truths and lay laughing before the reality of a sometimes disingenuous world. He does not miss a beat baring his own reality in this mix.

1-
Karma

The sociopath the experts tell us
has no conscience,
if not necessarily violent.
As a child, immortal,
I wished death on those who momentarily angered me.
"I wish, I wish, I wish you were dead!"
Had I a gun, I wonder,
might I have pulled the trigger?

Now I think twice,
afraid such expressions
could come back to haunt me –
justice is nothing if not irony –
reap what you sow, etc.

So utterly absent, negligent,
when it comes to genocide,
catastrophes, pointless pain,
death of innocents, infants,
God is yet said
to take cruel delight
in punishing wrongdoing.

Blows the smoke
from the barrel of the gun,
swaggers, self-satisfied,
through the middle of town,
Marshall Dillon down
the streets of Dodge City.

2-
The Sex Nerve

In Butterfly pose,
the yoga instruction manual informs me –
soles of the feet pressed together,
knees akimbo –
we exercise "what yogis call the sex nerve,"
as if promising some unspecified reward.

I remember the newspaper story
my friend sent me
when I told him about the yoga class
my wife and I were taking,
describing the swami
who introduced yoga to the United States
in the early twentieth century;
lascivious as Indra, or some other horny Hindu god,
he engaged in sex with his students,
pledging transcendental advancement as a result,
life on a higher spiritual plane.

The implication seemed to be yoga instructors
"only want to get into your pants,"
as girls used to be warned
about boys and their motives.

I think of my yoga instructor,
a lithe, lovely woman in her twenties.
Is she only trying to have sex
with a man over twice her age?
Yeah, right.

*In June, 2012, Time Being Books published my collection
of poems about missionaries in a leper colony in Vietnam
during the war, entitled* Fusen Bakudan *("Balloon Bombs" in
Japanese). I edit an online literary journal called The Potomac
-* http://thepotomacjournal.com/. *I am also a fiction editor for
The Pedestal –* http://www.thepedestalmagazine.com.

CHITRA LELE

Chitra is a poet I received submissions from in 2011 for my journal Heavy
Bear. I was instantly smitten with her understanding of God and its many
mysteries in the cosmos. I adore her captivating Indian charm and smooth
use of language, which coincidentally is not her first. Her work is refined
and structured; both in lovely symmetry.

Congealing Sights

> The railway station filled with clamor
> At times dons an unceasingly grim facade.
> Most of the times, we are dumbstruck
> At the architectural feat that railways signify.
> Although stations are eloquent symbols
> Of the city or town in which they pulsate,
> Peaking inside one realizes
> The grass is not always greener on the other side.
> Walking down the impoverished platform,
> I see many-a-congealing-sights
> Hitting hard at my mental tracks;
> I experience acerbic semaphores.

Reaching the junction of destinies,
I enter the tunnel of the dark world.
I am traumatized to witness
A continuous run of bereft beggars,
Abandoned elders with dilapidated hearts,
Threadbare clad children, hope viciously flirting with their eyes,
Virtually dead commuters taking shortcuts, heedless to warnings,
Sweepers taking siesta, with their brooms as headrest
And onerous porters dragging tired feet to fill their empty stomachs.

On the one side, the station signifies the mosaic of destiny
And on the other, the direst cross-section of humanity.
Reflecting on their lives offers me a passage to transformation.
In these constant push-pull forces of existence,
These strangulated souls never ever rail;
Hence they reach their station without fail.

Wonderful Words of the Inner Whole

Wonderful Words of the Inner Whole,
Gently I hear in my soul.......
Darkness will give way to sunshine,
Joy and happiness will be mine,
and by God's grace all will be fine.

Wonderful Words of the Inner Whole,
Gently I hear in my soul.......
Every problem will be solved,
every obstacle will be dissolved,
and every mistake will be absolved.

Wonderful Words of the Inner Whole,
Gently I hear in my soul.......
Every mental agitation will be crushed,
every anger pang will be made void,
and every serene emotion will be strengthened.

Wonderful Words of the Inner Whole,
Gently I hear in my soul.......
Every day is getting brighter,
every burden is getting lighter,
and every grip over the future is getting tighter.

Wonderful Words of the Inner Whole,
Gently I hear in my soul.......

Chitra Lele is a young record-setting author, keynote speaker and management consultant. Chitra has been conferred with the title of "A Versatile Writer" by the India Book of Records for penning maximum number of books in a short span of 18 months.

JOSEPH R. TROMBATORE

His rogue touches on words I know have been buried earnestly just for my uncovering. He is a new puzzle in how a thing works each time I am presented with it. Joseph is both fine chisel of tool towards the bulk of poem and the thing in progress as it makes haste of the intention. His mind movies about displaying for my edification how the world operates. A smooth pattern, juxtaposed with hilarity of being. There is something about Joseph that speak to my concern too; for just being still. I want to hold hands at the reckoning of poems he brings me. This implacability is delightful. His pastiche of vivid metaphor alone can drive the warmness straight into a thing. I am left with his truth, perhaps my own in the end too, for he has swayed my heart to sitting a spell and considering so much more in his quietude.

Joseph is a study in the presence of American poetry in the regular work a day life one must stay focused upon. it takes a lot of meditation to learn how to be present. Texan and fellow Southerner whose open-ness begs for you to tell him a story he has not heard tell of before.

The Striped Blouse
Edouard Vuillard, 1895

She busies herself with flowers
& get well cards.
Lives in fabrics: wild as lions;
of steeds raging across fields dancing in lightning.
She hangs upside down,
a Monarch butterfly
whose wings have not yet dried.

Her mother watches her every move.
Keeps piano keys dusted, sheet music crisp.
Wants a perfectly perfumed sonata
for her evening guests.

Fingers move from side to side,
like skaters on a winter's lake,
over brandy, cigars,
waiting for chrysalis,
morning eggs to crack;
that elusive octave range of sunrise into flight.

One more trip to the garden.
One more vase to fill with expectations.

The names of men she hides in her hair.

Originally appeared in: The Houston Literary Review

Untitled, 1968
Mark Rothko, 1968

So rich & luxuriant
I choose to leave you nameless
a number to memorize
a question & a comment
to amuse the crowd

I'll
paint over your supple skin
in layers so thin
they'll
think I found you at the beach

Your mouth
will become as the conch
I hold to my ear

keep to myself

You'll be as hidden
as a billboard
after a hurricane

&
only I will know
where to dig.

Originally appeared in: Poetry Friends

Joseph R. Trombatore *is an artist and poet whose work has appeared in: Travois:
An Anthology of Texas Poetry, Right Hand Pointing (online), Journal of the American
Studies Association of Texas, and elsewhere. His poetry collection,* Screaming at Adam, *was awarded the Wings Press Chapbook Prize in 2007, and one of his poems received
the 2011 Larry D. Thomas Poetry Prize (REAL, Regarding Arts & Letters). Other honors
include two Pushcart Prize nominations and a Best of the Net Anthology nomination.
Former Poetry Editor of: The Houston Literary Review (online) and Founder/Publisher
of the defunct online journal, Radiant Turnstile, he now resides in San Antonio.*

THE POETRY VI

LETTER TO SELF

While you count insects tap dancing across the ceiling
while your automobile smokes, sputters and dies
while you eat mustard sandwiches and potatoes
six days a week
while you get up at six am
to work the grocery stores
to serve the overfed
roaming the aisles like cattle
shuffling from the chute to slaughter,
they feed
while you atrophy.
While you fight fuck bleed
grind the gears, fight the storm
pull the sails and break the bough
curse the gods curse your ancestors.

While you wake up--in jail
the emergency room
the dew covered grass.

While you face another sun
in your translucent body
and face the darkness where your heart beat
keeps you awake with it's bell like demeanor
and your past is a million parasites
coming to devour you
from the inside out.

While your boss, an average man
with an average life
screams at you for a box
of Nutty Bars going stale.
You don't hit him
you take it at ten bucks an hour
only because rent is due
and it's winter outside.

Norman J. Olson

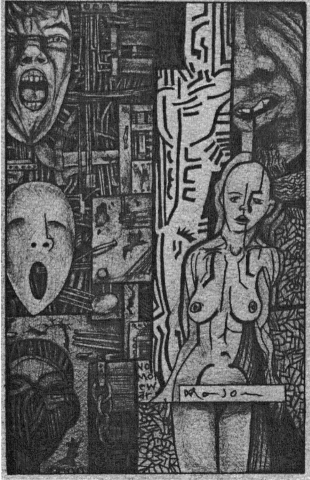

Remember the only thing
that has killed you so far is you.
Not the drugs the car crashes
the flood of 85
not the women and the men married to them.

Remember death has the patience of a child
run from the arms of it
just keep running
don't stop
don't look back
don't explain yourself
remember how to lift your wings
when the wolves come calling
remember your eyes as a child
when you could still make your parents proud someday
remember to keep a levity about yourself.

Remember that everything that has ever happened to you
will lead you to the place you saw yourself
when you dreamt
so climb back inside your head
put your words to paper.
Know it's all you've got.

Previously published in The Names of Lost Things
(LUMMOX Press, 2012)

Jason Hardung

Jason Hardung *was born and raised on the windy plains of Cheyenne,*
Wyoming. His work has appeared in numerous journals and magazines
including: Thrasher Magazine, New York Quarterly, Evergreen Review,
Chiron Review, Word Riot, 3 AM, Underground Voices and Monkey Bicycle.
He is also an editor for Matter Literary Journal. The Broken and the Damned
was his first full length book of poetry published by Epic Rite Press in 2009.

WE WERE KIDS NO MORE

I walk around
there's a sun out
and sirens in the street
because a kid got shot
and over there what's that
they're chopping down a 300 year old oak tree
cool
more room to roller skate
on top of the spilled brains of the blown away kid
what street am I on
oh shit it's just another American street
Central Valley Central District South Central
they cut down all the trees in Central Park
they cut down the sun from the sky
feed us marshmallows from wicker baskets
hook us like fish and bait us with ass licks
it's fun when you think about it
especially with a good script from the psych doctor
shoot me in the temple with extract of apple pie
switch on the mobile satellite
how many hits does it take to get to the center of the website
the mirror says it's your birthday today
subtract another candle from the cake
way to celebrate
in the future your brains will resemble scrambled eggs
a fine and beautiful mess not unlike
the tree house where you first jerked off
the parking lot where they found you shot in the head
the whole solar system at the edge of its seat
the universe in fact wants its money back
I walk around with the sound turned down
with my eyes closed
it takes practice

Jay Passer

Jay Passer's work has appeared in small press and online publications for over 20 years. His newest chap, Only Human By Definition, *is available from Crisis Chronicles Press, and a forthcoming chap from Corrupt Press is due out in late 2012. His native habitat consists of random carousing along the Pacific Coast, toasting the elements in size 12 loafers.*

step out

step out of
your cloud and
dance
rain will come but
it won't hear us
leaves will fall
yet the tree
remains
mountains
rise above
magnetic
green fields
still we step past
the deafening
light onto
the edge of
daybreak
a couple of
old souls
none the worse
for wear.

Jayne Lyn Stahl

*Published in Ygdrasil:
A Journal of the Poetic
Arts; December, 2010*

*Jayne Lyn Stahl is a
widely published poet,
playwright, essayist, and
screenwriter. She is a
member of PEN American
Center, and a book of
her poems,* "Riding with
Destiny," *is available
from NYQ Books, a
subsidy of The New
York Quarterly. http://
www.nyqbooks.org/title/
ridingwithdestiny*

VISIONS

Visions are meant for Preservation.
The city refuses to
Distinguish itself.
The hills roll into
Sandy mounds
Of wave-lapped beaches

Jeff Parks

*Jeff Parks lives in
Bellflower, California.*

That Other Path

Urban beatitude, the old embrace, is mine here
in this imagined Venice hotel room, rent unpaid.
Venerable old broad, I wear second-hand, embroidered silks,
washed threadbare. In my battered note book, in the language
of the street tribe on the corner, I have just scribbled another
poem in conversation with the freestyle flavors of graffiti
visible from my window. Falling in and falling out,
the writing brotherhood, journals in hand, stumble up
to my room from Venice alleys, (our free boxes
of voluntary poverty and voluntary madness). I honor
this life not lived, every detail, the frayed carpet,
exhausted wall paper, communal bathroom down the hall.
I can almost read those poems I would have written,
not bad, but not mine at all. Today deer wander past
my cabin window, on sunny days a red fox visits,
overhead, red-wings chase a hawk, otter swim in the bay,
and I think about how it is I wandered off that other path.

Joan Thornton

*Joan Thornton writes and creates artist's books in Inverness
Park, CA where she is active with two local galleries and
a poetry group. A passionate reader, she is especially
interested in the ways we create and then struggle to survive
our environments. She is currently working on a collection of
short stories, about the why and the why not.*

My Desert Flower

The glow of
Brilliant salmon,
Golden orange,
Vibrant,
Awe inspiring:

The Arizona sunrise.

Her display lit me up from the inside
As she brought to light the treasure of my
Desert flower.

Beauty,
Healing,
Exhilaration peeked
But then just as the sun drifts from the sky
So does the joy of the morning.

The intensity of the sun fades to the chill of the desert night
Revealing the emptiness of my arms.
I try to shade my desert flower from the dangers that surround
But like a scorpion it finds it's way in and attacks.
No matter how hard I try
I cannot keep my beauty from the storm.
Raw & bloody from the inside out.
Broken down to a crawl.
Strength so far off in the horizon it is blurry in the melting sun.
My body cries out for reprieve
But there is little refreshment to be found.
My feet long for solid ground.
My arms grow weary holding the hope of you,
My desert flower.
May the mountains console me and her
Comforting cedars embrace me,
But not alone,
Oh please,
Not alone.
She remains as a dream,
So real for a flash of a moment,
An oasis for my soul
Then like a mirage she is gone.
I drag my heart through the sand of the storm with strength I do not have,
Pulling from a well of Love that was dug deep by my Lord long before my time.
May each sacrificial drop bring me to the reunion of joy under the cedars of peace
That remains in the warmth of home.
Oh thrive my desert flower,
THRIVE!

Artist, Poet, Teacher, Friend, Believer, and Beloved to my husband who endured my longings for 13 years until we finally were able to bear a child. Which made it all the more heart wrenching to become a Mother 3 months too soon and watch my baby get sick in the hands of those who were meant to heal. Praise God, with suffering comes the opportunity for miracles which is exactly what we received.

Jody Balian

Skyline

It seems fitting how these smokestacks
Have names, only sometimes I wish
They weren't so absurd –
Winkin', Blinkin', and Nod –
The stuff of childhood,
Ridiculous dreamlike characters
Incongruous with the massive
Brick sentries I watched
As my parents drove us
Home from the Y,
My hair still damp because
I was lazy with the towel.
And as I watched them grow
Smaller in the distance,
I had only a vague
Idea of their power
And certainly no clue about
The smell they put off,
A dank industrial odor which
I never knew existed until years
Later when a visiting friend
Complained of the stench.
No, I wasn't aware
Of any of that,
Only their shape
On the horizon
And my eyes growing tired
Of keeping them in sight,
Their rhythmic blinking
The pulse of the city.

John Abbot

John Abbott *is a writer, musician, and English instructor who lives with his wife and daughter in Kalamazoo, Michigan. His chapbook "There Should Be Signs Here" is forthcoming from Wormwood Chapbooks.*

Cathedral of Assisi

The Sunday bells toll and
the Cathedral of Assisi birds
look down on the masks, gourds,
tapestries, pottery,
the sunlight finding
its way through the shaking leaves
to the street, forgotten conquistador's
name on cobblestone; the
wrought iron gates,
400 years of faith restored
after one night of rain, and
with a trip down stations of the
cross lane,
not hard to feel absolved of
most mischief.

Neruda said
poetry is the skin of the planet,
but faith is the marrow of stone,
monumental blocks of it
large enough to hold its weight
in ritual, its stained glass saints rigid
and beautiful in their
blind windows, the
rest of us down on the street
in the sun,
blistered by sin,

dwarfed by blue sky.

John Macker

John Macker*'s latest book,* Underground Sky *(the 2nd book in his* Disassembled Badlands *trilogy), is available at fine local bookshops. Other books include* Woman of the Disturbed Earth, Adventures in the Gun Trade *and* Las Montañas de Santa Fe *(with woodcuts by Leon Loughridge.). In 2006, he edited the Desert Shovel Review. After 17 years, he is in the final throes of remodeling an old stone and adobe house on the Santa Fe Trail near Las Vegas. The neighborhood coyotes, rattlesnakes and turkey vultures tolerate his presence and act as bemused muses.*

The Air Undressing

Turbine mist
above the river
like a bride
and her ghost,
I am colder
than the air
undressing them.
The poetry
that spoke to me
was consumed
in the maw
and searchlight
of its writing
on a stone top.
The cruelties
of disappearing
like an idea
remain after
the heartbreak,
I tended wires
to keep music
and endeavor.

John Swain

John Swain lives in Louisville, Kentucky. His work has recently appeared in BluePrint Review, Red Fez, Flutter, and Up the Staircase Quarterly.

dear john;

i'm sorry to say
the magazine's not going to happen.

that piece of shit
husband of
mine

left and took the money.

but your poems still sing to me.

so,
i'm returning them
knowing that they'll find a home
somewhere else.

i love your work.

send me
more,

and
if you can,
i sure could use

an extra
twenty bucks.

John Yamrus

Since 1970 John Yamrus has published 19 volumes of poetry, 2 novels and has had more than 1,400 poems published in print magazines around the world. His most recent book of poetry is They Never Told Me This Would Happen.

Passing on the Left

Blue herons in a crease of green
beside the highway, bald eagle
stationed in nondescript tree.
The farmer's house shredded
      by wind,
his crops blunt, shadow-tinged.

This our car, this our winter tongue.
Where miles change to kilometers
we take our cue
      from speed,
leave the border for other roads
beside which Anna Karenina's house
      sat out
the 20th century with no interruption.

Gauze curtains drawn,
blinds pulled,
      light the affect
of rooms never touched
by moon or sun.

In this, the difficult
          marriage—
a peripheral glimpse
serves to show how well, in rows,
the farmer's crop lies fallow.

If bulbs lie fisted
      deep beneath
glazed ice, they're certain
to hold entire skins
      swaddled, encrusted,
vein-laced and finely traced
by the kind of dirt no snow
will ever see.

    Judith Skillman

Claudio Parentela

Judith Skillman *has authored twelve collections of poetry, including* The Never *(Dream Horse Press, 2010) and* The White Cypress *(Cervéna Barva Press, 2011). A former editor of Fine Madness, Skillman has taught at City University and Richard Hugo House. www.judithskillman.com*

On Loneliness

There is something
about solitude in trees,
soft laps of liquid
against stone
and wood
and plant.

Revealed in moments
around dry landscape.
Hoarse cry of toad
Insistent birds looking for mates.

Sunlight splashes across
the shadow of my hand
reflecting my nature
upon nature.

Distant rush of traffic
on gentle breeze.
Faraway laughter
in spring.

Brown, gold, green
tapestry woven over lumps
and crags
and stuffed into gullies.

I've found the burial ground
of Egypt here.
Snakes instead of mummies.

Twisted trees beseech sky
for rain, yet weeds
tell of recent showers.

Peaceful and soothing
restoration of the soul.
There is something
about solitude.

K. Andrew Turner

K. Andrew Turner *writes
literary and speculative
fiction, poetry, and dabbles
in nonfiction as well. He has
been painting with words
since he was 12, imagining
how to connect worlds both
far and near. He is a creative
mentor and freelance editor,
and also teaches creative
writing.*

shrapnel around the heart

the boy sits
beneath the shadow
of the juniper tree
album splayed open
on his lap

his fingers caress
the pieces of his
collection

a friend joins him
an album of his own
tucked under his arm

and they fall into
comparing favorites

the boy proudly displays
rusted corkscrews,
shards of spark plug ceramic
two nails twined
into a crucifixion form
pulled from
the radiator of a bus
near the detonation of
a female suicide bomber
in Tel Aviv

his friend showcases
his own crown jewel
a ragged circle
laced with silver thorns
his father brought home
from work, last week,
pulled from the chest
of a five year-old girl

you can still see
the blood on it,
the boy marvels,
holding the disc up
to the fading sunlight

Karl Koweski

SPOTLIGHT ON KELL ROBERTSON

**KELL ROBERTSON and
OUTLAW POETRY: An Interview
of TONY MOFFEIT by ORION**

FOLLOWING THE DEATH OF KELL Robertson, this interview took place on January 20, 2012.

O: The poet Kell Robertson died on November 7, 2011. Can you talk a little bit about Kell and his place in outlaw poetry?

TM: If following your own way is first and foremost the main ingredient of the outlaw, Kell Robertson was an outlaw. Stubbornly independent and individualistic, he referred to himself as an outlaw, but wanted to keep it somewhat quiet. His reasoning was that the posse might not be too far away. Another reason was the living of the marginal life, the marginality of the outlaw. He died on the property he had lived on for the last fifteen years of his life, just Southeast of Santa Fe, New Mexico. It was one of his more stable stays, as he lived in an assortment of places in an assortment of cities and states, from San Francisco to Ocala, Florida to Austin, Texas to Raton, New Mexico to Santa Fe. He lived alone or he lived with his romantic partner, whomever she happened to be at the time. He was a vagabond. He was a loner. He was a romantic. He was a great communicator through two major means of communication: the letter and the cassette tape.

He was a poet and a country and western singer and songwriter. The poet Jack Micheline once told me, "Kell could make you cry with his singing and his songs." And Jack was right. The depth of the emotion coming through from that scratchy, downhome voice was extremely powerful. And his tapes were full of his songs as well as his poetry. It was through his means of communication that he was an outlaw. The outlaw communicates best one on one. Kell communicated best one on one. One on one

he was a communicator supreme, spicing his letters, tapes, and conversations with poems, songs, and bits of his own outlaw philosophy. He could make the reader, the listener feel a true intimacy. Because Kell Robertson was *real*.

O: What did Kell bring to the outlaw poem?

TM: The outlaw poet brings an innovation, a unique approach to the poem. What is it that Kell Robertson brought to poetry that was different? He brought a unique irony to the American poem. A unique irony that approaches a Zen-like quality. A unique irony that brings a form of enlightenment. Something goes off in your head. His twists of phrases, his rare, uncanny approach to life and language, turn the reader's or listener's mind upside down, and reveal a new way of looking at things. As an example, here is an unpublished poem of his:

Ada

They put you in
a plastic bag, tied at the top
a piece of tape said your name
on it- It was hard to open,
clawing at it while your friends
stood around in a circle
holding hands and waiting
while I tried to hurl you away.
Your brother's
ultra sharp hand honed knife
finally released you and
I whirled and whirled and threw
your ashes into the sleet laden wind
while everybody sang
"Amazing Grace". I was laughing
remembering holding you
in my arms as we two stepped
on that rough wood floor of the cantina
embarrassing them all, an old man
and an older woman, making fools
of themselves- The circle sang

Amazing Grace- some cried,
some wailed and some looked appalled.
After it was done, we went inside
the neighbors brought food, pies
and cakes and bowls full of hot chili.
Driving home we drank a quart
of good whiskey in forty miles
of bad roads- sleet turned to snow,
You were out there, not you but something else,
dancing with everything dead and
alive again, in some miraculous dance.

Kell tapped into the outlaw energy and he tapped into the ghost energy. His was an all-time classic description of what happens after death: "You were out there, not you but something else,/ dancing with everything dead and/alive again, in some miraculous dance." Just as naturally as sleet turns to snow. Or two stepping on the rough wood floor of the cantina.

Also in this poem one can see at work another Zen-like quality, the description of common, everyday objects and events with a secret, underlying mystical quality. As the poem progresses, the more commonplace the language, the more mystical, the more exacting the description, the more mysterious: "some cried,/some wailed and some looked *appalled*."

This poem exhibits another quality of the outlaw and outlaw poetry and that is an exceptional ecstasy, a metaphysical joy, a universal laughing dance. It brings to mind a statement of my own father when he learned he was dying of leukemia: "We're born, we die, and along the way, we just try to have a little *fun*." For Kell Robertson, and for the outlaw poet, the creative act conquers all, the creative dance conquers all.

O: In what other ways does Kell reflect the outlaw and outlaw poetry?

TM: Well, Kell was like an old Zen master. Gruff, he had no use for pretense. And like an old Zen master, you had to prove yourself, which wasn't easy. However, if he liked you, and respected you as an artist, he was extremely generous. He would send you endless poems, letters, cassette tapes, songs. His outlaw philosophy was wrapped up in these. He had no use for the computer or the cell phone. He typed out his poems on a manual typewriter. He recorded most of his songs on a variety of cassette tape recorders. If you were lucky enough to be a recipient of his letters and cassette tapes, you were in touch with a secret message or messages. His homespun philosophical ramblings were pure outlaw. His poems were pure outlaw.

In person he was full of a metaphysical humor. Buy him a beer and he would tell you endless stories. Once we were sitting in a bar in Santa Fe, The Cowgirl Hall of Fame, and he was flirting, as always, with a barmaid. As we were laughing at his flirtation, he told me the barmaid reminded him of a woman about whom a friend of his warned him, "You don't want to have anything to do with her. She's trouble. She will leave you the first chance she gets for another man. You can't trust her. She'll stab you in the back. She's about as bad as it gets. And besides, *I saw her first*."

Opening one of Kell's letters was always an interesting experience. He might say about his letter and an enclosed poem, "This is an experiment. And as far as life on this planet is concerned, it's still an experiment." And I might write him back and say, "Life can't get any better. If it got any better, you'd think it was a frame-up. If it got any better, it would have to be a conspiracy."

O: Do you have anything else to add?

TM: Kell Robertson helps to identify the outlaw. Kell Robertson said almost nonchalantly "If you want to call me something, call me an outlaw." And, he was immersed in the high drama of the poet, effortlessly. A Kell Robertson poetry reading was sure to be an interesting experience. His drinking, his asides, his performances were unpredictable and spontaneous. His best known poem, "A Horse Called Desperation," might be compared to Thoreau's line, "The mass of men live lives of quiet desperation." Kell's desperation was not quiet. It rang from the rooftops. His horse carried him "jerking and screaming through/the stark cold night and the flames." The outlaw takes the negative and through pursuing it obsessively makes it a positive. The outlaw is uncompromising. Kell was uncompromising.

Kell identified the outlaw poet in another way. He always approached the world, each day as if it were a beginning. Even in his early 80's, a few months before he died, he was working on a new book and he was in the midst of a new romance. His new book was to be titled "Slow Dancing On the Edge of Oblivion." As Kell said, "Hell, I'm trying not to fall into oblivion yet."

SOME POEMS BY KELL ROBERTSON

SONG (Christmas 1978)

Rain walk down through
Curtains of wet. Thin glimmer
of beer signs on the sidewalk;
"Louie loves Julie."
fingered into concrete
the date, 1947.

In Milio's bar
damp drunks lean
into hot brandies
and it's somebody's birthday.
The house gets a round
on the garbageman
With his arm in a sling.

Two hoods shoot pool,

scratch three times
on the eight ball,
laugh, curse God
in Spanish.
No harm intended lord.

A moth-eaten deer head
stares mournfully out,
his glass eyes
almost alive
in the flicker
of a dying neon light.

If we're falling
friends
let's sing the godamn thing
all the way down.

UNDER A WATERTANK

Under a watertank in West Texas
with a bottle of cheap whiskey
& a package of damp camels
watching the lights of El Paso
behind a curtain of rain.

I shared my whiskey with everything.

SONG

On the gravel shoulder
along one of those
great strips of asphalt

Sunrise

nobody here but me lord
& a lonesome bird
flickering in the brush
a can of pork and beans
heated over an open fire
a drink of cold overnight whiskey

chased with crisp creek water
my songs crackle
like brandnew dollar bills

a big truck whips by
the driver's eyes fixed
on somewhere beyond horizons
red eyed hauler of highways

there is an urge to sink into the landscape
crumple into those low hills

If I'm lucky
I'll make bakersfield tonight
wrap the warm taverns
around my eyes

things drop out of our hearts
you could kill a herd of Buffalo with.

GREASE

from the kitchens of Juarez
is soaked up by Mexico's huge sky

the odors of excitement
food booze women music
and death by the bucket full
carried by the living.

These people seem to leap through life
eyes flashing
like the sequins on the mariachis pants
or the suit of lights as the torero
arrogant in innocence
leans to face the bull
under the trumpets
the shouting crowds.

Death and grease
to feed the live
very real humanity
trapped and embraced
between the packed earth
the wide sky.

Orion is a poet, video artist, and singer who currently lives in Alaska. He is the author of Honky Tonk Heroes, a poetry tribute to Waylon Jennings and Willie Nelson, published in 2009.

THE POETRY VII

THE LAST DAY

"So whence the world's beauty? Was I deceived?"
John Updike – December 11, 2008

When I lie on that last bed
    on that last night, what
        might I wonder?

Whether I was deceived
    and, if so by whom?
        or was I my own Judas?

The one who pretends
    things are not as they seem,
        that there is no beauty
           in this devilish world.

I would have all the evidence
    any man could need if that
        is where I choose to look.

I confess to having traveled
    that stone-strewn road, the one
        awash in a cloudburst of sorrow, ruts
            cut deep from promises not kept.

Beauty has no address
    on this God-forsaken path
        yet we walk it, searching
            for the one house where
        regret no longer resides.

It would be easy to choose instinct,
    to run like a spooked rabbit caught
        in an open field, desperate for cover,
            the beckoning shelter of the tree-line.

Or I could remember watching
    my children burst from the womb's comfort,
        the sunrise on those days like none other,
            the moon those nights a sliver of a smile
                peeking between the silhouetted trees.

Krikor N. Der Hohannesian

Previously published in the Connecticut River Review

My poetry has appeared in many literary journals including The Evansville Review, The South Carolina Review, Atlanta Review, Louisiana Literature, Connecticut Review and Hawai'i Pacific Review. My first chapbook, "Ghosts and Whispers", *was published by Finishing Line Press in 2010 and nominated for The Pen New England Awards and Mass Book Awards, the latter selecting it as a "must read" in the poetry category for 2011. A second chapbook,* "Refuge in the Shadows", *will be forthcoming in 2012 from Cervena Barva Press. I also serve as Assistant Treasurer of the New England Poetry Club.*

WILDWOOD

I get on the El in North Philadelphia,
not far from Tulip Street
where Father died by
the posts of the ramps
to the Tacony Palmyra Bridge.
I sway with the clickety-clack of
the car pushing & pulling on the tracks
between closed windows
in the second story brick.

I want a woman with dark brown hair
to open one of those windows,
lean out with her breasts
brushing the fire escape,
and hand me a flower.
I want papaya & mango juice served
by the young man sitting next to me.
I want Miami in April,
and Wildwood in August.
I want Elvis on South Street,
and a big long car heading for New Orleans.
I want branches of magnolia
through an open window of
the St. Charles Street trolley,
cooked seafood in the hot wind,
and lips under the cream awning
of the Avenue Cafe.
I want to watch green grow under the door
of shotgun houses,
what pierces right through
and holds you there,
Jesse still in Tupelo.

I still want to be held in that way,
with mussels & oysters in the air,
to be wrapped in black shutters,
my hair flowing up a fire escape
to a Mansard roof,
a woman at the top of stairs
handing me a sweet southern rose.

I want tulips in North Philadelphia,
and the rhythm of the El
as it holds me between freeze-frames
of lovers in windows.
I want the reach of blue shell crabs
over the rim of a dented pot
as they are dropped into boiling water.
I want butter dripping down my chin
as I break open the shell.
I want Scott paper napkins
piled up beside my elbows on
a red checked tablecloth.
I want to ride in a convertible
down the curves of Fulling Mill Road.
I want the carousel and Ferris Wheel,
the tunnel of love and roller coaster.
I want the *Days of Wine and Roses*
at the Strand Theatre,
The Platters and Chuck Berry.
I want clams on the half shell and
crab sandwiches at the Shamrock Bar.
I want Wildwood,
the sweet Wildwood of my youth.

Kyle Laws

*"Wildwood" was previously published in
Caprice and the anthologies* POETS On the
Line *and* They Recommend This Place *from
the Women's Studies Program, University of
Southern Colorado.*

*Kyle Laws' poems, stories, and essays have
appeared in magazines for thirty years, with
four nominations for a Pushcart Prize. Books
include* Storm Inside the Walls *(Little Books
Press),* Going into Exile *(Abbey Chapbooks),*
Tango *(Kings Estate Press), and* Apricot
Wounds Straddling the Sky *(Poetry Motel's
Suburban Wilderness Press). She is editor
of Casa de Cinco Hermanas Press. www.
kylelaws.com*

Ceiling

Above Asilomar the cloud hangs planar solid glaring grey
It leans upon the wizened cedars, flattening their tops

The blackened hawk, in air compressed, just barely clears the scrubby dunes
To seek relief she glides as low as wash of ocean lets her go

At wet sand beach the seaweed sticks, pressed free of foam by heavy sky
The sky so planar solid glaring grey and motionless above Asilomar.

Lance Nizami

Lance Nizami has no formal training in the Arts. He is active in the world's most competitive profession, yet without an institutional appointment or income. He started writing poetry during a long airplane flight in 2010, and has written much since then in-flight.

Wringing Out the Mops

There are days you
don't want to see
your reflection in
the floor. But you
polish hard until it's
mirror-like anyway.

There's a little art
in anything done well.
This floor is a canvas.
Don't laugh; sometimes
art is simply caring in
a way no one else does.

Larry Rogers

Previously published in Samisdat, Vol. 49

Larry Rogers is a Fort Smith, Arkansas poet/songwriter.

Thumbing Through Envelopes

rebecca said
you put x-mas
on your
grandmother's
card

so?
i replied
larry
the woman's
been
a churchgoer
seventy years now,
she most
certainly keeps
the christ
in christmas

it's fine
rebecca
i wrote
merry christmas
on the inside
of the card

larry, she
ends her
phone calls with
god bless you dear,
i'd write out
a new envelope

well i'm not
writing
a new one

on account of
i keep the
christ in
jesus christ
this is
goddamn
ridiculous.

Lawrence Gladeview

Lawrence Gladeview is a barroom raconteur and foul-mouthed poet who lives in Boulder, Colorado with his wife Rebecca. His full length poetry collection, Just Ignore The Beer Stains *is available now from PigeonBike Press.*

COYOTE MASK

let sand
create
free flight
for the one:

aerial
in lodge shadow
of flights'
smoked-out confession
of seeing
the see through
eyes
where flames
take the desert
become sotol
or plumes
of sage…

wear outside
inside

it wore itself
and floated
until medicine shouted
banish it
away

that thing
that thing

casts too wide
a shadow for
a dancer
a beginner
here

Lawrence Welsh

Lawrence Welsh's eighth book of poetry, Begging for Vultures: New and Selected Poems, 1994-2009, *was published in 2011 by the University of New Mexico Press. A Southwest and El Paso Times bestseller, this collection was named a Southwest Book of the Year by the Pima/Tucson Library Association. A first generation Irish American and award-winning journalist, Welsh's work has appeared in more than 200 magazines.*

The Things I Most Desire

Yesterday you prayed
that I would heal,
but I am so cluttered
with last winter's dead leaves
tracked on the trail,
the job I lost,
and the friend,
I cannot find the stillness
to see the buds of forsythia,
--odd and jarring,
squat and symmetrical,
instead of free and new.

But after rainfall,
and the sun opening
things are sometimes
washed and shining,
resolved:
like a deer moving
through the woods,
safe, joyous.

Linda Benninghoff

*Previously published in
Kolkolka magazine in India*

Linda Benninghoff
*was published most recently in
Canary and Poets and Artists.
She published* Whose Cries Are
Not Music *(LUMMOX Press).*

Leftover Heartbeats

This man used to burst out with wild words
That tumbled faster than his breath.
Now he breathes through an oxygen tank,
Reminder of excess, nights of beer and laughter.

This other man who held a sword
Could not dodge the blows before him.
Now he wears scars of many wounds,
Incisions and encounters.

And this man whose heart walked the open road
Came finally to the place where his heart slowed down,
35 beats to the minute, trip almost over,
Until they gave him a wind-up machine
To make it beat on time again.

My heart, that raced so quickly after him
Would not stop racing. For that, there is a pill.
With my heart becalmed, I consider how
I could give him my leftover beats.

But he might construe that as romantic.
And of course, it is. How to deny it?
All these years separated, living our destined lives apart.
His heart ticking slower, mine too rapidly,
Until we meet halfway.
Listen to it, he says, feel it
But don't press too hard.
I put my fingers there,
reassured that wherever
there still is a heart beating
among our friends and ourselves
love has kept us ticking.

Lynne Bronstein

Lynne Bronstein *has written four books of poetry,* Astray from
Normalcy, Roughage, Thirsty in the Ocean, *and* Border Crossings.
*She works as a newspaper reporter for a Westside newspaper, has
written for numerous music magazines and web sites, has published
poetry and short fiction in numerous magazines (and web sites),
and was winner of the first runner up short fiction prize for Poetic
Diversity's Fiction Contest in 2006.*

**on trying to understand what it means to owe
trillions, what a trillion even is**

On reading that the national debt tops $14 trillion

I give up; stop searching the internet, dictionaries
and follow what I know in my gut....

it's the cost of an apple, the price of lettuce
I once worried about
that con ed bill that goes up with the temperature
the ac that breaks and must be fixed or replaced
but cannot keep out the heat

It's a debt that keeps increasing with
warnings of black outs if the bill isn't paid by a certain date
yeah, I finally get it...it's the process of subtraction,
not of dollars but breaths

nobody knows how many breaths they actually owe--
it's that coach some relative bought on the installment plan
and kept paying for the rest of his life because no one
told him to stop; it's a three room tenement apartment
the landlord coming for the rent...he did every month
                                        and
it's not exactly that my parents didn't have it,
it's just that they didn't have all of it
that there is no all of it to be had, it isn't something finite
soon, they kept repeating...soon...

a trillion is the highest point I can imagine falling off
a number so large it takes the breath right out of me
but I go on, everyone goes on, we keep on breathing
somebody's dirty air

Linda Lerner

Linda Lerner's *most recent collection,* Takes Guts & Years Sometimes (New & Selected
Poems), *was published by New York Quarterly Books, June 2011 http://www.nyqbooks.org/title/
takesgutsandyearssometimes. She's previously published thirteen collections of poetry. She's
been nominated twice for a Pushcart Prize. In 1995 she and Andrew Gettler began* **Poets on the
Line,** *(http://www.echony.com/~poets) the first poetry anthology on the Net. She's been published
in hundreds of journals, several anthologies and has read widely across the U.S.*

witness

for Charlotte Troesch

look at this ring
made for me by hands that worked in marble
I am monumentally clad from knuckle to phalange
my finger sheathed in silver tree bark
wrought with her magic
I wear this to shame the world

this pendant dangles around my neck
like Thor's hammer
swung on a chain of knotted silver
all her other work has been demolished
I wear this in sorrow for you
who never knew her

look at me
I extend my wrists to you
read the bones
I wish I had numbers tattooed on my skin
blue bruises inscribed by a despotic beast
then you would understand
why I am angry that I have survived
in a diminished world

> *Lorine Parks*

From an upcoming collection entitled Downey Noir.

Lorine Parks has just published her first book of poems, Catalina Eddy, *for which the Long Beach Press Telegram named her one of its Amazing Women of 2012. She curates the Third Thursday Poetry Readings for the Downey Arts Coalition.*

THE END OF POETRY

Give it up, poet!
surrender your images!
you've been demoted
to prose.

No more blissful strolls
among Monet's flowers,
or a bon-mot
which almost rhymes
-but not quite-
with 'sublime'.

Or agonizing
about which words
to save for the end.

To prose with you,
poetry...
you had your chance,
ecstasy raps at the door gently once,
and then it's memory.

> *LuíZxCam*p*Oz*
> o4//3o//12

*Dominican-born poet **Luís Campos** has been a member of the L.A. poetry community since 1969, when he joined the Venice Poetry Workshop, directed by John Harris and the late Joseph Hansen. He won first prize in the Bay Area Poets Coalition Contest of 1984; he also won the Unknown Reader Award of Electrum Magazine of 1985. His work has appeared in the Los Angeles Times, Venice Beachhead, Bachy 1, and other publications.*

MONTMARTRE

Haven't you wanted, sometimes, to
walk into some painting, start a new
life? The quiet blues of Monet would
soothe but I don't know how long I'd
want to stay there. Today I'm in the
mood for something more lively,
say Lautrec's Demimonde. I want
that glitter, heavy sequin nights.
You take the yellow sunshine for
tonight. I want the club scene
that takes you out all night. Come
on, wouldn't you, just for a night or
two? Gaslights and absinthe, even
the queasy night after dawn. Wouldn't
you like to walk into Montmartre
where everything you did or
imagined doing was de rigueur,
pre-Aids with the drinkers and
artists and whores? Don't be so P.C.,
so righteous you'd tell me you haven't
imagined this? Give me the Circus
Fernando, streets where getting stoned
was easy and dancing girls kick high.
It's just the other side of the canvas,
the thug life, a little lust. It was good
enough for Van Gogh and Lautrec,
Picasso. Can't you hear Satie on the
piano? You won't be able to miss
Toulouse, bulbous lips, drool. Could

you turn down a night where glee
and strangeness is wide open? Think
of Bob Dylan leaving Hibbing. A little
decadence can't hurt. I want the swirl
of cloth under changing colored lights,
nothing square, nothing safe, want to
can can thru Paris, parting animal
nights, knees you can't wait
to taste flashing

Lyn Lifshin

*Previously published in Iowa Review and
will be in her forthcoming book from New
York Quarter Books, A GIRL GOES INTO
THE WOODS.*

Lifshin *has published over 130 books and
chapbooks including a series from Black
Sparrow Press. Most recent books:* Ballroom,
All the Poets (Mostly) Who Have Touched
me, Living and Dead. All True, Especially the
Lies. *And just out,* Knife Edge & Absinthe:
The Tango Poems. *In Spring 2012, NYQ books
will publish* A Girl Goes into The Woods.
Also coming For the Roses *poems after Joni
Mitchell. For other books, photographs,
reviews, news and interviews please see her
website:* www.lynlifshin.com

---

one way

ninety-eight degrees of air
did nothing
to slow the steps
he took getting to her side
saying, "come with me"
and she did.
wiping sweat from her brow,
golden salvation swung
from a lopsided mirror that reflected
the valley along his neck and

he observed her as if
she were his personal Jesus
come to save his soul, so
he drove faster
than the scorching wind
visualizing scenes up ahead
on a cool platform
where they would perform acts
no hail Mary's
could forgive,

or would want to.

Lynne Hayes

*Lynne writes about what she lives
and observes. She is headed to New
Orleans & plans to finish her novella
on the banks of the Mississippi. She
also holds the reins at take-it-to-the-
street-poetry, a non-profit org.*

BITCH! L.A. *IS* POETRY!

TRUTH BE TOLD: L.A. ISN'T REGARDED as a literary mecca. With the notable exception of Charles Bukowski, the City of Angels is known for *TMZ* celebrity sightings, clogged freeways, earthquakes, surgically enhanced T & A, and, the Dodgers.

I know L.A. as a literary wonderland, as a far-flung community of poets (fallen angels in disguise), who, in various micro-communities, foster the written word at open mics, in local journals (both in print, and online), and, who have, unselfishly, given countless hours, days, weeks, months, and years to keep the poetry foundations strong and sure for those who are coming in, for those who are actively participating, and for those who move on, both geographically, and off this mortal coil.

The selection of poets I've chosen are those that I, as editor of *poeticdiversity: the litzine of Los Angeles*, have published, and, I am proud to be associated with; **Jerry Garcia**, whose cinematic poetry is as vivid and beautiful as his photography and films; **Deborah Edler Brown**, who's successfully helped many of her students transition from literary hopefuls to full-fledged poets and writers; **Eric Lawson**, a brilliant, funny chronicler of the L.A. human condition; **Charles Claymore**, a musician and poet who views L.A. as a mystical 21-century Constantinople; **Apryl Skies**, a writer who not only regularly promotes and publishes local poets, but whose own words brings a touch of old fashioned magic to the suspect glitz and glamour of L.A.; **BC Petrakos**, whose sorrowful brilliance is immediate and accessible; **Maja Trochimzyck**, an artist and modern-day mystic who finds beauty in the simple elegance of nature; and **Alex M. Frankel,** who unflinchingly shares the deepest, most vulnerable parts of himself to the bravest who will read, and remember his words.

I started *poeticdiversity* to capture the wonderful diversity that is our collective history. I've done a modest job, but, I wouldn't have been successful without the efforts of those who started before me, like RD Armstrong, whose journal, *Lummox*, is an awesome, and inspiring labor of love. I hope, you, The Reader, will remember that poetry is the most personal or all the Arts, and will continue to support those of us who, for the love of Truth, and the Word, keep working to strengthen our piece of the Left Coast literary legacy.

Marie Lecrivain

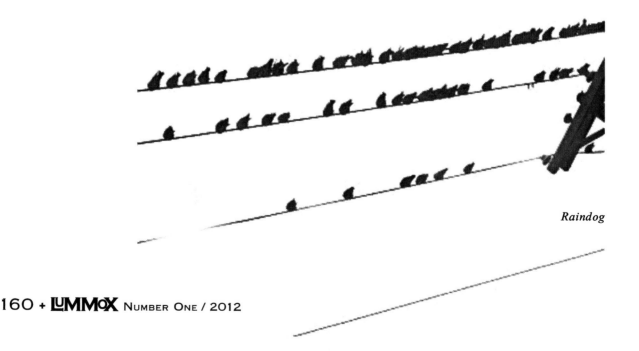

Raindog

MARIE LECRIVAIN

Keep Asking

You inform me that I left behind a trio of items
in your car; a black cloak, a diary, and some money

in an envelope marked "holiday in ___" The last
two items are my gifts to you. Everyone needs

a vacation, as well as the tools to get started. I mention
someone has upset me, which precipitates the joke

that you'd like me to bring you to heel with a ruler...
metal or wood... 12-inch or yardstick... you don't care.

Behind the humor, I sense the urgent need for domination,
not necessarily by me, but by any woman ready to strip you

of your bad boy charm, who'll leave you naked, breathless...
and on the edge of oblivion. The cloak is for you, to warm
the scars that run through your heart and burn like cold flame.

*Marie Lecrivain is a writer, photographer, and the editor/publisher of **poeticdiversity: the litzine** of Los Angeles. Her work has appeared in various journals, including Haibun Today, Illumen, The Los Angeles Review, Poetry Salzburg Review, and others. Her short story collection,* Bitchess *(copyright 2011 Sybaritic Press), is available through Amazon.com and smashwords.com.*

JERRY GARCIA

Toward the PCH of Divinity
in the 1970's

We found ourselves in a Dodge Dart
rattling 62 mph on city streets,
Jack Daniels hand over fist,
skunkweed fragranced the air,
passing headlights punctured dilated pupils.

Four mustachioed men in polyester prints
and double knit bell bottoms—brothers of ethos,
pace in and out from The Oar House to Buffalo Chips,
crossing Main Street in a chance of traffic,

nose powder glistening in street light exposure.

Merlin McFly's hosted cherry drink blondes
of college persuasion who kept an impenetrable huddle.
So we descended upon the discotheque on Admiralty Way
like it was our right to Travolta the floor,
a bunch of morons with no rhythm, style or moves.

Lights too bright, shadows too dark, we couldn't see our own drinks.
So we rabble-roused the parking lot and stripped gears down Sepulveda
toward the Wild Goose because Big Daddy's disco was a washout.

A strip club of modest means became a little bit of Vegas in Lennox.
Bachelor party boys looked lost among G-strings and pasties
—while my buds were just drunk and crazy.
Davy's nosebleed made Rorschach patterns on his disco shirt.
Stage lights triggered another one of Harvey's acid flashbacks.
Thrown out before last call, we sat on the curb and howled
at motorists passing on Imperial Blvd.

Slow-paced, off-freeway maneuvers to avoid cop bust
and drunker than we drivers,
we snaked Sepulveda to the Moulin Rouge of Lincoln Blvd-
—Van de Camp's Coffee Shop.

Sunday morning we watched sun up from the Santa Monica Pier,
hung over and weepy in the Hallelujah of a fisherman's church.

*Jerry Garcia is a poet, photographer and filmmaker from Los Angeles, California
who earns his living as a producer of television commercials and motion picture
previews. Jerry has been a co-director of the Valley Contemporary Poets and
served as a member of Beyond Baroque's Board of Trustees. His poetry and
photography have been seen in various journals including The San Pedro River
Review, poeticdiversity, Chaparral, The Chiron Review, Askew, Palabra Magazin,
and KCET's Departures: Poetry L.A. Style.*

CHARLES CLAYMORE

LA: Under the Guise of No-Thing

*"A million poppies gonna make me sleep.
But just one rose, it knows your name..."*
—Cracker, Low

0

Feverug

Sitting in a house with no lawn
watching the flamingos pogo by
on those new, high speed 'things'
they've just come out with.

And there were many, many distractions,

But I managed to just keep staring.

Pool of sweat a rug between me
and its back.

They say there's a place like this
where dwell many Angels.

That it's much like this.

1

Axes

First came the good times I beheld as bad.
Next, the good times I knew were good.
Then, the bad times, that, fooled, I appraised as good.
When came the blindness from dazzlement of the Light.

Now the pier withstands the tide's rip, and I grip the rail
behind, and wait...

As sight returns, I realize no need.
Desire, however, burns.

I feel the pull.

2

A Study

I look at her and I wanna say
give him everything you wanna give
and accept everything he wants to give
but I know it's selfish to tell anyone
how to live so I just look away

but I don't wanna, I don't wanna,
I don't wanna, I don't wanna,
I don't wanna, I don't wanna,
I don't wanna, I don't wanna

Stars on my wall,
Stars in my head,
Stars in my fall,
Scars on my bed.

I don't wanna, I don't wanna,
I don't wanna, I don't wanna

Oh, I look at her and I wanna say
give him everything you wanna give
and accept everything he wants to give
but I know it's selfish to tell anyone
how to live so I just look away

but I don't wanna, I don't wanna,
I don't wanna, I don't wanna,
no, I don't wanna, I don't wanna,
I don't wanna, I don't wanna,
I don't wanna, I don't wanna,

Stars on my wall,
Stars in my head,
Stars in my fall,

Scars on my bed.

Stars on my wall,
Stars in my head,
Scars in my fall,
Stars in my bed.

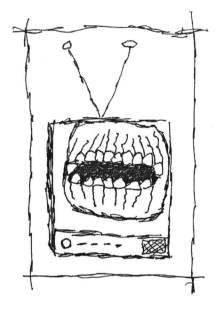

Mark Hartenbach

Charles Claymore

Charles Claymore *is, continues to be, or has
been, some of the following things: a circus
trainer, animal tamer, cook, traveler, librarian,
dj, artist, landscaper, archer, husband,
counterman, alchemist, musician, hunter,
flatworker, wing forward, racer, student, fling,
pain in the ass, priest, and poet. He has written
songs about people and vice versa. He lives,
and quite thoroughly enjoys, LA*

BC PETRAKOS

In Part

The part of me that is missing
Was funny
Quick witted
Open minded
Laughed and believed
The part of me that is missing
Was hopeful
Honest
Kind
That piece
Taken in midnight's violent stupidity
By selfish strangers
Scoring the road in blood-drenched escape route
Taken in silence lonely howl
That piece
Waits for me with lions and lambs

Explains mysteries
Says look again
The clock
Is not king
The pain a new door
Open it at risk
Always at risk

BC Petrakos *is a writer/performer
whose work has been published
in various journals, including:
poeticdiversity, Falling Star Magazine,
Red Fez, Duke University Press, Huston
Literary Review, and, others. She has
performed in the U.S., U.K., Scotland ,
and Spain, and, she also writes stuff for
Hollywood but thinks very little of it.*

ALEX M FRANKEL

Aubade

Time to drag my bloated kidney
elevated triglycerides
lattice degeneration
average IQ
below-average prospects
into the glare again
armed only with Wellbutrin
Cozaar Aldactone Lipitor

Sunup with its well-planned bourgeois vistas
its quiet and its shrubbery and its rules
should reassure me
the fastidious dogwalkers I pass on the drive to work
should reassure me
I call "I miss you!"
to a dog long dead I can't let go of
I reach an L.A. campus that's born again
with rich Mongolians   rich Chinese
I speak sense to a circle of noses necks   eyelids
in a haze of Mondaymorningness
to which my contribution is
deplorable posture
a grizzled head
impressive passive feet
that beg for the pleasures of a hot water bottle

Such tired sleepiness to handle a day
A half-century just bangs you up

Time was when I let in the sun
let it pour through the open blinds
power up my fountain pen and Smith Corona
to fill fifty sheets a morning
child novels   verse plays   naïve little odes

Can't stand the pitiless business of daylight
its monolithic will to go on no matter what

As I awoke from uneasy dreams
a sewer rat was squirming in a glue trap near my bed
legs   fur   tail   whiskers   sick on a soupy tray
pointy face abashed in the sickness
watching me

Alex M. Frankel was born in San Francisco in 1960, went to college in New York, lived in Spain for many years and in 2006 got his MFA from New England College in New Hampshire. He hosts the Second Sunday Poetry Series in Pasadena. His poetry, fiction and reviews have appeared in The Comstock Review, The Antioch Review, The North Dakota Quarterly, the Gay and Lesbian Review and Cider Press Review, among other publications.

ERIC LAWSON

After Last Call, Before First Light

My eyes are nearly devoid of all moisture
Why do I torture my nubile mind like this?
Why do I insist that I'm missing something?
My eyes can barely take in anything more

And yet,

I have seen may things I cannot un-see

Sweat pours from the bodies that are
mindlessly shuffling down Spring Street
at four-thirty a.m. heading nowhere fast
And me?
I'm fasting from boozy kicks via the ATM
The air is heavy
It had been a dark and stormy night like
all the other ones from clichéd rejection
letters clogging the arteries of Los Angeles

A tramp vomits into a nearby sewer
A hooker actually turns down a trick
A cop looks the other way on a meth deal
An innocent man is swallowed by the city

I am enveloped by the California night
But this is not hustle and bustle club hopping
This is not rescuing orphans for burning buildings
This is not saving the world from corruption
This is just here and now
Here could be anywhere
Now could be any time before sunrise

This is the time of the street urchins and hustlers
That magic time between one and five a.m.
While the dreamers are all fast asleep,
the hustlers are out making ends meet
or thinking up new ways to con the naive
or putting a new spin on cons long forgotten

And me?

I'm not in any hurry to get home just yet
but my old haunts have all denied me
The liquor store closed--
Damn those without second winds!
The paper stand is closed--
Screw tomorrow's tales of woe!
The bus is still off line--
To hell with your snails-paced coffins!
I hail a cab to ease my itching burden
The only thing waiting for me at this hour
is an empty apartment,
one glass of whiskey,
and no ice

*Eric Lawson is the author of three chapbooks
of poetry and two comedy collections. His
work has appeared in such publications as
Hennen's Observer, Subtopian Magazine,
Falling Star Magazine, and The Houston
Literary Review. He resides in Los Angeles.*

APRYL SKIES

this quiet burn

silence burns
parchment turns to ash
punishment serves no purpose
without redemption

reticence ignites
structures rust beneath torrid winds
elements corrode hollow walls
to wayward distance

silence ablaze
melting ice of another day
washed away, a brackish lake

white noise marks its place
searing hush turns over like tide
as archways burn
trust rusts between the lines
of inaudible destruction

silence burns precious days to ash
banishing a sun's simple ray
treasures lost, washed along
deserted shores

bridges decay beneath our feet
quietude cold,
sheets of relentless snow
and sudden flame.

Apryl Skies is a Los Angeles award-winning filmmaker and author of A Song Beneath Silence *and* Skye the Troll & Other fairy-tales For Children. *Her work has been published worldwide and she has been a featured guest reader throughout L.A. As the Sherman Oaks Poetry Examiner & founder of edgarallanpoet.com; which features poets and writers from across the globe, she is dedicated to preserving the integrity of poetics in art, culture and community. Skies expresses her devotion to the written word with a quiet intensity and is a superbly visual and telling writer, whose work holds merit among authors both classic and new.*

DEBORAH EDLER BROWN

Jerusalem

Jerusalem, earth-spirit mother,
are you true wife or harlot?

you nurture so many
you spawn ghosts like guppies

whom do you love?

three men have come to you
left seed in your womb

it burns in their imagination

see how the children squabble
they are their father's children, throwing rocks

do you care for any one
or do you sleep in the sun of ages

turning gold?

in your hills do you mourn them?
somewhere in your desert hills does water flow?

Deborah Edler Brown is a poet, performer, journalist, teacher and author. She was the 2005 winner of Kalliope's Sue Saniel Elkind Poetry Prize, the 1997 National Head-to-Head Haiku Champion, and a member of the 1998 Los Angeles National Slam Team. As a journalist, Brown was a stringer for Time magazine, and she is co-author of Grandparents as Parents: A Survival Guide to Raising a Second Family *[Guilford Press, 1995]. She was born in Brazil, raised in Pittsburgh, and lives in Los Angeles, where she writes and teaches creative writing.*

MAJA TROCHIMCZYK

Among the Lilies

-- after Claude Monet's Water Lilies at L' Orangerie, October 2011

Water Lily I

Etched under my eyelids
The water lilies rest on the surface
Of Monet's pond at Giverny
Intense blues and greens of his palette

Fill me with color he invented

This, I want to see – his *nenufary*
This I want to be – a lily among his blossoms
With my golden hair
In a halo of sunrays, above aquamarine
And celadon

My crystal necklace
Sparkles like the pond he made
Sunlit, translucent
Like stained-glass windows
Lined with birdsong

Water Lily II

Clouds measure the stillness of water
Cerulean breeze dances in the grass
He starts a new canvas
Turquoise into aqua into mauve
The secret of water lilies

Born in iridescence
His garden drinks in
The dark vertigo of the sky, swirling
With opaque strands of mist
Dawn air chills his fingers

Maja Trochimczyk, Ph.D. is a California poet, music historian and non-profit director, born in Poland and educated in Poland and Canada. She published four books of music studies, two books of poetry and two anthologies, Chopin with Cherries *(2010) and* Meditations on Divine Names *(2012). Over 120 of her poems appeared in online and print journals and anthologies by Poets on Site, and others; she writes a monthly poetry column for* The Voice of the Village *community paper. She is a former Poet Laureate of Sunland-Tujunga and a dedicated volunteer - managing Polish-American cultural groups and teaching arts and ethics in jail.* www.trochimczyk.net

THE POETRY VIII

NOT SO TENDER

I.

In the rain
the exiled homeless
next to a garage
of million dollar cars

II.

The bus drifts
into the Tenderloin –
bodies sold
for a roof
of drugs

1/11/11

Cruel eyed blonde
has the latest handbag
of death

2/16/11

the attractive
speedy energy
of the gaunt
peroxide boy,
face a riot
of piercings

12/21/10

Marc Olmsted

*Allen Ginsberg said "**MARC OLMSTED** inherited Burroughs' scientific nerve & Kerouac's movie-minded line nailed down with gold eyebeam in San Francisco." Olmsted's book,* What Use Am I a Hungry Ghost? – Poems from 3-Year Retreat *(Valley Contemporary Press, 2001), has an introduction by Ginsberg.*

Condoms on the handlebars
of a rusted bicycle

three sneakers are dangling
from the braided fiber optic line
parabola pole to pole in the sky
as we crash over pothole craters
in the pod of a restored rear-engine
Volkswagen Beetle on a back
street that looks like Dresden after
World War 2 as we disembark
into a forbidden quadrant to poke
gingerly with salvaged pool cues
from a fire bombed corner whiskey
bar at burial mounds in this artifact
rich free garage and yard sale
in abandoned homesteads and hulks
of chop shopped automobiles
recalling biblical Noah with his white
dove and olive branch but drunk and
naked in a tent at the end, while
we separate clothing from data

cable, cobbles, and condoms on
the handlebars of a rusted bicycle
in glory where the grips should be.

    Mark James Andrews

First published in Word Riot.

Mark James Andrews *has had a full and
checkered career as a gravedigger, inspector
at a defunct auto plant, jail librarian and
public library director. He is the author of
two poetry collections,* Punkpomes pleeze
and Burning Trash. *His poems, stories and
reviews have appeared in many print and
online publications. He continues to live and
write just outside the Detroit city limits most of
the time and claims no guru, no method and no
PHD at the moment.*

VACATION POSTCARD

    I scattered lost thoughts all over the streets of Paris
    Like rose petals, bread crumbs or cookie fortunes
    Hoping they would float down the Seine
    Beneath the ancient bridges
    Past the summer homes of Communist poets
    All the way to the sea

    There they would conspire
    With ghost vehicles of exile
    To slip through the Panama Canal
    Unnoticed
    And meet me in San Francisco

    Mark J. Mitchell

Mark J. Mitchell *studied writing
at UC Santa Cruz under Raymond
Carver, George Hitchcock and
Barbara Hull. His work has
appeared in various periodicals
over the last thirty five years. He
lives in San Francisco with his wife,
the documentarian and filmmaker
Joan Juster. Currently he's seeking
gainful employment since poets are
born and not paid.*

NEWBIE

Eric was kicked
out of Hooters
for saying something
to a waitress.
He's one of our
new cab drivers.
He's dumb enough
and mean enough
for the job.
If he'd start
slobbering out
the side of his mouth
he'd be perfect.

Mather Schneider

*Mather Schneider is a
42 year old cab driver in
Tucson, Arizona. He has a
few books available.*

A Dull Ache

Your head
is caught
in a vise,

just like
the one
in your
high school
shop class.

Every morning,
before making coffee,
before getting dressed,

you give
that steel lever
another
half-turn.

It's not
that
painful.

Not
really.

More like
a dull ache.

It's not
going
to kill you.

Matt Galletta

*Matt Galletta lives in
upstate NY. He brews his
own beer so he never has to
leave the house. Contact him
at www.mattgalletta.com*

Raindog

THE ROCKY MOUNTAIN HIGH

by Mike Adams

James Taylor III, Jared Smith, Jerry Smaldone, Karen Douglass, Phil Woods, Captain Barefoot & Mike Adams

WHEN RAINDOG INVITED ME TO WRITE something about the poetry scene here in Colorado and showcase some Colorado poets, I was at first flattered that he would ask; but I quickly began to have second thoughts; it seemed like such a daunting task. I decided to leave writing about the poetry scene here for another time, and focus on showcasing some poets. But I'm familiar with the work of a lot of Colorado poets; how would I choose? Literary critics always seem to have pretensions to some sort of objective criteria to rate the quality of a poet's work. But taste is a largely personal thing, and changes with ones age as well as with the times. There are a few greats whose work is timeless – Whitman, Dickinson, Yeats, Keats. But many other fine poets seem dated years later, or simply fall out of fashion.

There is nothing objective in my criteria. The six poets I've chosen here are all people I know well and whose work I admire. I have read with each of them, some of them many times. James Taylor III, Phil Woods and I, along with musician Jim Sheckells, are the Free Radical Railroad, and have published two books together as the Railroad and performed extensively. The work of all six poets moves me. What they share in common is an essentially narrative style, a belief in words as real and substantial, attention to craft while never (or almost never) allowing craft to overshadow the soul of the work. And indeed, all of their work has soul, by which I mean a belief that they have something to say that is worth saying, and the courage to say it. And, as in soul music, their poetry often merges the earthy, even profane, themes of the blues with the uplifting and spiritual themes of gospel. None of these six have allowed their work to be eviscerated by being beholden to one school of poetry or another. Beyond that, they are all quite different.

The poetry of **James Taylor III** is spare and honest, sometimes even brutally so, reflecting years of teaching in some of the poorest, most violence-prone schools in the country; and equally years of roaming the deserts and canyons of the American west. At the same time there are kernels of humor and lightheartedness scattered amidst hard tales of poverty, violence, and the simple stumbling errors that a man makes as he moves through life.

Jared Smith writes poetry wide and deep in scope, poems of long rolling lines and powerful themes of struggle and triumph. He explores the same strong river of verse traveled by Sandburg, Whitman, and Williams. Smith's poetry is as fearless as that of these predecessors. If you ever get a chance to hear him read, don't pass it up. As someone once said of some famous senator or another, he could read the phone book and make it interesting. Smith's poetry weaves together beautifully the tiny, the essential detail, with large society-wide themes.

The poetry of **Jerry Smaldone** asks questions about family, community and place that we all wrestle with in one way or another: What brings a place to life? What human elements imbue land, sky, streets, and buildings with soul and love? Smaldone's poetry is strongly grounded in the northwest Denver neighborhood where he grew up, and in the mountains and plains surrounding Denver. Read Smaldone's poems about Denver and you may well fall in love with the place even if you've never been there.

Karen Douglass' poetry is pointed and imagistic, infused with strong emotions without being sentimental or nostalgic. Douglass goes right to the essence of things without burdening her poems with either generalizations or unnecessary detail. Each poem tells a story, complete in itself.

Phil Woods is the most narrative of the poets I've selected. Many of his poems are unashamedly political, displaying his fiery passion for justice and freedom. Others are tender homages to family, friends and community, while others honor his love of the blues. It is easy for a poet who ventures into politics to become preachy and didactic. Yet the poems selected here show that Woods is able to walk the tightrope between lyrical poetry and rhetoric.

Captain Barefoot is one of the finest performance poets I've ever known. Short and stocky, he possesses a deep booming voice that belies his size, and an expansive and flamboyant delivery. An unrepentent hippie, he can stand on a busy urban street corner and hold an audience spellbound. The words on the page don't do justice to the thrill of a live performance by the Captain. The selection here stands on its own, though the best way to appreciate Captain Barefoot's poems is to read them aloud.. Roll the words around on your tongue, feel the heft and weave of them, chew on their solidity. Enjoy the sheer sensuality, the red rock sheen of them.

JAMES TAYLOR III

Poem for Olowan
died 2-10-05

The headlines broke by word of mouth
matter-of-factly over the moccasin telegraph
another kid murdered
strung up in his own backyard.

A quiet third year freshman
chillin' until something happened
and it did
tangled up
beer blind or meth charred
pissed off the wrong
hazards this time.

No one is talking
but the bragging will not
be silenced for long.
The retaliation
only a bad night away.

…

Old cottonwoods of the world
close to the muddy banks of the Little White River,
Corn, Horse, Sage or Spring Creek –

Black Elk instructs
how a five point star will appear when the upper limbs
are crosscut for prayer or endurance,
a dance of strength before human frailties.

…

Head bowed,
beaten so badly his knees buckled,
and unable to support his hundred and twenty pounds
of history ;
the sacred hoops and circles
became empty spaces to fall through.

And in the middle of nowhere
it was just another school night
punctuated
by loss.

James Taylor III writes occasionally and has just completed his Resignation Poem announcing his permanent departure from teaching high school Language Arts. We are not sure he will be any more prolific, but we're hoping he's not such a curmudgeon. He is the author of a few short books including Fresh Leather: The Buffalo Poems *and* Forty Years and Twenty Paces. *He is also a founding member of* **Family Breakdown** *and* **The Free Radical Railroad**.

JARED SMITH

Equinox

A grasshopper crawls over the twisted steel rail, rusting
within a hand's reach from where I sag down on haunches,
tumbles on its head, flails its feet on the rotting wooden ties
and takes to air tick-wickering the way grasshoppers do.
My fingers reach out to the yellowed aspen leaves,
testing their resilience which is not much, then dust.
I don't know why I have come to the end of this rail
way track that lies abandoned behind houses and rocks.
The sky has never looked so blue or the sun so dappled,
and my lungs are filled with the first cold air of autumn
from deep down where the wildflowers hold their roots.
Oregon grapes grow bitter but big in blueberry memories,
their thorny leaves strung in holly garlands along the ground.

The world ticks again, whickers, and wings fill the sunlight,
across our alpine meadow. The suits hanging in my closet
have so filled with time that they do not fit any longer. There
are dark men standing in the midst of forests all across our land.
They have their calloused hands out, calling silently.

Laying my hands to the steel bent and rusted, narrowing
toward home I feel still the hard hands of men who made this rail
a way of transitioning things that bring change from cities; those
hands torn lifeless now but not so long ago holding wars in Europe
between plantings of the seeds that grow around us now, and I
hear the winds of winter gather above our peaks, whipping
down wind and water carved canyons and through the aspen.
The mountains groan along that line of time, and space is
the opening of time between each leaf upon each trembling limb.

Each blade of grass, each leaf of sedge is sharp to the fingers,
cutting away the seasons of growth that gave it green,
each slender stock tinged toward tomorrow with yellows,
browns, reds intertwined. And the air is bright with the
scent of an old lady's Depression era spice cabinet.

In the dark pools, the hidden riffles far above Boulder
in the off-road unmapped Indian Peaks Wilderness, the
sun is rising inside brown trout and smoking inside their sides
with all the colors of the mountainsides where no one sees.

They bend into the rocks themselves spending their spawn
into the fusillade of color that gives life to time, flesh to flesh,
encasing themselves in bright red eggs that are the dawn of everything
dark beneath the water that feeds upon the songs of crickets,
and I wonder what this rail is still doing here, scarring
this seam of land. I think at times I know.

This poem first appeared in **Poetry Bay** magazine

Jared Smith is the author of ten books of poetry, including The Graves
Grow Bigger Between Generations *(Higganum Hill Press, CT, 2008);*
Looking Into the Machinery: The Selected Longer Poems of Jared Smith
(Tamarack Editions, PA, 2010) Grassroots *(Wind Publications, KY, 2010);
and* The Complete Poems of Jared Smith: 1971-2011 *(NYQ Books, NY, 2012).*

JERRY SMALDONE

Allora

In the presence of death
the barely felt breath
of life

What is left when the milk
is separated from the cream
the glue that holds us together
that keeps everything from flying apart.

The eyes of strangers that do not see
the darkness in the center
Here lies fleeting time like a sleepy dog
calling, chi 'e, who is it? this look I give you

When the sun and moon rise at once
and carry my blood away your dark eyes say
Play your flute, lonely man the night is deep
and soon you'll sleep.

Like the insects that sing
in the dry fields I sing in my unborn sleep
barefoot broken branches are burning in the dawn
as I pray for unrecognized desires for what, I don't know.

We drink wine and crack nuts complain
because there's little else to do
We trust the angels to guide our passions,
to protect our beds inside these four bare walls.

voices echo in the barren square
doors open just a crack

the songs, like a horrible howl
of a soul beaten into dirt.

You have to have energy
to eat, to sleep, to hang
I, like a gutted goat
waiting to be skinned

great dry canyons flanked by standing stones
wait in sun and rain and when I protest
I am not human they only scream louder

I feel bad for them I have no life
to give them only pain.

I belong to no party
it is against my vital breath
my heart beats for freedom
only a free man can be just

every farmer knows it's wrong to take
someone's land every walk in the snow
begins with a song.

Lay a card of St Gerard
on my sick bed as I groan my way
toward eternity

Let the angels sing me home now
one last time let me hear
the women's cries and
my sweet lover's scream.

*Jerry Smaldone writes from Denver, on the themes of Denver,
family, ethnicity(Italian), blue collar blues and self(eternal spirit). He
has published a dozen chapbooks over the last forty years. The most
recent was* All Flesh Shall See It Together *(Turkey Buzzard Press,
2010), available from the author at gsmal33@comcast.net.*

KAREN DOUGLASS

The Healing Tree

A child born ruptured in Dartmoor,
"passed through" the trunk of an ash tree,
split and wedged open. Three times
mother and father at dawn
handed the infant east-to-west
through the gap in the tree. Wounds bound,
baby and tree lived. Better, the father said,
than "sloppin' water in a church." Perhaps

the growing girl sat leaning against
her healing tree, dreaming
of a life that would split her open,
bearing her children into the world,
whole and hardy as a forest.
I would like to meet such a tree
and its daughter, but it's late
and our faith in trees is dying.

Karen Douglass' books include Red
Goddess Poems; Bones in the Chimney
(fiction); Green Rider, Thinking Horse (non-
fiction); Sostenuto, (poems) *and* The Great
Hunger (poems). Two-Gun Lil (poems), *is
scheduled for publication June, 2012.*

PHIL WOODS

Ray Charles

Do you remember the first time
you heard Ray Charles?
That throaty voice, that stutter-step,
hurry-up beat, man that guy
knocked me out every time.
Even when he did country
with violins & the whole big production
that voice like warm butter on hot toast.
I mean the guy touched you
someplace in your chest.
I remember seeing him on PBS
live at Montreaux. Whole bevy
of jazz greats ready to back him up.
Dizzy, Ron Carter, cats like that that,
& Ray smiling & those guys
trying like hell to hang with that
quirkiness that was Ray's signature.
They could do it, but nobody could chart it
or make it regular. You have to lose
your sight in Georgia, learn Braille
far from family, have your personal way
of marrying the sanctifying gospel sound
with that cat at midnight, barrelhouse boogie,

pure blues creeping sensuality
that makes for the set-you-free rhythms
we call soul. You can't buy it; you can't fake it.
Either you can testify because you've lived it
or you can't. Ray could testify all night
& never be done. Take patriotic cliche
& kitsch of America the Beautiful
& make even a square-assed honkie
like Nixon want to get down
on his knees & pray.
We won't see another like him.
"What I say? Hey, hey."

Phil Woods received his MFA from the
University of Oregon in 1983. He has been
writing poetry since 1967 and has published
nine books including: Original Mind *[Turkey
Buzzard Press, 2008]*; Lucid Dreaming
*[Turkey Buzzard Press, 2010]; and two books
in collaboration with poets James Taylor III
and Michael Adams, as* **The Free Radical
Railroad***. Phil is a retired high school history
teacher and an active member of the organic
theater group,* **The Romero Troupe.**

CAPTAIN BAREFOOT

Addicted

Chocolate to morphine. Acid to ecstasy.
I could jones on you forever.
Your taste on my tongue.

Sure, at times we trade tit-for-tat.
Give or take. But ultimately
both of us get taken away.

You say, Pay attention to my clock.
It's on Tibetan Tantric Be-Here-Now time.
But what I hear are the crazed

bees of electricity's angst
humming in the wires
& the sweet drawl lisp of your voice.

Love's a dented circle
pierced with arrows. I bring you
a heart of rough-cut alabaster.

Take my anger & polish it
to a sheen where at last
my own scuffed self can be seen.

Time to dance, I shout
Hooping & hoofing it while we can.
Give me a hand, darling,

Let's do a Tarentella Napoletana
under the slickrock black of our Anasazi sky
looking south to Lone Cone.

Once more I'll ignore the stars to stare
into the polished juniperberry
blue of your eyes.

Glazed. Longing. Hungry for
the grip of the other. So here now
we're gone.

Previously published in the Broadside Union of Street Poets, Vincent St. John Local / Colorado Plateau / Aztlán; Kuksu Brigade (Ret.) / San Francisco 2012

Captain Barefoot *is an unrepentant hippie living in the wilds of western Colorado attending Rainbow Gatherings, occasional Burning Man gatherings, and marching to the beat of a peace drum in a nation perpetually at war.*

MIKE ADAMS

One Woody Guthrie Song

Talking with my friend Phil
about the state of the world –
bad and only getting worse,
all of us rushing headlong
into the flames, ranting,
flailing at shadows.

I tell him about an interview I just
read with Gary Snyder – now 80 –
old wise bard, scholar and mountain climber.
Gary said towards the end that the state
of the world is dire and sometimes the only
thing that works is laughter.

Our dear old friend Dolores,
who lived her life ringed by mountains,
would say when we started to discuss
the Big Issues, like saving the world,
that it's hopeless, so let's all
chant, and sing, and dance.

Phil relates how the deep ecologists would sometimes
talk and talk until all that was left to do
was tell jokes,

Says that's all
that matters, that
and making music.
Phil is in his mid-60s
and is learning to play his first
musical instrument ever, the guitar.

He tells me, I want to be able to play one
Woody Guthrie song before I die.

Michael Adams fell from grace years ago and came to rest just east of the
Continental Divide in northern Colorado. His most recent books are Steel Valley
(LUMMOX Press, 2010), and If You Can Still Dance With It *(Turkey Buzzard*
Press 2012). Michael is an accomplished clawhammer banjo player and a
member of the poetry and music performance group, **The Free Radical Railroad.**

THE POETRY IX

Confessions Of An American Outlaw #167

The muse flies around the room
With the lights from the disco ball
I felt her wind pass by me
Caught her scent in the air
Pheromones seducing me
The muse she fucks me good
Leaves me satisfied
Comes around only when I make time
What a fucking woman
& she's easy too
No drama about her
& she understands why things have to be this way
She wants it this way. She has many other lovers.
That's all we are are lovers
Right now she skanks around the room to The Clash
There she goes
Out the window
The only woman I could love

Michael Grover

Originally published in Zygote In My Coffee #37

Michael D. Grover *is a Florida born poet. As a wanderer he's traveled and lived all over the country. He currently lives in Toledo, Ohio. His work has appeared all over the literary underground. Michael currently is a resident artist at the Collingwood Art Center in Toledo. He runs the Covert Press. His newest chapbook "americanEyes" is available on Propaganda Press. His first full length book* A Shotgun Does The Trick *will be out on Tainted Coffee Press. Michael is the current head poetry editor at* www.redfez.net.

Haunted Boat Ride

My haunted boat ride
Runs up and down Wilshire Boulevard at midnight,
As the undead, ravage trash cans
With caravans of lost shopping carts,
Sometimes two in a row,
Warming themselves on the flaming remains
Of what used to be a career at Camarillo,
Or Rikers Island.
They hold out their hands as I pass,
"Change?"
Says one of the burned-out inmates
As he spews bad breath
And the foulest B.O. that has ever gone
Up my nose.
His eyes are dead and hollow
And I think that maybe, this ride is just for me,
It's not real, I'm supposed to learn something,
But I'm not learning, I'm just not getting the message.

There are hundreds of them,
Some are even magic sages.
They tell you things that no one else could possibly
Divine or know, like,
"You need to eat more fruit,"
"They're going to kill you—with a gun."

A woman, with a beautiful but weathered face,
Powdered with white makeup, walks up and asks me for 50 cents,
A dollar will not do, it must be 50 cents!

The limousines circle around and around,
Dropping off visiting landlords and widow manipulators
Of vapor, bad paper, shit-ass rental stucco,
And some show business movers and shakers
At a French restaurant so close I could spit,
And hit the window,
Or the hot tin roof,
Of a black-and-white that passes by,
But never stops,
Until someone is
Over, under, around...or through.

Michael Meloan

*Michael D. Meloan's fiction
has appeared in WIRED,
BUZZ, Larry Flynt's Chic, L.A.
Weekly, SuicideGirls.com, and on
Joe Frank's NPR program. He
is coauthor of the novel "THE
SHROUD," and also a Huffington
Post featured blogger.*

looking for a muse

1

I suppose this cockroach will do
jumping from the counter, buzzing
shortly before landing
on the scattered pages
of my journal

2

hidden under the exoskeleton
it holds the wrinkled star
chart – the first edition –
fading each time
its body chemistry
is forced to adjust
to environmental changes

3

when it molts
it doubles in size
expanding
like a new universe
collapsing back down
to burn a little
stronger
eating its replica
repeating this until it has wings

4

if you allow one to sleep
on your tongue
you'll hear its soft clicking –
imagine the suck and pop
of blattarian dreams

– you may learn their true names
– you may learn the first language

5

be careful if you bite down

you'll hear the soft crunch
and it'll vibrate the senses
that trigger nausea and panic

but don't worry
the white gush
isn't blood, nor is it poisonous
it's pure protein, useful, nutritious

remember this when in dire need
of food

6

they taste like shrimp

7

if you allow one to crawl
into your brain
you'll be better for it –
your primitive brain will
remember plants
and shrubs that scientists
can only speculate existed

and like the cockroach's
yours will grow like a root
through your body –

your sexual life will be more
intelligent, yes, your genitals
will be cognizant

Michael Spring

Previously published in Mudsong
(Pygmy Forest Press, 2005)

Michael Spring *is the author
of three poetry collections:* blue
crow *(LitPot press, Inc., 2003)*
Mudsong *(Pygmy Forest Press,
2005) and* Root of Lightning
(Pygmy Forest Press, 2011).
Root of Lightning *recently
won an 2012 Eric Hoffer Book
Award (honorable mention).
His poems have appeared
in numerous publications,
including The Atlanta Review,
Chiron Review, DMQ Review,
The Dublin Quarterly, The
Midwest Quarterly, NEO and
Steelhead Speical. Michael lives
in O'Brien, OR. He is a natural
builder, a martial art instructor,
and a poetry editor for The
Pedestal Magazine*

Man Down

When you see a beggar on the street asking for a hand out, who is the beggar?
I give from my warm pocket straight to his hand because it is I who needs to feel less beggardly.
It is I who needs to be fulfilled, not him.
Most probably he will continue to beg every day, in heat, in rain, and in the cold.
These are the days that inevitably will fall upon him.
Right off the freeway, into the vast underbrush lies his
lady,his companion, in this dread existence.
Devoid of cleanliness. Devoid of teeth. Shoes flip flopping with only one flop that is connected
and the other loose and broken like all the dreams and orgasms not experienced.
Is he a man of color or a man dark with dirt ? Dirt caked within crevices and folds of what might
have been a decent looking face.
Who is this Thrown out man?
Was he a man of character, was she delicate and flowery in her youth ?
Ah, perhaps she is still in her youth and never became a delicate flower.
Add them up society, add them up.
Hundreds, maybe thousands ! Here in the U.S.A.
Where is their profit? Where is their Cayman Islands?
Where the hell will they eat, bathe, sleep, or defecate tonite?
Again as before. the burger joint closes and teens throw out the balance of today's vulgar food.
Greasy fat amid the smell of decayed flesh from animals recently slaughtered.
They will swallow as the night before and the night after whatever fills their belly so the pain o
hunger is put on hold.
Vomit behind the bushes. Hide it from your partner so she is not ashamed.
It is my shame, this beggar I see.
It is my hand that should reach out.
It is my shame, my hunger, not his.
I am the beggar......

Mitchell G. Cohen

*Chicago, IL born, raised and educated. U.S. Army. Disc Jockey, Newscaster. Writing since
14years of age. Married for 50 years to my Bride Barbara*

THE MAN WHO SEES COMBAT

he dances through dust storms
hurls bottles into a bruised sky
shattered glass sand-weathered glints in his yard
he won't uproot volatile sumac
plants acanthus and castor bean in rich ravine soil
he wanted to be a fireman cooks chile rellenos
swings the pan so egg and salsa decorate kitchen walls
he taught me long drives up the coast sleeping in fields
names of plants and birds I never can remember
we flew gliders off cliff sides soared

until he lurched out of the theater where
guts splashed on screen doctors joked
my car tracked his hunched body home
through deep puddles gasoline exploded on wet logs
he ran roaring back out into the thunder
I didn't know his love of sushi and sumie
began in the Philippine jungle
with the grenade he threw
at the Japanese soldier about to shoot him

this whiskey God/Bhairon
rubbed with betelnut decked with flowers
I see him curled up with his bottle television aflame
how can I judge his worship
that grunt's eyes broiling his brain

   Nancy Shiffrin

Previously Published in Game with Variations

Nancy Shiffrin's collection of poems GAME WITH VARIATIONS is available at http://www.unibook.com/ en/Nancy-Shiffrin/GAME-WITH-VARIATIONS. Her website is http://home.earthlink.net/~nshiffrin/ nshiffrin@earthlink.net

GRAVESIDE

Kneeling unsteadily near the head stone
he unfolds the clean cotton handkerchief
from his breast pocket and carefully cleans
the lenses of his eyeglasses, wiping
away the loess of their past life as fine
and dry as powdered bone;
the thought of her
under the freshly turned earth so weighty
that it bends time under its mass, curves light,
warps reason;
surveying adjacent plots
nestling restless aroused souls close by,
nearly hip to hip and thigh to thigh,
pressing obscenely against her on each
side, ghostly frottage in a vulgar crowd.
he conjures up a prayer but lets it fall
unspoken onto the sod, into the
soil, jealously hating heaven after
death where strange souls are urged to love his love,
and briefly hoping for hell for her, where
no love survives the crucible, where she
melts in the heat of his lust forever

Ned Randle

*First appeared in EMERGE LITERARY
JOURNAL, June 2012*

Ned Randle *resides in Southern Illinois. He
writes fiction and poetry. His short story, "The
Amazing Doctor Jones", recently appeared in
the Cigale Literary Magazine, Summer 2012.
His poems have appeared in a number of
literary publications such as The Spoon River
Quarterly, Poydras Review, Emerge Literary
Journal, Barnwood International Poetry
Magazine and The New Poet.*

The Melt

The magpie flew
right out of my heart
to you, my sons.
Even now I am weeping.
The melt is starting,
icicles falling.
There is talk of bluebirds,
of mating flights,
la primavera.
The sun is warm on my body.
I feel you with me.
I feel your youth,
your strength,
your love.
I want to live
the rest of my life,
each day,
as good and honest as possible,
find the grace to stand tall,
always kind, gentle, helpful to other creatures,
always grateful and humble in my heart.

Peter Rabbit

From the book **ORNITHOLOGY** *by Peter Rabbit
© 1982, Minor Heron Press, Taos, NM*

Peter Rabbit, *nee Peter Douthit, was born 10-8-
36 in Bradford, PA. Graduated HS in Owensboro,
KY. Attended several colleges, Black Mountain was
useful. Married, with 3 children. Has written &
performed poetry since his teens. Has been a has
been at least 3 times, bohemian, beatnik, hippy.
Has performed & lectured at colleges, universities,
museums, jazz clubs, bars, supermarkets, strip
clubs, festivals, etc., all over the U.S. & Canada.
Published 6 books of poetry. He was founder-
director, with his wife Anne MacNaughton, of
Taos Poetry Circus 1982-2003. He's lectured
& published extensively on alternate lifestyles,
appropriate technology & architecture &
expanded states of consciousness.*

Anniversary

I watched you sleeping
After a night of sexual chaos
Breathing contentedly
The sounds of the world filtering
Through the open window
Along with the gray light of dawn
It was the best thing in my life
So right
So unreal
A piece of silk floating on the black lagoon
Blown in by the ongoing tornado
That is this crazy life
We call home

I could scarcely move for fear
That you would bound away like a startled doe

I didn't know if I should laugh or cry

But then that moment was lost
Crushed and absorbed into the hungry maw
That was either your insatiable need for
Validation or the ongoing tornado
I really can't determine which

Now I sit here
Amid the ruins
Another error
In the grand scheme of things
Another
Told-you-so moment

Two years forward
And still spinning

RD Armstrong

Published in Muddy River Poetry Review.

RD continues to try to elevate the craft of poetry as a written form of expression. Like Don Quixote, he knows it's an impossible dream, but still he can't/won't stop. He has 7 books and 12 chapbooks and has worked on 8 anthologies. He lives near the L.A. Harbor, where he waits for his ship to come in.

Postcard To Myself, Syracuse New York, 1979

A few notes to the boy
I didn't leave behind:

After fishing that day on the Erie Canal
don't let the fish drop off the chain

hanging from your bicycle
on the way home.

The image of the live fish breathing
on the sidewalk,

somewhere in the middle of town
will haunt you for years.

Don't even fish.
Just go to the canal and wish them well.

Don't let them put you in the locker.
Don't hit the girl.

Take your clothes off more;
You'll know when.

Don't ask the boy at your birthday party
if he was invited.

Don't go to your best friend's birthday party
with socks as your gift.

You will not have the chance to apologize
for this for thirty years.

This is the first sign your mother
is not well. There will be others.

Burn the golf pants.
DO NOT TRADE YOUR COMIC BOOKS WITH TOMMY NOJAIM.

If it is ever twenty degrees below zero
it is okay to not deliver the newspapers.

Throw them away. No one needs the news
under those conditions anyway.

Whether you like it or not
you are moving to California.

Judaism isn't so bad.
Don't lose your great grandfather's watch.

You will find her.
I'd say, wish you were here,

but you will be soon enough.
Far too soon.

> **Rick Lupert**

Rick Lupert has been involved in the Los Angeles poetry community since 1990. He served for two years as a co-director of the Valley Contemporary Poets, a non-profit organization which produces readings and publications out of the San Fernando Valley. His poetry has appeared in numerous magazines and literary journals. He is the author of fourteen books. He has hosted the long running Cobalt Café reading series in Canoga Park since 1994 and is regularly featured at venues throughout Southern California. Rick created and maintains the **Poetry Super Highway***, an internet resource and weekly publication for poets.* PoetrySuperHighway.com

St. Germaine District, Paris, 1949

My dad sets up his easel
in the ruins of St. Germaine
and I get to amuse myself
in the post-war debris.
Concrete slabs and twisted rebar
throw mad shadow in the morning sun.
My dad takes a charcoal stick to the blank
canvas, roughs out
what's left of an apartment building.
Stained canvas becomes a battlefield
The hand and the stick depend on tension.
Six steps lead up to nothing,
fascinating to me or to someone
who studies destruction.
There will be no finishing touches
on this new order.
We try to imagine the noise this
would have made but the kids
went blind
before they were deaf,
went senseless before the skin peeled away
from the shock of fire.
Theory and speculation no longer matter. There
is disregard for the form and content debate.

There is no counting of ambiguities;
it all goes up in a flash and
it all goes up as one.

But this is about art,
illusion that sustains us.
Dad puts up the one piece
that is still recognizable as wall
while I break rock and
darkness falls.

Rick Smith

First published in Rattle #16, 2001 and later in Burning Bush online, 2004.

*Rick Smith writes & plays harmonica for **The Mescal Sheiks** (see mescalsheiks.com). He is a clinical psychologist, specializing in brain damage and domestic violence, working in Rancho Cucamonga, Calif. He has two titles out with LUMMOX Press:* The Wren Notebook *(2000) and* Hard Landing *(2010).*

a magpie

stops its mimicry
just long enough
to swoop
under a bridge
amid the vagrancy
of human dander
and spent tobacco
just long enough
to trek-peck along
towards a shiny bit
that caught its eye
it flies away
the novelty cast
into the river's wavelets
alongside other slices
of regret
forgetfulness
or fancy
a magpie
sings the same damn song
again

R.L. Raymond

R L Raymond is just a storyteller. His work has appeared in dozens of print and online journals here, there and everywhere, including most recently Epic Rites, Existere, Envoi, Carousel... His first collection "Sonofabitch Poems" is out and available. When not writing, he runs PigeonBike Press.

Decoy

We are sitting by the pond

as the sun slides into the trees

snags on the braided branches.

You point at the far bank,

almost hidden in shadow,

where a slash of white

balanced on one leg

leans into the pond.

Its yellow diagonal bill

tips toward the surface.

Bluegills and bass feed

unafraid in the reeds by its feet.

But from the air, even egrets

can't tell their own from a decoy.

Robbi Nester

Robbi Nester lives and writes in Orange County CA. She is the author of a chapbook, Balance *(White Violet Press, 2012), and has published poems in Qarrtsiluni, Inlandia, Victorian Violet Press, Philadelphia Stories, Floyd County Moonshine, Caesura, and has poems forthcoming in Jenny and Poemeleon.*

Because AIDS was slaughtering people left and right,
      I went to a lot of memorial services that year.
There were so many, I'd pencil them in between
      a movie or a sale at Macy's. The other thing that
made them tolerable was the funny stories people
      got up and told about the deceased: the time he
hurled a mushroom frittata across a crowded room,
      those green huaraches he refused to throw away,
the joke about the flight attendant and the banana
      that cracked him up every time.

But this funeral was for a blind friend of my wife's
      who'd merely died. And the interesting thing
about it was the guide dogs; with all the harness
      and the sniffing around, the vestibule of the church
looked like the starting line of the Iditarod. But
   nobody got up to talk. We just sat there
and the pastor read the King James version. Then he
      said someday we would see Robert and he us.

Throughout the service, the dogs slumped beside their
      masters. But when the soloist stood and launched
into a screechy rendition of *Abide With Me,* they sank
      into the carpet. A few put their paws over their ears.
Someone whispered to one of the blind guys; he told
      another, and the laughter started to spread. People
in the back looked around, startled and embarrassed,
      until they spotted all those chunky Labradors
flattened out like animals in a cartoon about
      steamrollers. Then they started too.

That was more like it. That was what I was used to:
a roomful of people laughing and crying, taking off
their sunglasses to blot their inconsolable eyes.

     Ron Koertge

*From GEOGRAPHY OF THE
FOREHEAD, U. of Arkansas Press.*

Found Art

To spot a diamond bit
among crushed beer cans
and rusty cars
is to find truth
in this man-made world.

    Roseanna Frechette

*Roseanna Frechette is
a longtime member of
Denver's thriving poetry
community. Former
publisher of Rosebud
Forum magazine, she
has great passion for
the power of small press
and the beauty of spoken
word. Her integrative
style reflects both a
love of nature and an
appreciation for
urban culture.*

*Ron Koertge is the author of a dozen or so books of
poems. The latest are FEVER and INDIGO, both from
Red Hen Press. A prolific writer, his new crossover book
for older teens/adults is LIES, KNIVES, AND GIRLS IN
RED DRESSES. He is also a dedicated handicapper of
thoroughbred race horses. More at ronkoertge.com*

"KIND OF LIKE THE SOUTH, BUT NOT"

OKAY, GET OUT YOUR MAPS: MY "region" is a little hard to define. It seems to center on Tennessee (especially, in these poems, the Western end – more especially Memphis and its little cousin, Jackson), although there's one in here from North Carolina, about 500 miles and a mountain range away. Maybe a name would help. Ten years ago, when I first moved here, I heard a local newscaster use the term "Mid-South." At the time, I thought it was just a way to keep people from confusing this patch of ground with the classic Deep South – you know, Mississippi, Alabama, Georgia? "Kind of like the South, but not," as a co-worker un-helpfully explained. Later, I realized that the phrase "Mid-South" serves equally well to separate us from the Mid-West where I grew up. And I can confirm that Jackson, Tennessee isn't like any place I saw in Ohio as a kid.

Sadly, that's about as far as I can get on my own: telling you what this place isn't. As for what it IS, I will refer you to the writers whose poems follow. All of them have put in considerably more time here than I have, so they've got the qualifications. Before I turn you over to them, however, I'd like to point out a few things I noticed, some subject matter which these poems share and which, as I think about it, might start to tell us something useful about this place: music, vegetation (that's right, plant life), and the lingering presence of the past – in memory, of course, but also in the living world around us.

Memphis, of course, is one of the birthplaces of American music. And in the first stanza of "Whatever Happened to Robert Johnson?" poet **Michael Adams** sketches that nativity scene, down in the Mississippi river-bottoms claimed by kudzu. As Adams renders it, though, the "green flood" could either be that infernally fertile, choking vegetation itself, or the river that gives it life. Or both. And the river, rising and falling "in three-quarter time," is of course the

music as well. Like kudzu, like the Mississippi, Memphis music inundates the landscape around here. It's as much a part of our day-to-day reality as the tugs, the barges, or the splattering fryers at Delta Donuts. It's also filled with good old carnal heat, as **Debra Tayloe** tells us in her "Making Music, Memphis Style," where the audience's "liquored tongues" are commanded not merely to lick, but to "pluck" each other (like guitarists' fingers on the strings?), and where the verbs "sing" and "moan" are pretty much interchangeable. Don't believe them? Come on out to the "Blues City Café" some night and see for yourself. But don't forget your galoshes.

Back to local flora. Of course, kudzu isn't the only vegetation hereabouts, just the most insistent and obnoxious. Less menacing, certainly – although just as tenacious – are **Rebecca Yancey**'s "Southern Blossoms." No cliche symbols of fragile female purity or civilizations gone with the wind, these blossoms are dogged survivors: "outlasting us all," as Yancey contends, continuing to bud and bloom beneath their wrap-around porches long after the women who planted them, like the speaker's own grandmother, have vanished into memory and old-fashioned cameo portraits.

Or are those women really gone? Biologically speaking, the living granddaughter is no less a product of her forebears than those "buds of the coming year" are growths from the original planting. As our Deep South neighbor, Mr. Faulkner, put it, "The past isn't dead. In fact, it's not even past." As if to prove that point, Yancey's speaker travels back through her own memory, resurrecting an earlier self "stretched out over the front steps" as "the scent of honeysuckle and clean sweat / settled around me with summer dust": a moment as fully available to the mind as any in the present moment.

A more analytical kind of time travel is recorded in **Justin Luzader**'s "Rapture," where the remembering adult is still trying to figure out why a neighbor girl was so mesmerized by the way boys piss. Then there's **Justin Langford**'s "Stuck in Line," with its sardonic comparison between present-day facts and a fictionalized past: between a shopping cart filled with this week's "microwaveable gourmet goods," and the airbrushed culinary heritage purveyed in an issue of Southern Living magazine. The illusion is masterful – "steam from home-cooked dishes / rises from the page" – and yet so remote from the speaker's own experience that he can still wonder "what / an oven-baked dish even looks like."

Speaking of the line between fact and fiction, I'll leave you with my personal theory that there's not a dime's worth of difference between the limo driver in **Garrett Crowe**'s "Oh, Father" and whoever (or whatever) brought Robert Johnson back from the crossroads in Michael Adams' poem. And that brings me right back to where I started, which is as good a place as any to stop and let you get on with the poems themselves.

Me? As mentioned earlier, I'm originally from Ohio, but I've just finished a book called *Body and Soul*, a kind of novel in verse set partly in New Mexico. My main character, Cassandra, sees the southwestern landscape and herself as nearly interchangeable, hence the blurring of human and natural intent in my poem "Re-Mudding."

Ryan K. Guth

MICHAEL ADAMS

Whatever Happened To Robert Johnson?

Old man Muddy never stopped rising,
falling in three-quarter time down to the gulf.
Kudzu grows fast enough to watch.
The green flood chokes Mississippi bottoms.

I saw Robert wait in dusty, old
shoes for a ride back from the crossroads.
Saturday came to collect
the night he hit that strychnine whiskey,
took to bed three days, and passed.

Mornings, now, at the intersection of 61
and 49, they fire the fryers before sun-
up at Delta Donuts, keep the coffee warm,
pouring for the locals.

A few miles west, tugs push their barges down
stream. The river bubbles white in their wake.

Michael Adams was born and raised in Somerville, TN. He completed his undergraduate and graduate studies in Creative Writing at the University of Memphis in 2008 and 2012, respectively, as well as a graduate certificate in African American Literature. Michael currently lives in Memphis. His creative works have appeared in Heiroglyph and In Pieces. He recently had a critical essay published in Black Magnolias. The selections published in this volume are from Michael's MFA thesis, White Trash Griot, a book-length collection of poems born from his experience growing and existing in the Delta.

GARRETT CROWE

Oh, Father

Before I met them, I rode in a red limo
and wasn't alone. That's right.
Tinted windows, so dark,
no in or out. Upholstery lined with pentagrams.
Fin-antenna on the trunk of the ride,
pitchfork-shaped, picking up snow signals
that barely told us where to go next. Beside me,
he smoked a cigar that smelled like hands

of childhood with dirt in fingerprints,
waiting to be washed, but kept filthy just because.
There was also a mask. Two bloody fangs,
long waxy gleaming wig. Same mask I wore Halloween '96 –
Lexington, Tennessee. It scared me then, but I didn't have to see it.
I wore it and ran through neighborhoods with the latex sweaty as
it coolly stuck to my face. That same holiday
I took toilet paper to my homeroom teacher's
fall-dead magnolia. And the wind
hit the thin paper like a harp. Defacement was fine.
Me and him, we were fine as we flew by deserts
in the air-conditioned limo. It felt good.
I got older and it felt like drugs. We went beyond
Death fucking Valley, dead on. Parts
unknown, can you believe it?
All the while, the limo's interior lights shined on
his slick black dress shoes
a moonlight white, the moment before
gray. And gray is a moment before
black, and black is what happens
to us all.

I'm in a four-door Toyota Camry. "Just perfect
for the economical family," that guy told me. He had
a tie with an angel on it. Damn.
I had a new car. Now I could drive past the
same young streets of '96, Huntingdon and Dogwood and Hinson.
There will be more magnolias and flags on mailboxes
pointed up to let heaven know that this is my
address. And I'll end up so far from Hell, some people
call it something else.

*Garrett Crowe lives in Chattanooga, Tennessee, where he earned
an MA in Creative Writing from the University of Tennessee
at Chattanooga. His poetry and fiction have appeared or are
forthcoming in Workin' Nights, Peeks and Valleys, Breadcrumb
Scabs, and elsewhere. Garrett is also a fiction reader for Drunken
Boat. You can follow him at twitter.com/crowegarrett.*

JUSTIN LANGFORD

Stuck In Line

People in neutral, waiting patiently
with hands on carts, on magazine pages,
on the black conveyor-belt, on carefully
cut coupons, making abrupt conversation
with meaningless glances –
anything to interrupt the mundane
routine of their daily/weekly/monthly
buying extravaganza.

"Shopping Eden with buggies," I think.
a copy of *Southern Living* catches
my eye. The pages are glossy and shining.
Docile smiles cover every advertisement
and the steam from home-cooked dishes
rises from the page. Deep-down country living,
like Rockwell's "Freedom from Want," sends
the unwelcome message of the classic
American lifestyle that few rarely
have and never really need. I wonder what
an oven-baked dish even looks like as I
peer into my own cart filled with
microwavable gourmet goods/dishes/mock-meals.

*Justin Langford was a resident of Jackson, TN
for 28 years. Holding a BA in English from the
former Lambuth University, where he contributed
to the university's poetry journal & various
creative writing classes, he also joined the
Griot Collective (headed by fiction writer James
Cherry), published his own zine with friends,
played music, and posted blogs and other writings
to the Internet. Justin is currently living in a
small hovel in Elgin, Illinois where he works with
students at the local community college and has
contributed to a local pop-up poetry project. In
his spare time, he is an ESL teacher.*

JUSTIN LUZADER

Rapture
Kings Mountain, NC

Back when a summer's day was the *clocking*
of the screen door against the doorjamb of a house
I've since misplaced:

we do striptease
behind the barn. Our parts not worth discussing
with parents or ourselves. The summer birds maintain our silence,

save occasional throat clearing.
She is the oldest by three years & has us neighbor boys
piss in the same spot because she is interested in accuracy.

She *ah*s & the streams meet
at mechanically perfect angles, fractal
into formations of holy visages as white

light's refracted through. She is awed
because for her it's school again & the boys are too young
& there's something complicated here she can't finger –

but she pictures her mom
wearing the same play dress she is & struggling
her legs into the rubber diaper of a child's swing.

We expect this is what moved her.

Justin Luzader is an MFA candidate in poetry at the University of Memphis, where he also works as assistant managing editor for The Pinch journal. Poetry of his has recently been published in The Broken Plate.

DEBRA TAYLOE

Making Music, Memphis Style

taste the salty sea
called blues
feel the rhythm
bump and grind
pluck each other
to the bone
with liquored tongues
sing and moan
this hot sauce music
ours alone

Debra (Higbie) Tayloe was born in California in 1952 and grew up in the farmlands of Ohio, but has lived all her adult life in Tennessee. In addition to writing poetry and being a "regular" at the University of Iowa's Summer Writer's Festival, Debra is an accomplished visual artist and "teaching artist" who brings a multi-disciplinary approach to the many arts education residencies she has conducted across the state with the purpose of helping others construct meaning through doing. She is also an avid conservationist, gardener, hiker and reader.

REBECCA YANCEY

Southern Blossoms

Late sun filtering through magnolia
lights up the hydrangeas' blue fringe.
In the damp earth nearby, dogs
doze to the drone of bees.

They only bloom off the old stalks,
leaves breaking through, and then the buds.
Even under a glaze of ice, bare stalks
warm buds of the coming year.

The old ones are strongest, outlasting us all
in beds framing our wrap-around porches,
blossoms nodding under the weight of rain
or brightening lace cloths at an afternoon tea.

My grandmother in her high-collared dress
held these flowers against her face.
With her far-away look, she was like her cameo,
her skin ivory with delicate lines.

And as I stretched out over the front steps,
legs tan against blue blossoms,
the scent of honeysuckle and clean sweat
settled around me with summer dust.

*Rebecca Yancey was born in Memphis but
now lives in Jackson, Tennessee, where
she taught composition and literature at
Jackson State Community College for many
years. Although she learned about poetry
mainly through exposure to the works of
great writers, she has attended many writing
workshops, in particular with poets Vivian
Shipley and Howard Nemerov. Poems of hers
have appeared in "Forked Deer," "The Old
Hickory Review," the "Anthology of Tennessee
Writers," and "The New Laurel Review."*

RYAN K. GUTH

Re-Mudding

Once a year
you fill a tub with red-brown yard dirt,
mix in water and straw

then, handful by cool handful,
smooth it on
over every inch of each wall –

building back
those wind-scoured corners,
healing rain-scars and sun-cracks, leaving

nowhere a perfect plane or edge
unless
this is perfection: human touch,

human thought and movement
bodied in a structure
that remembers

it is still the earth?

Arroyo Hondo: 1977

Ryan K. Guth *was born in Dayton, Ohio,
earned a Ph.D. in Creative Writing from
the University of Cincinnati, and currently
lives in Jackson, Tennessee, where he
teaches English at the University of
Memphis Lambuth campus. His first full-
length poetry collection,* Home Truths,
*was published in 2006 by the Alsop Review
Press, and he is finishing up his second
book, a novel in verse set partly in New
Mexico. Poems of his have appeared in
various literary journals, including Iron
Horse, Solo, Bryant Literary Review, and
Third Coast Review.*

What We Earned

    earned so much more than a fat spliff
my boy Slumpie rolled—really that was his nickname, given to him

because he never stood up straight, kept his hands in his pockets
when he walked on a late afternoon in August

for no reason I can name I hear him strumming
that cheap Fender, playing an Aerosmith solo, spooling exhaustion

after we'd stood side by side washing dishes
at the Memory Lane—those long nights smoking grass, reading Whitman,

the leaves of his hands opening the air

with each riff he hit that guitar we were train
tracks that criss-crossed wrists, blue notes

borrowed from scratchy vinyl discs.   Slumpie
was missing part of what kept us numb.

Those days we'd hitchhike to the Goffstown trestle,
leap the forty feet into the river down below,

the hard smack like the hand of his father—
drop outs, stoned, raking minimum wage.

How long since I thought of him in that tenement
on a side street a block from the mill, that blue room

where his sister found him—what was her name?   The voice
of that loss—*her name was Lily*—, bowed as a lily

(as a broken spine) and stains like the pollen
after cutting the stems, when we wipe

our hands and reach to touch one another,
the way I'd reach for Slumpie's shoulder

after a long shift and sing *the roof is on fire*
---and he'd scream, *we don't need no water*

Let the motherfucker, burn—

Sean Thomas Dougherty

Sean Thomas Dougherty is the author of 12 books including the forthcoming All I Ask for is Longing: New and Selected Poems *to be published by BOA Editions. He works at Gold Crown Billiards in Erie, PA and teaches creative writing part-time at Cleveland State University.*

Her Smell

hangs in the bedroom

like fat
dollops

of come

soaks the sheets
seeps into
my closet

full of clothes

cloys at
my mind

tilts my marriage

Sheryl L. Nelms

Sheryl L. Nelms is from Marysville, Kansas. She graduated from South Dakota State University in Family Relations and Child Development. She has had over 5,000 articles, stories and poems published, including fourteen individual collections of her poems. She is the fiction/ nonfiction editor of THE PEN WOMAN MAGAZINE, the National League of American Pen Women publication and a recent Pushcart Prize nominee

*

Ankle deep it's Spring, these stones
already green -- to keep from falling in
he's taught himself to limp, stutters
while I bathe the invisible dog
that clings to his chest, whose fur
bristling with gooseflesh half at the controls
half iron pail for the drinking cup

--he must dread the splash
is trained to wade slowly and where
the waves are buried, where these stones
harden, climb to that same altitude
they once flew --a sky
still slippery, filled all at once
with 12 dark-green stones

and he looks up, says my fingers
as if the spray reminded him
how his first breath is now too matted
though it tries to leap, its huge jaw
licking its paws --a few months each year

he wobbles into a water
that's falling off the Earth and he says
his fingers are too heavy, says
hold him, save him.

Simon Perchik

Simon Perchik is an attorney whose poems have appeared in Partisan Review, The Nation, The New Yorker, and elsewhere. For more information, including free e-books, photo, his essay titled "Magic, Illusion and Other Realities" and a complete bibliography, please visit his website at www. simonperchik.com.

HENRIETTE AND THE HUNTER

It was the last day of summer, a hot day,
and only the trees trembling
in no wind
were thinking of winter.
I'd been gathering kindling when I heard
one shot and saw a bird fall like a single
dark drop from the sky. It was so sad I wanted
to throw myself into the sun. Instead
I walked half dreaming to the place
where the bird fell and found,
as I'd felt I would, a man in the green jacket
and yellow boots of a hunter.
I knew he spent his winters alone, knew
that with the wind shaking his door
he would make a fire and sit down to watch
the flames fly around the iron pot.
He told me he killed only what he needed
to live, then he drew me towards him
as if it were he who dreamed all this,
not I. As the sun dropped, the air
began to whisper. It was the whirring
of mayflies, the inaudible
panic of moths.
We lay down knowing one of us
was just game,
just one more wounded, we didn't
care who.

Suzanne Lummis

On the Trembling Earth

Too long we sit in volcano's roar,
here on the trembling earth.

Not, not ourselves,
but ghosts we bear so lightly,
those invisible cloud balloons.
Know yourself and your flag, be ready
to mark it on your forearm

with a knife. Even then, you will probably
forget, when the meat arrives, steaming
on a white tureen, bedecked with parsley

and ringed with new potatoes hot
and brown. A feast you won't
recognize, feeding the lava mouth of dawn.

Steve Klepetar

*Steve Klepetar teaches literature and
creative writing at Saint Cloud State
University in Minnesota. His work has
received several nominations for the
Pushcart Prize and Best of the Net.*

*Suzanne Lummis came out of the famed CSU
Fresno program where she studied with Philip
Levine. She is the founding director of The Los
Angeles Poetry Festival, a board member of
Beyond Baroque and California correspondent
for New Mexico's Malpais Review. Heyday
Books published her collection "In Danger" as part
of The California Poetry Series. Her poems appear
in the Knoph "Everyman's Library" anthologies
"Poems of the American West," and "Poems of
Murder and Mayhem," and in Ploughshares,
The Antioch Review, Hotel Amerika, The New
Ohio Review and other magazines.*

Raindog

California Streaming

"Strange trees," the teacher snipes,
staring at my painting,
disgusted.

He's never seen sycamores
in all their
twisted glory.

"Water's the wrong color," he complains,
eyeing my dun-shaded
channel with despair.

He's never seen a stream in summer,
when river life flows
beneath us.

"God didn't make yellow skies," he snorts,
jabbing his pencil
at my golden blaze.

He's never looked through eyes that savor

value, color,
and complement.

"And where are the buildings for scale?" he asks,
pointing at my tranquil
creekside fields.

He's never seen…anything.

Terry Sanville

*Terry Sanville lives in San Luis Obispo,
California with his artist-poet wife (his in-
house editor) and one plump cat (his in-house
critic). He writes full time, producing short
stories, essays, poems, an occasional play, and
novels. Since 2005, his work has been accepted
by more than 150 literary and commercial
journals, magazines, and anthologies including
the Picayune Literary Review, Birmingham
Arts Journal, and Boston Literary Magazine.*

AN INTRODUCTION TO THE WORK OF TIM PEELER

by Carter Monroe

I FIRST MET TIM PEELER MORE THAN a dozen years ago. Ironically, it was not through his poetry, but a short story published in an online journal. I emailed him a complimentary note and thus began a correspondence/ friendship that endures to this day. At that time, he directed me to some of his poems that were published online and to a website that displayed his first perfect bound collection, "Touching All the Bases." I knew in an instant that this was someone I wanted and needed to know.

Since that time, I've had the opportunity to see a real poet work and continue to hone his craft on an almost daily basis. Plenty of poets work at writing. Not many work at improving every phase of their writing. Though he works primarily in a narrative vein, he understands that equations are not always a necessity in terms of the narrative or the poem in general. Few poets, outside the realm of "same old/same old" narrative, work as diligently in terms of the consideration and possibility of line as Tim. His work is as crisp as a piece of fresh celery and as tight as the strings on his tennis racket.

Another and very endearing part of his personality is his willingness to work harder for poets in whose work he has strong beliefs than he does for himself. This is because his focus is strictly on his work and not what the work can ultimately do for him. He lets the chips fall and goes on from there. In short, he's a poet who doesn't define himself as such. When we visit we'll exchange books we've found to be of interest since our last interaction, but we're just as apt to discuss a variety of things non-literary.

In recent years, he has begun to adapt the Spicer "books" theory. That is, thinking of poetry in terms of books or series. A great example is his very fine and critically acclaimed book "Checking Out" Hub City Press 2010. Tim draws from his years in hotel/motel management and the many characters who crossed his path. Poets as a whole tend to look beneath the surface of everything. Oftentimes, Tim is looking underneath what's underneath. Poetry is always about seeing what isn't obvious. Tim Peeler processes it all and the results are always spot on. He is not subject to the small press adage, "His best work is as good as anyone's" because it's all good. Even after years of writing, he is the rare poet who doesn't write because he has to, but because he still wants to. He continues to find pleasure in the arranging of words to match his ideas just as we continue to find pleasure in his end results.

Carter Monroe

Carter Monroe lives and writes in The Provinces of Eastern North Carolina. He is the author of a novel, a collection of short stories and essays, and five books of poetry, the most recent of which is THE NEW LOST BLUES - Selected Poems 1999 - 2005 *(Thunder Sandwich Press 2005.)* He has received both Pushcart and "Best of the Web" nominations. He founded Rank Stranger Press in 2001 and has since published over 20 books including poetry, short stories, and novels for poets and authors across the country from Wilson, NC to Los Angeles CA.

Henry River Poems 5

Mother league of dreams,
You feel your bones tip
As if the ship's about to,
Kettles and jugs on the porch,
Wind leveraging maple limbs,
You hear the buzzer, then
The serious man on the TV
With the warning voice.
Sky black, she taught you
To fear God disguised as nature,
Disgusted with simple man,
Old Testament thunder,
Perilous in the apple orchard;
You hear the barn door let go,
The tin on the tractor shed,
And she prays Lord if it
Be thy will, then the hail
That ruined everything
Fell.

Henry River Poems 6

He could not verbalize
The oddity of his feelings, and
She could never understand
His obsession with the cards,
Meeting under the old bridge
After church with the boys,
The week's grease scrubbed
From faces and hands,
Gray-suited, hobbled by brogans.
Sometimes he'd draw a pistol
On Shoehead's old man,
Or Childers in his goofy pointed hat.
But the afternoon was loaded
With sunshine, and his playful smile
Could never pull the trigger
On any game sane enough
For her to abide.

Henry River Poems 13

There was a hum you could hear some nights
As if the looms in the old brick mill,
Overlooking the river and dam,
Had enveloped the entire hill
With their deafening chatter
And you no longer heard passing cars,
Barking dogs, crescendos of crickets,
Even your neighbors in the darkness
Talking and smoking on their front porch.
At supper, you watched your wife's lips move,
And you knew she was telling you
Something about her mother, yet
All you heard was the sound of the looms
Spinning away the hours.

Henry River Poems 19

After the great storm
The river rushed through and over the dam
Like a cannon ball's exit wound
Of brown blood, broken pine limbs,
Car tires, the ragged flags
Of a snapped clothesline
Somehow still pinned;
The dam locks gulped and gurgled
Rath Burton's drowned calf,
A belly up hound dog
Still dragging its chain,
And as the last drops descended,
A rainbow arced peacefully
Across the hog shoulders
Of Baker's Mountain.

Tim Peeler is the Director of the Learning Assistance Program at Catawba Valley Community College in Hickory, NC. He is a winner of the Jim Harrison Award for contributions to baseball literature. He has authored six books of poetry and three regional baseball histories. His poems have been anthologized by Time/Life Books and have been used in an HBO documentary. His latest books are Checking Out *(Hub City Press)*, a book of narrative poems related to his eleven years in the hotel business and Waiting for Charlie Brown, *a collaboration with poet Ted Pope available from Rank Stranger Press.*

THE POETRY XI

A Poet, to Himself

Strange night.
No sirens.
Quiet streets.
No weather to speak of.
Good night to write.
But no, I can't get up for adventure.
I feel a kind of dullness.
My head is in a puddle.
My neck turns.
My cartilage moves.
I don't like the sound of my bones.
Strange, atomic night.
The dogs in the neighborhood are
going crazy, running in circles.
Loneliness, so alive, so big
that it is almost a creature on it's own.
I have slept alone all week
reaching across the sheets
to find loss, not warmth.
I take myself into the night.
Walk the streets for rapture.
Now early rising moon,
pour into me.
I can't breathe without you.

Tim Tipton

Tim Tipton *was first seduced by the craft of poetry when he read the "Panther" by Rainer Marie Rilke. His poetry that has been featured in ART/LIFE, Askew, the San Gabriel Quarterly, and the on-line journal poetic diversity. Tim is a graduate of California State University of Northridge where he received a Bachelor of Science in Sociology. He also received a degree in Substance Abuse counseling.*

Get Wide

"I don't get high;
I get wide."
- John Thomas (R.I.P.)

I think I was high
pretty much every single time
I saw John Thomas, and we met weekly,
on Tuesday nights, for years. Back then
I was looking for an escape, for some way
to jar my brain from the straight-line thinking
I had been born and raised with. From school
to more school to job after job after job
I felt my entire life had been spent behind a desk.
I'd been living in someone else's schedule for
my entire thirty years (at that time) and
I got high to fill out the rest of my brain.

I could, and can, do whatever the masses are told to do.
But, by getting high, I also did more. I released
the outsides of my brain, the areas that weren't
getting any exercise in my life of
rise, work, eat, sleep, repeat.

We're all trained to be good, to do what They say,
buy what They think is important and to keep it together
at all costs. But we're never shown how to listen to ourselves,
how to appreciate our own thoughts on how to live. And it's
fucking sad, because if we listen to Them we're doomed to die
sad deaths with excellent credit ratings and no adventure.

For years I tempered my hatred of all the systems with drugs
and alcohol. Since they offered me an escape (via lay-off
and the worst economy since The Great Depression) I no longer
get high. I get wide and I've changed. My cycle now goes:
live, love, write, believe, repeat.

Previously published on Todd Jackson's website www.oddwitha-T.com

Todd Jackson

Todd Jackson *(aka Isaac "Zack" Edwards) was born in Story City, Iowa,
and lived in a trailer on the outskirts of town. He no longer lives in L.A. or
Detroit or Minneapolis and is the co-founder of Slow Collision Press. His
writing can be found at www.oddwithaT.com*

Red are Her Lips

A tomato seed stayed stuck on the slicing board.
To wash the dishes and cutlery in the warm clear water of my dreams
the fringes are so thin and the shelters so permeable – another scoop of ice cream.

I sliced the tomato and my finger, it bled on the bamboo wood slicing board.
Beetroot mixed with tomatoes and dressing made of olive oil and balsamic vinegar
Sherry flavour, cheerio, cherry red, blood drips and the kitchen knife is at another turning point of
its existence.

Depressed the shrink shot a bullet in his head. I remain alone, left aside, on the pavement of the
doubtful moments, the harsh times of the forthcoming days.
Will you spend you day in bed again when all we need is some light in our shed?
Anna sings for me, deeper and darker than the red-haired woman used to, still does, from time to
time.

Plaster on my finger to prevent more blood to flow away and leave me bloodless, exsanguine, livid
and dead.

Walter Ruhlmann

Walter Ruhlmann *works as an English teacher. He has been publishing mgversion2 datura
(ex-Mauvaise graine) for over fifteen years. Walter is the author of several poetry chapbooks
and e-books in French and English and has published poems and fiction in various printed and
electronic publications world wide. He is a 2011 Pushcart Prize nominee for his translation of
Martine Morillon-Carreau's poem "Sans début ni fin, ce rêve" published in the January 2011
issue of Magnapoets. His blog http://lorchideenoctambule.hautetfort.com*

Easier Come

The managing editor of the local
print deemed newsworthy
claimed she did right by me,
reciting an "up-yours bitch" policy,
and my complaint was forwarded
to the phantom publisher;

a twisted game of Monopoly without a
get out of jail free card where letters
to the editor are carefully selected for
a captive audience inside the trash can;

so I peddled my signed books for four
unadvertised hours, fluorescents playing
off old rhinestone brooches and new sequins
—just one degree shy of chic—
while re-reading Jason Hardung's
the broken and the damned
wishing I could toss down naked in the street,
didn't have to be a lady all the damn time;

behind the library stacks an audio book
quoted Bible verses while Hardung
promised to talk God up in one of his poems;

I got up to stretch my legs
remembering the sour-grape verse
someone I didn't know
had referenced me in, and reflected on
this easier-come brand of buzz.

Wanda Clevenger

*Wanda Morrow Clevenger lives in Hettick, IL.
Over one hundred pieces of her work appear
in online and print literary journals and
anthologies. Her debut book* This Same Small
Town in Each of Us, *a collection of this and
that and some other stuff, released on October
30, 2011. She never dreamed advertising book
signings was going to involve warring with the
local newspaper.*

Watching You Fish in the Ganges

Watching you fish in the Ganges,
I'm astonished that the fish speak
Hindi, Bengali, or English
to beg for their lives. Merciful,
you return each to its habitat,
which (because of its frequent

and seriously, deeply unwashed
human population) feels thick
and gelatinous. I don't believe
in holy waters, but this river
does offer the unexpected,
like the rowboat we found laden

with hides of animals no one
could identify. Or the corpse
floating with empty eye sockets
that burst into a Gilbert
and Sullivan medley before
abruptly sinking like an anchor.

But watching you fish with a star
bright sapphire as bait saddens
as well as amazes me. Why catch
fish you'll only return with ripped
and bleeding mouths? Do you need
so badly to hear them speak human

with species-specific accents?
Their scales look rough and crude,
like those of Koi. But their jaws
suggest gar or northern pike.
Their pastel coloring shivers
as you hoist them into the air.

Their attempts to breathe outside
water render them pitiful.
Too bad India's a dry nation,
or we could retire to a pub
and leave the fish conversing
among themselves. Let's settle for

tea in some prissy little post-
British tea shop, where men
chew over local politics
in Hindi, Bengali, English,
and don't waste their time fishing
for creatures no one can eat.

William Doreski

*My work has appeared in various e and
print journals and in several collections,
most recently* Waiting for the Angel
(Pygmy Forest Press, 2009).

Here with the Rest of Them

It's at the corner of Turk and Taylor,
maybe you know it.

I was going to say
the saddest bar in town
but it's a place beyond sorrow;

a netherworld of the lost,
a waiting room for the void.

The junkie next to me is
way far gone

and stares with abandoned eyes
at the television screen.

She laughs an empty laugh
and says,

Hey, you wanna do some harewin?

I say, No, thanks, I've got
a beer,

and she says, O, I thought you looked
like the type.

I shrug and I smile
and guess maybe I do,
because I'm here
with the rest of them,

here on a Wednesday afternoon
in this place where life
is turned away at the door

and death just can't
be bothered.

William Taylor, Jr.

William Taylor Jr. *lives and writes in
the Tenderloin neighborhood of San
Francisco. His poems and stories have
been widely published in the independent
press in publications including Poesy,
The Chiron Review and The New York
Quarterly. He is the author of the poetry
collections* Words for Songs Never
Written *(Centennial Press 2007) and* The
Hunger Season *(Sunnyoutside, 2009).*
An Age of Monsters *(Epic Rites Press,
2011) is his first collection of prose.*

Didn't Mean to Write a Book

in 1998
you decided to roam
and our home became
two feet less than perfect
I laid out a spiral bound
wrote some words
drew breasts and labia
over the pages
later I heard
your dream came true
and a young woman
tasted good for you
that year
I wrote more, then
drew cunts
and cut them into shards
to line the drawers of your old desk
by November
lanced pages had red smudges
atop drawings of
broken hearts
didn't mean to write a book
but nothing worked better
in 1998

Winnie Star

Previously published in Deuce Coupe

*Winnie Star lives in California,
glad to have been transplanted from
New York (a long time ago). In her
straight life, she holds out as a nurse
practitioner and principal co-author/
editor of several award-winning
textbooks in women's health. Creative
writing of poems and short stories
started a few years back when she
discovered the other side of herself.
Her poetry has been published in The
Permanente Journal, Mystery Island
Magazine, and several ezines: Juice;
Warm Angel Whiskey; Deuce Coupe;
and Rusty Truck.*

Untitled

It was the first time I'd been inside a bottling plant in twenty years. The manager showed me to my locker and then toured me through the facility. The mixing room, the filling station, the conveyor belts that snaked their way through the plant like a massive tapeworm. I'd taken my shot at immortality, and lost. Now here I was, restored to the Earth, dwarfed by the hiss, clank and clatter of meaningless machinery. Back in his office, he turned to me and asked, "So, did anything in there look familiar?" "Yeah," I said, "the look of fear in everyone's eyes."

Wolf Carstens

Wolfgang Carstens lives in Alberta, Canada with his wife, five kids, two cats and a dog. His first book of poetry, Crudely Mistaken For Life, *was released by Epic Rites Press in 2010. It has since garnered outstanding critical reviews, was placed on the "recommended reading list" at Small Press Distribution, and is presently stocked on the shelves of numerous North American libraries.*

Costco, Mother's Day 2012

There aren't many more
mothers here this day.
A handful of additional fathers,
but not mothers. I notice this as my mom
youngest brother and I stroll
the produce and meat sections
grabbing hot link, salmon, hamburgers
strawberries, blackberries and blueberries
for the BBQ at my parents' house.
We sample the free samples,
Normally I'd pass, but I've kept hungry
all morning in anticipation for the gluttony
of the afternoon. I notice out in
my slight glance a man in the deli section
crying above sliced turkey.

Zack Nelson-Lopiccolo

Zack Nelson-Lopiccolo is a guy from Long Beach who is one of the founding editors of Bank-Heavy Press, but he hangs/tapes drywall to pay the bills. His work can be seen in his chapbook Dancing with Scissors *as well as small press mags such as The Mas Tequila Review, Carnival, and Short, Fast and Deadly among others. He offers foot massages for a mere .50 cents.*

THE INTERVIEWS

These two interviewees were chosen because they have been instrumental in pushing the craft of poetry (and its presentation) forward for over 20 years. A third poet/promoter was to be a part of this but he pulled out due to a conflict of interest. -- Editor

G. MURRAY THOMAS Interview

Q: Like Rick Lupert, you came from the east... what brought you to the L. A. area and why did you stay?

A: Why does anyone move to SoCal? Beaches and sunshine. I grew up in Rochester, NY, and by the time I was twenty I had had enough of winter. Even so, I still lived in a couple more places -- Massachusetts and Idaho -- with nasty winters before I got here. So, yes, the weather brought me here. I stayed for the poetry. Seriously.

Let me back up a little here. I have always been a writer. Before I could even write, I would dictate stories to my mother. My primary interest was, and to a degree still is, fiction. I got a BA in Creative Writing from Hampshire College (Amherst, MA), primarily by writing three novels (all of which suck). While my professors thought I might (emphasis on might) have some potential as a fiction writer, they let me know I was certainly not a poet.

Anyway, in 1987 I moved to Laguna Beach. I was, at the time, deep into another novel. I started going to Laguna Poets just to meet other writers. But it wasn't long before I wanted to get up in the front of that room and read something. My first "poems" were descriptive paragraphs out of my novel, chopped up into short lines. But I was soon writing real poems, and getting enough encouragement to keep going. I discovered something. The novel was taking forever (I had already put in about five years), but I could finish a poem. So the novel went into a drawer, and I became a poet. At that time (about 1990) the SoCal poetry scene was pretty thin and scattered. But there were enough readings to keep me interested, and enough to get me out on the freeways, and driving across town. (To be honest, I was petrified by the freeways when I first moved here.) About the time I started to get sick of traffic, smog and urban sprawl, I was hooked enough on the poetry scene to stay. (In case you're wondering, I did go back to that novel some years later, and I finished it. Then I spent a couple of years shopping it to agents, got a couple of tiny nibbles, but nothing more. So it's back in the drawer again. Any agents out there want to take a look?)

Q: There's a lot of talk about legacy these days... What is it that you hoped to accomplish both as a writer and as a promoter of poetry? Do you think you have been successful?

A: I think the primary goal of any writer is simply to be read. I feel I have accomplished that, at least to enough degree to feel some satisfaction. I don't think I'm bragging to say I have fans. I get to read regularly. I've sold at least a couple hundred books, probably more. Maybe that's not a lot, and I could certainly wish for a larger audience, but it's enough that I feel accomplished.

A secondary goal, which follows from the first, is the ability to make a living as a writer. That one is a lot farther away. I've reached a point where I'm actually making some money, but it's mere pocket change. (Hear me IRS? Mere pocket change.) But it is enough to make me feel like maybe, sometime, it will actually help pay the bills. (BTW, you can order my books through my website: gmurraythomas.com.)

As for my ambition as a promoter, that has always been to share my love of poetry. Especially with people who aren't poets, who may not even think they like poetry. To show them that poetry can be entertaining, can be a positive, meaningful experience. I think that poetry is much more accepted by the general public now than it was 20 years ago, but I doubt I've had anything to do with that.

That was much of the motivation behind Next…, the SoCal poetry calendar/ newsmagazine I published from 1994 - 1998. That was why it was a magazine, and not just a calendar. And that was why I wanted it to be free. I wanted to create the possibility that some nonpoet would pick it up, read something they found interesting, and be inspired to attend a poetry reading. I have no idea if that ever happened, but that was the idea.

But it did accomplish a secondary goal. That is, it helped to connect, and strengthen, the SoCal poetry community. It inspired poets to go to readings on the other side of town. It introduced them to other poets they may not have been familiar with. It encouraged collaboration and cooperation among poets. So in that I was successful. (Blatant plug #2: If you want to see more of what Next…was about, you can order a copy of *News Clips and Ego Trips: The Best of Next...* from Write Bloody Publishing -- writebloody.com)

Q: Explain your type of poetry…has it evolved over the years? In what ways? Who are your influences?

A: Oh, great. The dreaded "what kind of poetry do you write?" question. I used to say something like "performance poetry," just to give them something to hang onto, even though it really only described part of what I did. Still, much of my poetry is, if not specifically written to be performed, shaped by the process of reading it aloud. But even that is less true these days. I have two books out: *Cows on the Freeway* (iUniverse, 1999) and *My Kidney Just Arrived* (Tebot Bach, 2011), and there is a huge difference between them, both in style and subject matter.

Cows on the Freeway is more performance oriented. Much of it is humorous. I would describe it as observational poetry. I would see something, often something I found absurd, and write about it. It was heavily influenced by my being new to SoCal. I would joke that when first I moved here, I wrote about two things: the ocean and the freeways. But to a great degree that was true.

My Kidney Just Arrived, on the other hand, is very personal. While not exactly confessional, it is directly about my experiences, specifically my experiences as a dialysis and kidney transplant patient. I was on dialysis for seven years, finally got a kidney transplant in 2010. All of the poems in the book were written during that period. Even the poems not directly about the experience were influenced by it. For example, there ended up being a lot of poems about waiting. That inevitably lead to a more direct style of writing. Less imagery, more storytelling. I leave it up to the reader to decide which style they like better.

As for who influenced me, if you want a recognizable name, let's say William Carlos Williams. I really like his directness, the idea that plain language can be poetic. But the truth is that the people who influenced me the most are mostly unknown. They are the people I hear reading all over town. Early on, when I was learning, and most open to influence, it was people like Gary Tomlinson, Lawrence Schulz, Ron de la Rosa, Eric Brown -- people who showed me how much energy can be put into a poem. That was an important realization.

I can name a number of poets I really admire right now -- Brendan Constantine, Mindy Nettifee, Daniel McGinn, Rachel McKibbens to name a few. But I don't know how much they influence me. I'm sure they do, but it is a on a much more subtle level. Part of it is that I have formed my own style, and I am less inclined to try to copy what someone else is doing. Still, I'm sure some of what they do seeps in.

Q: *What are your thoughts on poetry these days?*

A: I think poetry is in a pretty good place right now. I hear, and read, awesome poetry almost every day. There is so much of it out there. Also, as I mentioned above, I think the general public is much more accepting of poetry now than they were when I started out. I mean, maybe my neighbor or co-worker still isn't going to come to my reading when I invite them, but they no longer look at me like I'm some sort of weirdo. They might even be impressed that I'm a poet. Also, and I know there are plenty of people who will disagree with me on this, but I feel the battle between academic poetry and performance poetry, which seemed so important ten years ago, is largely over. Sure, there are still disagreements over what constitutes good poetry (or even what constitutes poetry at all), but the divisions are not nearly as clear. There is much more of a spectrum these days. I hear poets with MFAs doing stuff that would have been considered pure performance, and I hear poets with no formal education writing poems as finely crafted as anything out there. Maybe it's not all liked, or even appreciated, but it is all accepted as poetry.

Q: *Last thoughts?*

A: I continue to be pleasantly surprised by the vibrancy of the SoCal poetry scene. I am constantly hearing amazing poetry, and meeting amazing poets. It's still what keeps me here.

G. Murray Thomas *is best known as the editor of* Next... Magazine, *a poetry calendar / newsmagazine for Southern California.* Next... Magazine *was published monthly between 1994 and 1998. Thomas currently edits a monthly listing of poetry events for Poetix.net, the source for information about SoCal poetry. He is also the Reviews Editor for Poetix.*

Thomas' first full length collection of poems, Cows on the Freeway, *was published by iUniverse in 2000. He has also published five chapbooks,* Death to the Real World, Opposite Oceans, Poetry Spilled All Over the Carpet, A Rare Thing, *and* Songs of Inappropriate Desire. *In 2005, iUniverse reprinted* Paper Shredders, *an anthology of surf poetry Thomas first published in 1993.*

Thomas' poetry has been published in numerous literary magazines, including Chiron Review, Pearl, Caffeine *and* Spillway. *Recent publications include* Sage Trail, The Poetry Super Highway *and* Beggars and Cheeseburgers.

In 1992, Thomas founded Orange Ocean Press, dedicated to publishing poetry anthologies on "unpoetic" topics. Orange Ocean Press published three anthologies, Paper Shredders, *about surfing (republished by iUniverse in 2005),* Polluted Poems, *a collection of environmental poetry, and* Kill the Opossum, *about dead opossums. Orange Ocean Press also published collections by Tom Foster, Lawrence Schulz and poetry cartoonist Walt Hopkins.*

In addition to poetry, Thomas writes poetry, fiction, political commentary, literary and music criticism, and anything else that comes into his fool head. He has had articles and reviews published in OC Weekly, Panik, *and* Skratch, *as well as the websites* Poetix, Ground Control, Poetic Diversity *and* The Independent Reviews Site. *He writes two regular columns on rock music: "The Aging Punk" for Ground Control, and "A Personal History of Rock'n'Roll" for Poetic Diversity.*

Thomas received a B.A. in Creative Writing from Hampshire College, Amherst MA, in 1980.

RICK LUPERT Interview

Q: *You came from the east, as well...what brought you to the L. A. area and why did you stay?*

A: I came to Southern California on August 17, 1982, an anniversary I consistently remember weeks after it has passed. My mom and I travelled from Syracuse, New York for three days straight on a Greyhound bus. I was thirteen years old and believe I wore the same pair of golf pants for the entire trip. (I have never played golf.) I was really just along for the ride here as my mom was moving us to California to pursue a law degree at a local school. I started ninth grade, the first year of high school, a few weeks after arriving which begin the truly formative years of my life. By the time I was an adult a few years later I considered myself to be an Angeleno much more so than someone from the east coast. I've been here thirty years now...I travel a lot but Southern California is my home.

Q: *There's a lot of talk about legacy these days... What is it that you hoped to accomplish both as a writer and as a promoter of poetry? Do you think you have been successful?*

A:

Scientists say
our sun will burn out
in three billion years;

all life on earth
that ever was,
gone.

With this in mind
it is my policy to not make
long term plans or

worry too much
about my
legacy.

(from my poem
"On My Eventual Death")

As a writer my main interest is writing poetry that I find interesting and entertaining with the hope that others will too. I've had a lot of good feedback from people who have read my work and have expressed that they have found it both interesting and entertaining...as well as people who have said that they don't like poetry but they like my poetry. Having reached an audience composed of a fairly disparate groups of people, I feel pretty good about my success so far.

As a poetry promoter on the web and producer of a weekly reading series, my mission has always been to expose as many people's poetry to as many other people as possible. Through my work creating and running the Poetry Super Highway website (http://poetrysuperhighway.com/) I have published 2 poets online almost every week since 1997 from all over the world inclusive of every style of poetry you can imagine. The weekly reading I've hosted since 1994 at the Cobalt Cafe in Canoga Park, California (http://poetrysuperhighway.com/cobalt) has attracted almost everyone in Southern California at one point or another as well as numerous touring poets. I publish a broadside for each of my featured readers (all of which are available online after the reading) which created a way to compensate the poets for their reading. I also regularly invite other individuals and groups to select and present the featured poet (which always includes an open reading with a very generous seven minute time limit) widening the sensibility of who is presented beyond my own. Since I started creating broadsides in 2003 I have (almost) not repeated a featured reader...and the variety of featured readers has also been quite diverse.... from touring and local "spoken word artists" to individuals who have had pieces published in revered literary magazines to newer poets who've given their first featured reading ever on the Cobalt Stage. The open reading is also an essential component to the series...seven minutes is highly generous and allows a poet to almost put together a mini-featured reading and really give the audience a sense of who they are as a writer. So through these two projects I think I've had good success servicing my mission to expose as many poets to as many other poets as possible.

Q: Explain your type of poetry...has it evolved over the years? In what ways? Who are your influences?

A: I tend to write narrative, humorous and observational work with the occasional delve into the surreal...the idea is to make the mundane spectacular...calling out the tiny details in the every day experience through my own filter with the hope that others will see those things in that new way and find it interesting, enjoyable and maybe even funny.

I definitely think it's evolved - I remember when I first started going to open readings my main goal was to make people laugh. There was a lot more sophomoric work and imagery. One newspaper review actually said after one reading that it seemed I wrote poetry specifically for "college sophomore males." I certainly can't deny that this imagery appeared in earlier work... now that I think about it I can't deny that I don't go back there periodically with my writing. I'm a fan of shock-value and blue humor and it comes out sometimes. But the feedback which has been most meaningful to me is when people say they consistently find my work entertaining, but with an undercurrent of something more serious.

I'm constantly being influenced by the many poets I encounter at readings on a weekly basis... though my original influences are Richard Brautigan for his humor, simple accessible writing and deep insights to the every day human condition; Douglas Adams and Monty Python for their easy swings back and forth from slapstick to dry-wit humor, along with modern poets Jeffrey McDaniel and Brendan Constantine for their abilities to write and engage every conceivable type of audience member and reader.

Q: What are your thoughts on poetry these days? In your opinion, is it going in the right direction? Is there room for improvement? If so, what would you like to see done?

A: I'm not sure what this means...if we're talking about actual poetry, as in the words written by poets in the form of poems then I'm quite confident that the many different directions it's going in, by the wildly different individuals doing so are absolutely the right ones to be going in. There couldn't possible be a wrong direction as everyone's path, style and artistic sensibility is different. I firmly believe, at an open reading for example, that for every poet who takes the stage, there is at least one person in the audience who doesn't like their work and who wishes they would wrap it up...and at least one person who loves it and wants to hear more. I believe this non-school of thought can be applied to any aspect of poetry...poetry reading styles (as in the events where readings happen, how they're run etc...), the poetry "community" or "scene" (if such things even exist) along with the type of poetry being written along with its perceived quality.

I would like to see people continue to do what they're doing...to not write off one reading or individual or style or school of thought...but rather expose themselves to as many of these things as possible to both foster an appreciation for what it is on its own terms as well as to continue to develop their own voices and styles.

Q: Any final thoughts?

A: Yes. In the interest of science, world peace and the betterment of humanity, I would like everyone reading this to send me eleven dollars. Thank you.

Rick Lupert *has been involved in the Los Angeles poetry community since 1990. He served for two years as a co-director of the Valley Contemporary Poets, a non-profit organization which produces readings and publications out of the San Fernando Valley. His poetry has appeared in numerous magazines and literary journals, including* The Los Angeles Times, Rattle, Chiron Review, Zuzu's Petals, Caffeine Magazine, Blue Satellite *and others. He edited the anthologies* A Poet's Haggadah: Passover through the Eyes of Poets *and* The Night Goes on All Night - Noir Inspired Poetry, *and is the author of fourteen books:* Death of a Mauve Bat, Sinzibuckwud!, We Put Things In Our Mouths, Paris: It's The Cheese, I Am My Own Orange County, Mowing Fargo, I'm a Jew. Are You?, Feeding Holy Cats, Stolen Mummies, I'd Like to Bake Your Goods, A Man With No Teeth Serves Us Breakfast *(Ain't Got No Press)*, Lizard King of the Laundromat, Brendan Constantine is My Kind of Town *(Inevitable Press) and* Up Liberty's Skirt *(Cassowary Press). He has hosted the long running Cobalt Café reading series in Canoga Park since 1994 and is regularly featured at venues throughout Southern California.*

Rick created and maintains the **Poetry Super Highway**, *an internet resource and weekly publication for poets.* PoetrySuperHighway.com

Currently Rick works as a music teacher at synagogues in Southern California and as a graphic and web designer for and for anyone who would like to help pay his mortgage.

Mark Hartenbach

THE ESSAYS

The Yuppiefication, Bourgeiossification, Commercialization, Industrialization, Leveling, Degradation, Proletarianization and Desacralization of Poetry: or, Notes on A Recent Sociology Of Poetry, or:
The Coming of the YUPOETS

by Steve Goldman

RECENT DECADES HAVE SEEN A KIND of (slight, not enough of an) increase in the prominence, visibility, production and distribution of poetry. This is an amplified interest in and concern with poetry; which though not even faintly "mainstream now" was largely banished from serious consideration in popular arts circles heretofore, - and even then mostly of concern amongst scholars and a few devotees. Hallelujah! But unmitigated jubilation is alas, premature: this progress is largely distorted. Because with clockwork reliability in this culture, the slightest success of a new or long suppressed, neglected or ignored art form, now a fad, encounters the commensurately growing danger of its being appropriated and co-opted by the *Commercial Narcissist Monstrosity Dept. of the Great American Bullshit Machine*: now infused with considerations of celebrity, money, commerciality, unbridled nigh-manic careerism, "showbiz", egomania, and offensive yet pathetic narcissism: ME! ME! ME! Etc. There are many mutually entangled skeins to this degradation. What follows are notes on just a few of the ranker elements.

CARREERISM

Far and away the worst most flagrant element is the rampant and utterly rapacious careerist ambition practiced by increasing numbers of poets and would-be poets, a kind of relentless, compulsive self-promotion, which if it weren't so damaging would be almost comically ludicrous. I mean a heated incessant concern; unabashed status seeking, seen in such activities as bombarding publishing vehicles, a kind of industrialization of one's work, with computerized running tabs on submissions; continual seeking and cultivating reading opportunities; reading twice or even more in one day in widely distant locales; (or should I say "venues"?). Internet access; personal multiple self-promotional web sites; intense conferences in restaurants talking only "shop"- which these days means comparing strategies to get published; which poetry "prize" to pursue; taking every available workshop and of course sucking up to celebrity poets. These "name" folks are cultivated to 'get ahead'; attending no readings except your own and those of certified eminences and the *ne plus ultra* of this utter betrayal of the traditional poet's stance: contriving to secure a co-featured reading with the big-shot poet. No angle is left unexploited in the quest for self-publicization, e-mail, web site, etc. I haven't looked up in the sky lately, but if I saw skywriting advertising Joe/Jane Schmuck's reading, (or worse yet demands to be given one,) I wouldn't be surprised. In a word, we are witnessing the *Day of the Yupoet.*

OK, so what's wrong with that? It seems innocent enough, and what's more it can be said to forward or spread poetry, a *desideratum* which this writer passionately argues for. Well, this is what is wrong, what is very wrong with all of that.

The recently late and incontestably great Octavio Paz said, *"Poetry is important, the poet is not"* [1] This means the sacred priority of poetry as an institution, a practice, but most especially as a product is geared to

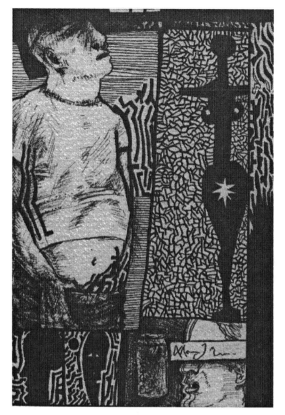

consciousness change for the better, - over and above that of the ego of the producer. And further that the poetic endeavor has an implied politics – or rather a meta-politics unto itself, which the kind of nauseating careerism described above is utterly contradictory to. Accordingly, it is ruinous of that meta-politics, as regards the furtherance of a broad authentic poetic movement, the purpose of which would be no less than like furtherance if not salvation of society and sanity, even love, let alone the suddenly urgent matter of the very survival of life on this planet.

So just what is that meta-politics? It's axiomatic, such that it underlies anything that actually is poetry. Poetry's implicit ethical responsibility, its very axiom, is surely about *the spiritual in some broad sense at least.* What else could it be about? Most ironically, it is "pro-life"[2] Arf Arf Arf! (Thank you, Popeye)

Poetry is among other things about love, transcendence, peace, war, death, pain, betrayal, dignity of the individual, the sanctity of the soul, protest against the inhumane, the evil; beauty, children, and oppression and victimization, the "biggies". And while *devoid of specific doctrinal requirements of course* – it is about: the politics of spirituality. And poetic yuppieisim, narcissism really, is diametrically opposed to all of that. Again, while no topic is required or forbidden to it, nor any style required or forbidden to it, one plank of poetry writ large is celebration or grieving, (Thank you, Harry Northup) – which can be and often is, critique of the cultural status quo or degenerative tendency, not the adoption and advocacy of it. And rampant rogue ambition on the part of the individual (yup) poet is just that: a component of what far-sighted shrinks call the pervasive social drift toward 'character disorder'.

Poetry as a practice is spiritually communal, not isolative of the individual. 'Agape', not 'loose cannon". Poetry as social phenomenon is contra any "star-system"[3], and the narcissism and exploitativness that underlie same, let alone the sheer selfishness of the aspirant. The Talmud says: "We are all born to save the world" and poetry, i.e. the poetic endeavor, individually and world-culture wide - is a way, or at least a perennial effort to do just that. Poetry is about spiritual transcendence, personally and culturally, not "stardom." And, although there is no correlation between the quality of a person's poetry and how savory a personality he or she may be, the persona of the poet has been traditionally at least been conceived of as giving, sacrificing, not selfish. It's the sacrosanct role of the poet (outlaw, willful outsider, seer, visionary etc. spiritual pathfinder) that is being prostituted by Yupoetism.

Ultimately, the poet's calling is a shamanic office, that is: he/she is a kind of priest, not a celebrity for its own sake. (The prehistoric shaman raving and dancing at the front of the cave, just behind the roaring, dancing, sputtering fire, the shadows bounding and dancing on the cave walls, is the first poet.) One of "the unacknowledged legislators of society" as Shelly (not Shelly Berman) put it. A prophet, not a rock-star, not a media idol, aspiring or otherwise. Put another way, the job of the poet is to do poetry for it's own sake, to be a poet-among-the-people, or a poet-for-the-sake-of-the people, (loving spiritual metapolitics again) and to 'live poetry' - in his or her offhand remarks, and hopefully by rendering it at births, weddings, funerals, bar mitzvahs and various other consecrations and wherever else informally. The *bardic* function, if you will. At this point in American cultural history, that job should involve more of infusing poetry into more events and aspects of life than in its 8 tolerated ghettoized venues: the coffee house, the college or university, the precious little literary group, the workshop, the library and the bookstore or museum. It is adamantly not to become a celebrity by marketing campaigns of self - manufacture; i.e. the merchandising of one's ego-as-commodity and one's poems as well. That is violative of the poet's office, the bourgeoisification and commercialization of poetry, and destructive of its priceless and indispensable gift. Let's listen to Paz again: **"We have lost our poetic sense, and with it our humanity."** And "yupoetic" narcissism and status seeking, facilitate just that. The poet needs distance to discharge that "seer" (that is: see-er) gift, here specifically (albeit not uniquely) the "seeing" and articulation of the cultural pathology. Distance, perspective, not immersion in banal and obscene striving. Goddamnit, the poet needs a certain perspective to become the poetic vehicle, and to achieve that he/she needs to be *an outlaw, not another "certified" middle class professional.*

But instead we see the "professional-ization"— of the calling and the trade, with all the paraphernalia of the "professions": advanced degrees, conscious analyses about how to "locate" oneself in poetic history, (read "get famous, become historically important"). What the fuck next, licensing? Whatever happed to writing spontaneously, from one's heart, one's soul, one's agony, one's life, one's conscience (did I say 'conscience'?), one's wry comedy, one's love, at least from one's wits, calling 'em as one see's 'em, or "hears 'em) i.e. being open enough to listen to the great "Horn In The Sky", the source of all poetry - devising or adopting whatever devices or styles are needed to transmit the message as one goes, without regard to the aforementioned unhappy and self defeating stratagems? What ever happened to:

> "In my craft or sullen art
> Exercised in the still night
> When only the moon rages
> And the lovers lie abed
> With all their griefs in their arms
> I labor by singing light
> Not for ambition or bread
> Or the strut and trade of charms
> On the ivory stages
> But for the common wages
> Of their most secret heart..."?

I don't know, Dylan.

This is but the tip of the iceberg, to coin a phrase.[4] Again, there are many tangled strains (to mix metaphors) in this monstrous prostitution of poetry. Some examples merely in passing: the conversion of the reading from "secular church" to show-biz hype; precious little "poetry cabals" dedicated to the "advancement" of their members; pernicious influences on the very language of poetry itself, that is to say the "leveling" of 'high poetry'

(Thank you Roger Taus); bizarre forms of the workshop and the reading, the vexed matter of the MBA in Poetr... uh, uh, whoops the MFA in Poetry [5], the revised but now mangled (thank you, Raindog) conception of the identity of the poet. These are just a few. The list goes on and on. For now, here's a closing note on the last mentioned.

So to sum up, here - today there is an antagonisticpolarityoftwocompetingmentalities motivating the poetic endeavor: that is: opposed rationales for a personal poetic career. On the one hand there is the "capitalist" or narcissist mindset: (fame, money, narcissism, Show-biz, awards, careerism, flattened didactic language, fragmentation, rage: ME! - and on the other the "communist" or communal consciousness: (agape, transcendence, abnegation of ego, spiritual and elevating language, inclusion, lyricism, love: ALL!) These are the mutual antitheses that characterize the poetic landscape today. Admittedly, this is a sweeping and categorical judgment, and individuals harbor both impulses in varying ratios, but it does serve to illustrate the competing tendencies. And let it be said that along with the broader spectrum of cultural deterioration, it is the former that is in the ascendancy. God help us.

NOTES

A PROPOS THE YUPOET UH, MOVEMENT IN GENERAL:
Nothing succeeds like success. (Proverb)
Power corrupts, total power corrupts completely. (Tom Jefferson)

[1] Paz also said that in other times and in other places, poetry was at the center of society, now it is at the outskirts. This he calls the exile of poetry: "el exilo de la poesia". Here and now, it is being further attacked *while in exile.* (Thank you, Octavio)

[2] To life: "L'Chaim!"

[3] Great poets are not "stars".

[4] This article is but a fraction of a sprawling rant I have produced over the years, frankly in self-defense..

[5] Francois Villon did not need an MFA, and neither do I.
"We doan neeed no steeenking MFAs." Arf Arf. OK, OK:
It's hard to bust someone for undertaking an advanced course of study so as to earn a living teaching about what she loves. But "let's put it where it is": the MFA is a "union card". And real poetry does not come from the Academy. It comes from the confrontation of the nakedness of the poet's soul with 'being-in-the world'.

SOME SQUIBBITS TO PONDER IN (R)ELATION TO THE ABOVE.

"....All I have is a voice
To undo the folded lie..." '(Thank you, Wystan Hughie)

"...For poetry (is)... a way of happening
A mouth ... (Thank you again, W. H..)

...Irish poets learn your trade, sing whatever is well made, scorn the sort now growing up all out of shape from toe to top... (Ahh, sure 'n thanks darlin' Billy Y.)

"People wish to be poets more than they wish to write poetry, and that's a mistake. One should wish to celebrate more than one wishes to be celebrated."
(Thank you, Lucille Clifton)

Steve Goldman *exists*

Towards Printing The
POETIC IMAGINATION

GUESSING, BY MY WORK, IN ESSENCE, I could be construed as a messenger of generally bad tidings. I cannot, even, consider myself an inspiration towards anybody's search for cathartic hallucinations, etc.

I don't believe in Poetry as therapy nor do I have any truck with pandering to the "oh-don't we-love-poetry-so" fan-clubs.

I suppose it's important to point out, that since the Selected Poems subtitle, in 1998, I've insisted the words "Poems "or "Poetry" be, purposely, omitted from cover graphics on either my recordings or print documents. I even have trouble referring to myself as Poet. I let others call me those names far too honorable to be misused.

There's a sense that, over recent years, those genre words have been so maligned and so abused by those to which I, in no way, feel genetically connected: the chip and dip poetry society hierarchy who poison Poetry every time they breathe on it.

I do not identify with the self-promoting parasites with the poetry prize union cards in their wallets. I refuse to use "poetic" license to fish for recognition and rewards nor deal with the art form as a self-serving competitive warclub.

I'd be hopeful if scanning my work will, somehow, pave a road for anyone who has the inclination to decide on a metaphoric destination for themselves.

I don't think of myself as a be-all-end-all conveyor belt of wisdom capable of teaching people how to write. I could very easily guide them into using tools and techniques which will allow them to teach themselves; all of which is to emphasize that I never thought of myself as an innovator but, always, had the feeling of being a participator: more like being a member of the street-roaming mammal search and finding diverse methods to sharpen my tools of observation.

My approach to language art has been divided into examinations and interpretations of what I call psychic geographies: which include the media maps of film culture, music culture, as well as the disturbing alienation histories of art and architecture. And this is, essentially, the scope and focus of my creative process. Too many poets s believe what their idolaters and sycophants have convinced them to believe: that their poems are delivered from on high; that the Olympian gods have anointed their precious prize-winning petrifaction.

You might be better off accepting what is, by its very nature, the foremost obligation of any writer: to make very good friends with your wastebasket: developing an uncommon perception of what works at the time and what to wad-up and consign to the incinerator.

As a practitioner of contemporary poetry, certainly, you must recognize the necessity of advising yourself to stand on the imagery brake, once in a while, to once-in-a-while get off the right brain bus and recognize a need for engagement with an alternative logic by, quite simply (paraphrasing Fredrich Nietzsche} writing dangerously; it's the only way to write at all.

Michael C Ford
(El Paso, Texas 2011)

Michael C Ford was born in Chicago. Since 1970, his catalog of approx. 26 volumes of published work include books, chapbooks, broadsides, pamphlet editions, both vinyl and compact disk spoken word recordings. His Brainpicnic Productions in association with Hen House Studios produced a poetry film documentary paying tribute to Kenneth Rexroth... His most recent print product is a pamphlet edition of modern music-related poetry entitled Atonal Riff-Tunes To A Tone Deaf Borderguard. It is published by Lawn Gnome Books in Phoenix.

On
POETRY

by Jack Foley

A short talk given at Laurel Books, Oakland, 4/18/08 for National Poetry Month

As we emerge from the fantasy of unity
to the fantasy of multiplicity...

THANK YOU FOR COMING. WE'D LIKE this evening to be a celebration of poetry and a presentation of the kind of poetry Adelle and I write. Since 1996, April has been designated as National Poetry Month. The Academy of American Poets announced that their goal was to "increase the visibility, presence, and accessibility of poetry in our culture." That word "accessibility" is problematical when applied to poetry. Many people find poetry "inaccessible"—difficult to understand, at times perhaps infuriatingly "obscure," full of things which some people may understand but which are opaque to many. Why can't poets just say what's on their mind? Gertrude Stein—no paragon of "accessibility"—gave this as an answer. She was lecturing at the University of Chicago and she was asked about her notorious line, "rose is a rose is a rose." She replied,

Now listen. Can't you see that when the language was new— as it was with Chaucer and Homer—the poet could use the name of a thing and the thing was really there. He could say 'O moon,' 'O sea,' 'O love,' and the moon and the sea and love were really there. And can't you see that after hundreds of years had gone by and thousands of poems had been written, he could call on those words and find that they were just wornout literary words. The excitingness of pure being had withdrawn from them; they were just rather stale literary words. Now the poet has to work in the excitingness of pure being; he has to get back that intensity into the language. We all know that it's hard to write poetry in a late age; and we know that you have to put some strangeness, as something unexpected, into the structure of the sentence in order to bring back vitality to the noun. Now it's not enough to be bizarre; the strangeness in the sentence structure has to come from the poetic gift, too. That's why it's doubly hard to be a poet in a late age. Now you all have seen hundreds of poems about roses and you know in your bones that the rose is not there. All those songs that sopranos sing as encores about 'I have a garden! oh, what a garden!' Now I don't want to put too much emphasis on that line, because it's just one line in a longer poem. But I notice that you all know it; you make fun of it, but you know it. Now listen! I'm no fool. I know that in daily life we don't go around saying '...is a...is a... is a...'. Yes, I'm no fool; but I think that in that line the rose is red for the first time in English poetry for a hundred years.

Now, there's another problem we need to deal with as well. If we're going to celebrate poetry, wouldn't it be a good idea to tell people what poetry is? Surely everyone knows at least more or less what poetry is— but what is it exactly? What is its essence— what are those qualities we absolutely need to see if we're going to call something a poem? There are "poetry sections" in book stores. What is in them? I have been writing poetry in one form or another since 1955, and I have written many articles and even books about poetry. You'd think I'd have at least a glimmer of what poetry is. But, to tell you the truth, I don't. If we ask exactly what an automobile is, we can come up with some elements which might apply to any automobile—and without which you would have something other than an automobile. It has to move, for example. But poetry? The problem is that there have been a number of activities over the centuries and they have all been called "poetry." But very often they are quite distant from one another. Does poetry have to rhyme? In some periods, yes, but in others no. Classical poetry didn't rhyme. Can poetry be its diametrical opposite—prose? Yes. There exists a creature called the "prose poem." Does a poem have to have some sort of "form" which can be reproduced by other people?—the form of a sonnet, for example. Yes, but not always. And people have produced 14-line poems which they have called "sonnets" but which have no regular meter and no rhyme—usually defining characteristics of sonnets. The fact is that poetry has no essence. It can be—almost—anything. But if it has no essence, it does have a history. It is a name that has been given to a number of highly disparate activities which are in some ways related but in others not. Rhyme can be one aspect of poetry—but it doesn't apply to all forms of the art. Further: poetry is created for different reasons and purposes. There are poems which are self-expressive—this is what I feel—but there are also poems which have very little to do with self-expression. (For years people have been trying to figure out exactly who Shakespeare was by reading his poems and plays. Their efforts haven't been particularly successful. It may be that Shakespeare's poems and plays aren't especially "self-expressive.") Poetry can be used for idealistic purposes; it can be the conveyer of uplifting thoughts: "Life is real, life is earnest, / And the grave is not its goal," wrote Longfellow. But it can also be immensely cynical, satirical, like the work of Alexander Pope or certain lines by T.S. Eliot. There have been critics who believed that poetry was essentially irony—saying something like the opposite of what you mean.

So what are we celebrating? An ancient art form with an immensely complicated history which cannot be reduced to any particular definition. The minute you define poetry, poetry slips away from the definition and tells you, "I'm not that because I'm this." But to say this about poetry is also to say that poetry is free—not only free-floating but free. Any individual poem is a momentary definition of poetry, but the definition belongs only to that moment. The next moment, poetry will be something else. We poets are always trying to catch at the reins of Pegasus, which has its own kind of horse sense and will go wherever it wishes.

<pre>
honor the fire
which holds us—
sweet
talk,
light
that
flashes—
in the east,
mind
in the west,
mind:

nowhere
is
home
</pre>

*Jack Foley's radio show, **Cover to Cover** is on KPFA every Wednesday at 3; his column, "Foley's Books," appears in the online magazine Alsop Review. He has published 11 books of poetry, 5 books of criticism, a history of California poetry, and a book of translations of work by the French singer/ songwriter, Georges Brassens. In 2010 he was awarded the Lifetime Achievement Award by the Berkeley Poetry Festival, and June 5, 2010 was proclaimed "Jack Foley Day" in Berkeley.*

SCIENTIFIC THOUGHT AND POETIC VISION:
Seeking New Imagery And Metaphor to Involve The American Scholar

by Jared Smith

POETRY OF WHATEVER FORM OR school can be broken down into two significant areas of study, the combination of which establishes a poet's voice. One area of study is that of "*craft*," which might be briefly defined as the study of how a poet lays out his or her words on paper in such a way as to communicate the intended feeling or understanding in the mind of the reader. Within craft, one can further break the work down into more precise matters, such as line length, meter, imagery, symbolism, or others.

The second area of study that is required, however, is "*vision*." Of the two, vision is the more important and the harder to teach. It encompasses the sense of *being* that the poet possesses, along with his formal or informal philosophy as to the significance or lack thereof of any image, symbol, or metaphor as it relates to that philosophy. A significant poet's vision is vast, and may contradict itself, but its cohesion provides the material with which readers can dissect and analyze the poet's work. Vision generally involves the poet's understanding of art and the humanities, of existence and perception, of nature and human achievement—though these are often implied by context and juxtaposition of images rather than stated. Craft follows vision in poetry, just as form follows function in architecture, or in evolution.

Together, a poet's use of both vision and craft form what we usually think of as a poet's *voice*. The different voices that define a generation or a literary era are generally recognizable as being from that era by other writers, as well as by historians and scholars. A significant part of what makes them recognizable as being from one era or another is the furnishings with which the poet provides imagery and metaphor. What kind of social settings are described, for example, or what pastimes, or what technology? Technology is important because it represents what is newly perceivable or achievable because of an increase in general human knowledge. It significantly shapes or impacts the society and people living at that time. Thus, the technological framework of the 1920s could be used to provide a dissolute setting for "The Waste Land," or alternatively for the hearty exuberance of Sandberg's "Chicago." It could also be used as counterpoint for contrasting pastoral egalitarianism. In any of these examples, the technological framework opens doors to and illuminates the understandings of its time. And it provides a uniquely contemporary canvas or milieu for discussing new ideas and their implications across a wide spectrum of the educated public, providing a cross-fertilization of thought that extends beyond the craft of writing.

These thoughts on the importance of utilizing scientific thought and technological achievement in poetry are not entirely new. They were at one time endemic to our literature. Ralph Waldo Emerson first advanced the notion of "The American scholar" as a person of insatiable and wide-ranging interests and disciplined learning, along with a profound respect for literature. He was among the strongest early supporters of Walt Whitman's *Leaves of Grass*. And it was Walt Whitman who wrote within that work "Scientists, I welcome you. You open doors for me." Thus began the greatest expansion of U.S. literary growth to date.

Whitman lacked significant scientific or technological training, but understood the importance of such knowledge in trying to create poetry that could capture the full human potential for understanding the vision he perceived of an oversoul or universal spirit that infused all people. And, as in the quote above, he encouraged it. He understood that new scientific and technological discovery could provide powerful images that would lend fire to the public imagination, as well as an enhanced degree of proof for his own beliefs. Out of that understanding and encouragement of others, grew at least a century of advancement when poets became concerned with the intellectual examination of ideas within their work, in addition to their continued interest in imagism, meter, and stanzaic form. This initiated an environment that fostered the keen intellect of poets such as T.S. Eliot, the business experience of Wallace Stevens, the social understandings of William Carlos Williams, and eventually the entire spectrum of social groupings and voices that make up today's contemporary poetry.

Nor was the rest of society, outside of poetic circles, untouched by this sudden infusion of intellectual and scientific interest. T.S. Eliot's description of the gas works that he visited and the musings they nurtured, were close enough to the cutting edge of technological advance at their time that they captured the attention of

Robert Branaman

Robert Oppenheimer as he worked on issuing-in the Atomic Age. Richard Rhodes, in his 1986 *Pulitzer Prize* winning book **The Making of the Atomic Bomb**, notes several references to Eliot's work in Oppenheimer's notes.

Imagine that! A discussion of ideas and morality; of human consciousness and conscience between two of the nation's most respected people—a scientist playing with the act of creation or destruction, and a poet working along the same themes!

But, of course, gas works are today an almost-extinct technology; town gas sites across this country are now *Superfund* sites for toxic remediation. Already, by the time powerful poets like Anne Sexton and Denise Levertov and Sylvia Plath focused attention on the importance, strength, and vulnerability of the individual in technological societies, that technology had been replaced. Poetry remained vital because the conflict remained vivid between machinery that is designed to exploit human labor for the good of society, and the pressure the individual in such a society must confront when the good of the society conflicts with *personal* good or desire. This conflict, of course, led in part to the anti-intellectual rebellion of the Beats and of society generally.

That rebellion might be said to have helped open the doors for such writers as Robert Bly and W.S. Merwin, writing within the same generation as the above, who could draw upon as well as translate the experiences of nations and cultures perceived in a more mythic or nonlinear mode of thought than our own to highlight weaknesses within our society, where individuals were in danger of losing their connection with the natural world around them. Their work, along with increasing numbers of other poets from their time and ours, pulled with increasing frequency on nature imagery once again for its effect, because nature imagery remained common to so many readers across our intellectual and emotional landscape. Most of their writing, however, lacked an urban or technological imagery that could communicate viscerally with an educated general readership audience—as opposed to a more specialized poetry audience.

An exception to that statement about their work is Robert Bly's **The Light Around The Body**, which drew heavily upon the technology and weaponry of war to achieve a powerful effect not only among poets, but among the larger readership of the general public. But that exception strengthens the argument that technological setting is important. The book was a resounding success and helped further resolve feelings against the Vietnam War because the general public was so well able to visualize and relate to its contemporary imagery. The combination of that specificity with the more Shamanistic perspective that is a general component of Bly's work provides a wonderful breeding ground for what he himself refers to as "Dragon Smoke." It is where the poetry happens. Even so, there still remains, even in that book, an absence of any sense of wonder or discovery coming from scientific or technological progress. There are few *positive* new images or metaphors for the time.

This is not because of a lack of adeptness at poetic craft; poetic craft is, I believe, at as high a level as at any time in our history. Never before have so many writers come out of years of studying and applying craft for their MFAs. What is missing in much of our current writing is vital new imagery. The technological imagery of the past generation is no longer perceived as a common part of our shared human landscape. The science employed as imagery and as a door of discovery by the past generations is growing old. The technology from those generations is perceived as obsolete. And the metaphor, so well established and such a powerful tool for shaping society to the needs of the people, has been weakened.

This contributes to making poetry a weaker force than the shear number of its practitioners might otherwise suggest in contemporary society. One can no longer read the works of even our most widely recognized poets in the newspapers or wide circulation magazines, the way one used to be able to read W.H. Auden, for example. As Dana Gioia wrote in his book **Can Poetry Matter**, long before he became involved with the NEA, poetry even as it expanded in numbers of participants in the 1960s onward, started to become an area for learning that generated too many MFAs who were trained in writing poetry, rather than providing poetic or literary training for both MFAs and practitioners in other fields of endeavor. And, as Gioia suggested, the overwhelming number of MFAs overcame the ability of literary magazines to look toward other fields of knowledge to include with craft. He further proposed in that book that a large number of these MFAs were *not* trained in what he termed a "rigorous enough" fashion to publish in the scholarly magazines—despite the fact that "publish or perish" was the rule at all the universities. Thus, he surmised, the number of literary journals continued to expand, and the number of poets continued to expand, but poetry itself became seen by the general reading public as rather light fare due to the number of journals competing for a rather select number of innovative writers. Great writers were there, but the general public was having a very hard time finding them. And because of the degree of specialization our contemporary society began to require of any professional, whether scientist or plumber or poet, the scientists and plumbers who might once have been encouraged to write poetry as well—to enhance cross-fertilization of experience--found themselves having to devote more and more of the free hours they might have used in such pursuit just to stay on top of the swelling knowledge base in their field.

The standards accepted as publishable poetry by today's literary magazines are therefore increasingly established by specialized Masters of Fine Arts, not by physical or social scientists, philosophers, blue collar workers. Not by The American Scholar, nor even by students of the Liberal Arts, which encircle all of the above.

There remains a way back, of course; a way to draw forth new visions with all that that word implies. That way back calls for poets to welcome back the American Scholar, and to open the doors of human advancement once again to the province of poetry. It may call for inclusion of meditations on the implications of mapping the human genome, or of the heavy metals that make up our bodies coming only from the heart of super novas that exploded millions of light years ago to bring us together where we are. There are many, many dark, chilly places that we as poets have not ventured yet, despite receiving scientific fact that shows that over 90% of the universe is composed of dark matter and is not observable through our senses. One hopes that we will begin to do so, that we will step down from defending ourselves as definers and protectors of a language that has already expanded well beyond the words we work with as poets; that we will begin to think about these things and include current data in our musings, even as prose writers do.

It would be good to speak again as equals with the likes of Robert Oppenheimer and T.S. Eliot, and to drive forward new understandings that once again lie beyond the doors that science opens and can only partially comprehend; to be American Scholars rather than specialists. If we have unique knowledge of the Cosmos, and every poet of vision does, let us learn better to communicate with the imagery of our time.

First published in The New York Quarterly, Issue 62

THE REVIEWS

THE MYSTIC SMOKE OF BORDER FIRES:
The Poetry of John Macker
By Michael Adams

Books discussed in this review:

Underground Sky [Turkey Buzzard Press, 2010]
Woman of the Disturbed Earth
[Turkey Buzzard Press, 2007]
Wyoming Arcane [in Mad Blood #5, 2005
Winner of first Mad Blood Literary Arts Award]
Adventures in the Gun Trade [Long Road/
Temple of Man La Cantera Press, 2004]
Burroughs at Santo Domingo [Long Road/La
Cantera Press, 1998]
The First Gangster [Long Road/Mesozoic
Thumbprint Press, 1994] chapbook
    contact author for availability

JOHN MACKER LIVES IN AN OLD roadhouse along the Santa Fe trail, on the plains of northern New Mexico, hard by the Sangre de Cristo mountains. A hardscrabble land of cholla, turkey vultures, scorpions, boiling summer days and freezing winter nights. This, and the searing desert plains of southern New Mexico, are the landscapes that inhabit most of Macker's work. It's a land that demands a poetry that is spare, lean, and unsentimental.

Macker's most recent book is *Underground Sky*. It is a book in three parts, inhabited by characters who are part myth, part history. Think Ed Dorn's *Slinger*. Section 1, "Ghost Histories", begins with "Elegy"

    ...every memory has forgotten them...
    they're still fragrant with neglect
    & lost ranches, old
    timers safely spirited away behind
    unruly frontier grasses,
    in unsavory graves.

Interestingly, this poem is set not in New Mexico but in northeastern Colorado, up against the Wyoming border, a place his immigrant ancestors moved through, on the way, always, to a better life that never quite arrived. This section is elegiac, quiet and filled with loss and love, the work of a mature poet in his middle years.

"Song for Tony", a tribute to his friend Tony Scibella, is filled with grief as he buries his friends ashes:

    Everywhere, all about us in the air
    a whisper, a grieving, a memory that
    you can't hear, pawing the earth like

    a dreaming bear, as if his tiny bone shards
    scorched marrow & dust would reassemble
    & exist just for a moment for us in cool sunlight:
    exhale a poem or merely reassure us

    that the cosmos is not a threatening
    black thing after all but full of grace & dreams

There is a nice balance in this poem between the artistry of the language and the sentiment Macker wishes to express, no place more so than in "pawing the earth like/ a dreaming bear" to express his grief. In his earliest works, particularly *The First Gangster*, Macker's skill as a wordslinger often outshines what he is trying to say. Compare "Miles Does Porgy & Bess" from *The First Gangster* with "Miles Davis Played the Rainbow"

Jesus is coyote
fresh Catholic bebop roadkill
the Miles of bad road we've come
to know & love
the snow on the mesa is as
deep as faith-

come spring
Hark! the herald Ornette plays
                    Miles Does Porgy & Bess

The True Human Beings followed
the December, May & August of
the buffalo in acoustic rhythms
of long llano grass
as seductive as
the Birth of the Cool
while back in Denver Miles
led an all-white electric band
of smoking 24 year olds into
"Time After Time" ...

...Miles belayed the Second Coming
by laying the voodoo down on all of us
that seductive snowless April night emptying
everything but the Buffalo Moon out of
that horn, back turned to the music hall as if he
were a defrocked friar performing a post-modern
Last Rites in Comanche for the derelict agnostic
in all of us
                    Miles Davis Played the Rainbow

Now don't get me wrong; "Miles Does Porgy
and Bess" is a good poem, playful and punning.
But "Miles Davis Played the Rainbow" is far
better. Maybe its just me, a matter of taste, but
I get a deeper, longer lasting charge from depth
rather than surface.

As I get older, I find myself agreeing more
and more with Christopher Merrill, that poems
in which gesture and voice provide the main
charge interest me less than those that address
the questions that press on us. The best poems of
all are those that balance the two. John Macker

is adept at providing this balance, especially in
his recent works.

One of these pressing questions, one that we
as a people and a nation have never adequately
addressed – one that we have, in fact, actively and
often bellicosely avoided addressing – is our history
of conquest, genocide, and ethic cleansing.

I woke up at dawn under a Manzanita tree
damp, blood red bark glistening
in the sunlight...

Cochise sliced his way out of Bascom's
winter tent to freedom, accused
of kidnapping Mickey Free, 1861, the
inaugural morning of
                    Inevitable Hostilities.

In my dream I read Chemo Sabe's *Gran Apacheria*
again
as both sides refined effluvial notions
of abject behavior until
Abu Ghraib became an extension of
1860s white-eye Indian Policy.
                    Impressions of Chiricahua,
                    from *Underground Sky*

The tragic history and landscapes of the
American southwest run through Macker's
works. No place is this more fully developed and
explored than in *Underground Sky* and *Woman
of the Disturbed Earth*. "The Chihenne Feels the
Heat" blends these with a touch of myth:

In the trickster silence, there's no border, just
more or less Mexico.

    Standing in the shade of grandmother
    mesquite, sweating buzzards, Victorio
    believes in the sun-bleached fertility
    of hope because beneath all this
    revolutionary euphoria are starving
    families, disgruntled warriors,
    scalphunters.

    Fifty-year-old Victorio carries the blood

fate of a tribe on his back. Under his fingernails. The Mescalero families now immured at Fort Stanton couldn't understand the manifest destiny shitball craziness of the loco whites in Lincoln County. But the children could smell the gunsmoke.

William Bonney, Saturday afternoon horseplay, gunplay, loitering on some tequila boothill...pokes his mean six-gun through the curtain of all space and time. He aims, fires. Appreciates Victorio because Victorio has taken some of the heat off of him.

The Apache chief Victorio in the concentration camp of Fort Stanton in the 1880s, with Billy the Kid mixed in. But it could as well be Palestine or Afghanistan in the 21st century.

"Nana's Raid" is a concise history of the final months of the Apache Wars in 1881, while "Nana Rests Up Against the Firing Squad Wall of the Mission Church" provides a more mythic, post-structuralist look at those final days.

Woman of the Disturbed Earth is a lyrical work, the book that a man writes in his middle years, no longer young, not yet old, sadder and wiser at how little the things of the world change: "In my early twenties/ when a protest was still a protest—/ I listened with granola-hearted mothers/ to Corso read "Bomb"/ on mountain lawns/ of eternal light. When/ sitting on the railroad tracks/ of Rocky Flats was a privilege&/ necessity..."
[Blues for Parajito Plateau]. In this book Macker finds the sweet spot where combining politics and poetry is not tedious or preachy. Political poetry is rarely done well, and many poets won't attempt it, but this is avoidance, pure and simple. As Macker demonstrates, it can be done well and with nuance. The pen has power. Shouldn't we, who work with words, wield it? Isn't that our responsibility? Macker's answer is yes, we must. But with skill, understanding and a touch of irony.

"Jornado Del Muerto" muses on the 60th anniversary of the first atomic bomb test at the Trinity site:
through the deep heat haze
walking like the memory of
faraway thunder:
skinny Oppenheimer
as pale as the bloodless moon,
with the other boy scientists,
across the mesa ranch, into
the cholla, New Mexico dust like
burning pollen, upends
his pipe & sees the cinders of our hearts
broken into small shadows.

and on an immigrant crossing this journey of death:
She walks in slow motion
desert rhythm footprints in the sand,...
one gallon jug
of water, a straw hat,
napalm mango of a sun
a blistered echo on her tongue;/

we left mama on a homemade stretcher
on the border road, collapsed earl/
from the heat; the norte
americanos will find her at dawn.

A false hope, something she tells herself so she can go on? "If she lives they'll send her back to/ Hermosillo... if she dies her ghost will/ search for water." All of this under "... this same branding iron sky that/ lords over the river, the border, the mesquite,/ the fragrant sage in windblown/ congregations, the last of the/ hummingbirds pulled out at midnight, a better life."

This poem reminds me of the best of Kenneth Patchen's political poetry:

...We'd like belonging
Here, where sleep is not of city-kind,
Where sleep is full and light and close
As outline of a leaf in a glass of tea; but
Knowledge in the heart of each of us
Has painted rotten eyes within
The head: we have no choice; we see
All weeping things and gaudy days
Upon this humble earth, blending
Taxi horns and giant despair...

[We Must Be Slow, The Collected Poems of Kenneth Patchen, New Directions 11th printing 1998]. The styles are radically different, but both share the same awareness of how hope and despair, beauty and ugliness are inextricably tied to each other in the modern world.

Wyoming Arcane, which has not been published in book form, was the winner of Mad Blood's first annual Literary Arts award. It was inspired by the terrible beating death of Matthew Shepard outside of Laramie Wyoming in 1998. Shepard was pistol-whipped and crucified on a barbwire fence by two homophobes because he was gay. Macker explores how such an event shapes and twists the soul of a place, and interweaves it with an exploration of is own ancestors' difficult lives in Wyoming. In *Wyoming Arcane* one experiences the absolute dominance of space over the western landscape:

the architecture of primitive starlight over
a vast plain so (geometrically) flat
they forgot what they came West for
in the first place
so many deranged by the (philosophically)
formless pure emptiness of it...

The West —and by that I refer to the vast spaces beyond the tall grass prairies of Kansas and Nebraska and before the continent throws up its western shoulder in the imposing ranges of the Sierras and Cascades – has always been a land of space and light.

Charles Olson said "I take SPACE to be the central fact to man born in America...Large and without mercy."[1] The central role of space in John Macker's work is more fully developed in *Wyoming Arcane* than in any of his earlier books. Though it is a family history, the central character is the land itself – the Wyoming high plains. What is human grows out of it, shaped by the borderland where flesh meets earth and sky:

Out in the middle of nowhere
adolescent U.S.A. near the Medicine Bow River
lightning struck a plow. The plow
became a charred thing that begat
a post hole which begat a fence post
which begat a dry well,
a church steeple, then,
an American flag pole which
begat a missile silo
which grew into a human erection
This is the source.

And so it goes, the human and the earth.

There are "Only two living pasts – your own and the one we don't really have a good word for but let's call it myth."[2] In *Wyoming Arcane* Macker invites us to tie ourselves to the web that connects four generations of Irish Americans to the extended family of land and space. Myth and legend are central elements in all of Macker's books. *Adventures in the Gun Trade* is a mythic-surreal history of the American southwest. It follows the trail blazed by Ed Dorn in *Slinger* and wanders the hard heart-breaking soul wrenchingly beautiful landscapes of Richard Hugo in *The Lady in Kicking Horse Reservoir*. It is Billy the Kid as synecdoche for all western heroes/anti-heroes, the great amnesiac comic book pop culture of post-war America. It is a wonderfully ironic and highly idiosyncratic exploration of the American psyche. Yet, for my money, *Wyoming Arcane* is better than *Adventures in the Gun Trade*. It's a shame that it has never been published in book form. It's got a lot of heart and it's full of immediacy:

His dog star woman bride companion
    Celtic-Anna,
Wyoming daughter, her blue sea-grace
    softness once touched
her vision to his skin. Fingers aflame with
his frozen whiskers, she can't believe he'd
    slip to the
earth like that. A milky serenity floods his
eyes as she pries the mattock from his
    hands. She weeps.

The way that Macker plays language reminds me of the way that Charlie Parker played the sax – hot, cold, wild, violent or feathery soft. It's easy for someone so skilled to become so caught up in technique that the soul of the work never fully emerges. But good and balanced art emerges from the application of the right kind and amount of technical skill to the subject at hand. The language should match the land. Too much flash and the soul of the work is obscured. Here are two passages, the first from *Adventures in the Gun Trade* and the second from the Sonnets section of *Burroughs at Santo Domingo* that show that Macker hits the nail right on the head more often than not:

feeling the mystical smoke of border wildfires
filling the sky to the south
he wipes his eyes, making a point
to his morning warriors, greased up for
the day's belligerence, arms spread
    like
        THIS
standing arms akimbo on a pyramid
of boulder
s
When under the gun
become a shadow of yourself

Survive
He communicates with the sheer volume
of his presence. He speaks in metaphor
for an entire civilization wired to the desert.

Cochise: A Meditation

and

Something deep inside me loves the touch
of the word chamisa. I've seen August
    herald its
arrival like a line of new clothing. I watch
    my wife pray for
its rain kneeling on the fossilized veins of
    strong
Comanche arms. The blood runs deeper
    than
sunlight here...
Memory is more learned than fossils. In
order to remember fragrance, we twist the
    sage between
our fingers and imagine all of our senses
above the fray, beyond our dreams, under
    siege

Sonnet #6 for Annie

Like most poets who don't labor in the industrial MFA mills of academe, John Macker is unknown to the poetry establishment. That is the academy's loss, and in no way reflects upon the quality of his work. In fact, I believe that his work may be better for the fact that he is not shackled to the poetry machine, dragging a train of scholarly tradition behind him. It makes him freer; he can move like mystic smoke across the deserts and hazy blue mountains of the southwest.

* * *

Laurel Ann Bogen:

Washing a Language (2004: Los Angeles: Red Hen Press, 46 pp., $8.95)

A Review by Roger Taus

THE SIGNATURE INTELLECTUAL POET of a star-stricken dumbbell movie town with few poets of distinction, alors, but with Mississippi deluge of plasticized noirated botoxed celebrities maas Querading as artists, Laurel Ann Bogen emerges here with a less flamboyant bent than in her halcyon, aesthetically salad days with P. Schneidre's avant-garde Illuminati Press--her works of lyric genius comprise such as *Origami: The Unfolding Heart; Do Iguanas Dance, Under the Moonlight?* and *Rag Tag We Kiss—but* her poignard style of verse remaineth intact. Her unusual burnished love of Eliot's verse shines through the veil of words unabated in this collection of americano English poems of an impeccable diction and mordant bite. Yet I cannot help but propose that it is perhaps the early-surrealist French poet Robert Desnos who is better suggestive as exegetical link here than is Ol' Possum, with his verse of the hardened artery, the royalist bank account, and the smell of the law office.

Where hath thou gone, Wallace Stevens?

Take that, Paul Simon!

For Bogen's book here at hand smoketh apace, never mind its odd, pedestrian title and the front-cover rubbish gussied up as arte and executed by Red Hen as hyper-linked, gross, faux, a vanity view of Los Angeles from the window of house atop Hollywood Hills once owned by Veronica somebody for several months before it was commandeered by a richer lioness and repainted ochre. (This, gleaned from years of running the utility road around Lake Hoi on 3, 5 and 10 mile training runs with Arno and Esteban back in the day.)

"Washing a Language," in fact, is no title poem in *any* collection of Bogen's verse. It is a birthday card, humorous, likely written during a boring midnight laundry run absent bringing a good book to reed and not at all her mission of redeemed heartbreak and pillaged soul. Give the title "Washing a Language" to the Shelleyan W. S. (William Stanley) Merwin's next opus if you like, or to that industrial plague the languagers, who have scrubbed it down to lint, but not to Bo-gen's work.

"Slipping into Night's Secret Clothes" is one of a number of poems here that better serves as actuelle title poem because of the shimmering way it holds an universal loneliness up to the spotlight of moon, mystere, even madness, the loco motive of youth, age, fade, death. All life is suffering said the Budd, the original Beat, and

Bogen's arch wit and Quick dagger say so poem upon poem (see her book, *The Burning*). This is the author of the dark and classic poem, "Live Steam at 8:45," the outre "Jive Artiste Speaks Out on Frustration," and the signature Los Angeles poem, "Rat City." "Detective Supremo Meets Her Match" isn't exactly chopped liver, either.

> It is all revealed
> somewhere like the
> clue that eludes you
> each time you open
> a door pale blue and
> black orchid you twist

in that jacket
arms tied around your
waist as the night
mumbles strange
offerings that return
like a bounced check
you scan again and
again looking for your
name . . .

It's high time Bogen received her due in a fat collected, properly titled, edited, and proofed (Tomaž Šalamun, Hen, with two hačeks [pronounced "hat checks," page 18], the "ž" and the *"Š"; that's* what you get employing corvée labor known as "interns"). Few poets who stuck with Los Angeles have given of themselves to a World Wide Public Toilet, movie-crazed, barren public so much startling original verse, noir as bull, cut loose and at the mike ready to kick ass.

* * *

Charles Bivins: *Music in Silence*

(1994, Los Angeles: Heat Press, 129 pp.)
Another Review by Roger Taus

IN A DEFINITE LEAGUE WITH VERSE BY earlier but postbeat contemporary worthies d. a. levy, Stuart Z. Perkoff; The Vagabond Poet, Tony Seldin; and the great Bob Kaufman, the poet Charles Bivins' book *Music in Silence,* with its San Francisco O'Farrell St. Sequences, calls out United States imperialist America as special devil rival codex to Dante Alighieri's frenzied fourteenth century circular chthonic reticulated Firenzian serpentines. It is in exactly that genius that Bivins well serves his muse, for he renders impossible—that is, makes a stone lie of—the Mafia of Fine Arts (MFA) school of influence which currently holds sway over-or strangulating ownership of, if you prefer—americano poetry.

It is impossible not to conclude from a reed of Bivins' verse that this poetry of tech suffers from terminal constipation and that the stench is deafening.

Often clean, yet inscrutable as an effaced glyph, Bivins' poems radiate diamond clarity. As you will see, visionary line upon line builds toward an demonized americano state unlikely to be saved from dodder and demise by the wan fey rhetoric of recovering drunks with university teaching jobs who are regularly published by the capitalized, leveraged press of this rival codex looking out for and ensuring the security ever of its own cash register ass, sobre todo.

O'FARRELL ST.

1

half moon
sea gull
gin mill in the morning

2

no white switch
when spirit
spoke from the
water-pipe

3
does the patient thief this cruel night
await awakening in each heart

4

night of sable beacons
nothing to walk for
disappear down wet alleyway

There is nothing the numbing thwart of an iron grip censorship—The Big Ignore—can do about such poetry. (Do not be deceived you live in a free country simply because it is not czarist Russ or Heian Japan.) It is a poetry that proves the existence of the muse, the duende of the soul's cojones, as it were. Without it we are really lost, instead of merely in the dark. For if there is no light to illumine the smoky murk of city walk and schmuck unemployment and unhouse-ment and starvation on the boulevards, the barren goof of samsara has us by the throat. Aaaarrrggh, as my friend Steve H. used to say, on our five milers at old Lake Hoi.

I would compare Bivins' verse to none save Hart Crane's but without the violent suicide of throwing oneself to the sharks of the south Atlantic and much more important without Crane's mythologizing architectural hangup, excessive Elizabethan lingo betimes, odd idolatry of his own demons, overweening ambition in the po biz, and overall undesirability as your dinner guest were it 1930. See Geoffrey Wolff's stout bio of Harry Crosby (and Caresse and Josephine Noyes Rotch and Hart Crane), *Black Sun,* for an exegesis of the anomie of which we speak. As the great poet Kenneth Rexroth said, you cannot produce and bruit about and *use* the atom bomb and then expect to pacify us with Coca-Cola.

Bivins never went to Mexico and fucked Malcolm Cowley's wife and then jumped off the S.S. Orizaba but his end was no less grisly or sad. He died a pauper in early 2008 at hospice after a long siege; he was so little thought of, the attendant on duty when he died discarded his notebooks including his last work. A week later his brother Patrick committed suicide. Bivins had been scheduled—a rare appearance—to read his verse at Beyond Baroque that March.

His poetry is among the most remarkable of the day and beyond. He eschews the cheap money laundering of Bukowski all the while living—and dying of—the underside. From "POEM IN DIM LIGHT":

> i know these things go on. i
> live in an empire, a missile

fortress, a bloated reptile of a
nation, but still it seems
to be in some distance, some
other dimension than the one i
breathe & speak in. so i confront
these facts in this quiet night
just out of ear shot of screams,
just over horizons from wars. . . .

my stillness
is offered as no counterbalance,
my poetry is an opaque glasspane
tinged with the brittle perception of
these brutal facts.

And from "MUSIC IN SILENCE":

raindrops golden
crows heads in
flashlight searching the garden   you!!

Morpheus   strange
indeed are thy dictates

* * *

FOUR REVIEWS
by C. Mulrooney

The Missouri Review
Vol. 34, No. 3, Fall 2011.
Editor: Speer Morgan.
quarterly, $24/yr. The Missouri Review, 357 McReynolds Hall, University of Missouri, Columbia, MO 65211.

Hayden's Ferry Review
Issue 49, Fall/Winter 2011.
Editorial board.
semiannual, $25/yr. Hayden's Ferry Review, Box 875002, Arizona State University, Tempe, AZ 85287.

The Sow's Ear Poetry Review

Vol. XXI, No. 3, Fall 2011.
Editor: Kristin Camitta Zimet.
quarterly, $27/yr. The Sow's Ear Poetry Review, 217 Brookneill Dr., Winchester, VA 22602.

"GRAFFITI IS HARDWIRED INTO society," says *The Missouri Review*, citing Cleopatra, Julius Caesar, and Lord Byron to its thesis, more, it shows you pages of full-color spread.. On the other hand, "I just don't think any of the arts are really at the center of our culture right now." Can we speak of a position? "He thought about things."

Hayden's Ferry Review, too, has full-color spreads, photo-portraits of plastic surgery patients, also kids and critters, eccentricities and whatnots. "Life and art constitute a unity." "A few nameless poems, weary of their travels..." "Even the dead have dreams." "Already too late. Before I / get lost." "Our hands sort nothing but our own lies / and the unreachable Eid". "I'm interested in the various economies of the human imagination."

It's been said before, and it'll probably be said again, you can't make a silk purse of *The Sow's Ear Poetry Review*, not even with a feature on the Egg Money Poets, what with "If Plath Had Reached Middle Age" and "On the Day Fay Wray Died at the Age of 96", etc. "There is nowhere that is nowhere," says the editor, "here is no one who is no one."

The Hudson Review.

Vol. LXIV, no. 3, Autumn 2011.
Editor: Paula Deitz.
quarterly, $36/yr. The Hudson Review, Inc., 684 Park Ave., New York, NY 10065.

THE POETRY IS DESPERATELY BAD. "The most beautiful bird I ever saw close up / was a flicker, a kind of over-sized woodpecker, dead / on prairie spring mud behind the house where I wrote / all day. Birdscratch. Wordprocessor-slow. / Peck. Peck. The scarlet head I saw on a walk. // Folded wings a black-and-white pattern of feathers / like a royal cape. Its rosy-brown back. Feet / and underfeathers yellow. It lay on its side. / No blood anywhere. Audubon perfect. / Soundless as a page or a print when it's finished."

The prose is superficial and redundant, a defense of Frost against its author's own "uneasy feeling" occasioned by a silly misreading of "Two Tramps in Mud Time", for instance, though he gives all of "A Roadside Stand" and it's worth the price even if he reads that wrong, too.

* * *

LAST CALL: The Bukowski Legacy Continues

ISBN 978-1-929878-86-4 LUMMOX Press, San Pedro, CA $18. RD Armstrong, ed.
Reviewed by Ben Newell

IN HIS 1974 REVIEW OF CHARLES Bukowski's *Erections, Ejaculations, Exhibitions and General Tales of Ordinary Madness*, the great Lester Bangs describes Bukowski's face thusly: "This old fart is 55 and has one of the ugliest slag-slugged mugs I ever seen" (59). And Bukowski himself addresses the topic in Glenn Esterly's 1976 *Rolling Stone* article: "The shot of me they used on the cover of *Erections* has done a lot to sell that book. The face on that cover is so horrific and pasty and completely gone beyond the barrier that it makes people stop and wanna find out what the hell kinda madman this guy is" (33). Let's face it, Bukowski will always be a writer known as much, if not more, for his persona and wild exploits as he is for his prodigious body of work.

But it is most definitely the work itself that inspires the pieces in *Last Call: The Bukowski Legacy Continues*. Conceived, edited, and created by RD Armstrong, the man behind LUMMOX Press, and a poet and short story writer to boot, *Last Call* is a Bukowski-themed anthology featuring, according to its editor, "writers whose work shows the influence [of Bukowski], though not necessarily in style or form, but in the *feelings* that their pieces (especially true of poetry) evoke in the reader." This is an apt description as Bukowski's influence is certainly felt throughout the pieces: forty-seven poems, five short stories, and six essays.

Without question, the poetry and essays are the book's strength. Among the poetic jewels are Ben Smith's "Poetry Money" in which the narrator is treated to a hand job the morning after his first poetry reading: "I heard Praying Mantis

/ eat their mates after making love; / God knows what they do to a hung over poet, / after a hand job" (30). Doug Draime's 1976 poem "Small House On Winnona Boulevard" is rife with the seedy atmosphere of Bukwoski's East Hollywood: "I walk by his court apartment / going to my job at the porno bookstore, and I salute / him from the darkness of Carlton Way. I / salute the famous poet of East Hollywood" (56).

Armstrong's "Poetics" exemplifies the humor that set Bukowski's work apart from so many other writers associated with the counter-culture as its narrator, while buying groceries, is mistaken for the Dirty Old Man himself: "Yeah / I told the checker / I get that a lot / Me

and Buk / Go way back / That's cool / She says / As she gives me / A deal on the Jif / Peanut butter I just bought / At last my association with / Bukowski / Is finally paying off" (71-72). Neeli Cherkovski's "SHOSTAKOVICH CAME TO VISIT" is one of the few pieces written by a Bukowski friend and contemporary: "and we were glorious smoking cheap / cigars from Ned's Liquors, and the / Russian composer battled it out" (75).

In addition to the poems, notable Bukowski scholar Abel Debritto's "Atomic Scribblings from a Maniac Age: The Artwork of Charles Bukowski" is a strong piece of scholarship about the many doodles, sketches, and cartoons the writer produced throughout his life. Claudio Parentela and Henry Denander contribute wonderful black and white drawings that supplement the text nicely.

If you're looking for a heaping of short fiction in the tradition of *Erections* and/or other Bukowski collections, you'd best look elsewhere. If, however, Bukowskian poetry is your thing, you can't go wrong with *Last Call*.

Works Cited

Armstrong, RD, ed. *Last Call: The Bukowski Legacy Continues*. LUMMOX: San Pedro, 2011. Print.
Bangs, Lester. Rev. of *Notes of a Dirty Old Man* and *Erections, Ejaculations, Exhibitions and General Tales of Ordinary Madness*, by Charles Bukowski. *Creem* Oct. 1974: 59. Print.
Esterly, Glen. "Buk: The Pock-Marked Poetry of Charles Bukowski; Notes on a Dirty Old Mankind." *Rolling Stone* 17 June 1976: 28-34. Print.

(Endnotes)
[1] Olson, Charles Call Me Ishmael from Collected Prose of Charles Olson (University of California Press, 1997)
[2] Olson, The Present is Prologue, Collected Prose

THE ARTISTS

CLAUDIO PARENTELA
Born in Catanzaro (1962-Italy) where he lives and works...Claudio Parentela is an illustrator, painter, photographer, mail artist, cartoonist, collagist, journalist free lance... Active for many years in the international contemporary art scene. He has collaborated & he collaborates with many, many zines, magazines of contemporary art, literary and with comic [books] in Italy and in the world...& on the paper and on the web...some name amongst the many: NY Arts Magazine, Turntable & Blue Light Magazine, Komix, LitChaos, Why Vandalism, Thieves Jargon,180 Mag, Braintwisting, The Doors of Creativity Anthology, Lo Sciacallo Elettronico, Inguine, Stripburger, Lavirint, Komikaze, Mystery Island Magazine, Monoclab, Mung Being Magazine, The Lummox Journal, The Cherotic R(e)volutionary, Sick Puppy, Malefact, Gordo, and johnmagazine to name but a few.

ROBERT BRANAMAN
Beat Generation painter, poet, and film maker Bob Branaman continues to make avantgarde art today. Branaman joined the Beatniks in San Francisco in the 1950s, part of the Kansas Vortex, which included Bruce Conner, Charles Plymell and Michael McClure. He showed his paintings at the seminal Batman Gallery in San Francisco (1969 -1965) He presently lives and works in Santa Monica, and is the Artist in residence at the Beyond Baroque Art Center.

NORMAN OLSON
Norman J. Olson, the artist, writer and poet lives in Maplewood, Minnesota. His images have been reproduced in dozens of art and literary magazines and publications throughout the world. Longing for quiet and stability, Norman avoids personal contacts with the public. His art is driven by the compulsion and obsession of a man who prefers his own company.

JAMES McGRATH
James McGrath is an artist and poet living in Santa Fe, New Mexico. He has had numerous national and international one-man and juried shows since the early 50s. He is a founding member of the Institute of American Indian Arts.

MARK HARTENBACH
Mark Hartenbach lives in a small rust belt town along the Ohio river.

BILLY JONES
Billy Jones was an artist, poet and emotional expatriate born in Camden, New Jersey in 1935 where Walt Whitman died. He quit high school, joined the Marines, then went back to school on the GI Bill majoring in American Literature at LA State. He migrated to Australia from Stockholm in 1967. He kept a journal of drawings, paintings, poetry and every day events since June 28, 1975. He was working on volume 167 (ME & MY GANG OF ALTER EGOS) when he died ---100,000 pages, 4500 illustrations. Overall title: THE ILLUMINATION OF BILLY BONES.

RAINDOG
A failed artist who at one time tried to get into Art School, Raindog has been dabbling in the arts ever since. He is best known as a poet and former café singer. His alter-ego, RD Armstrong, is renowned for his work as a publisher. Visit www.lummoxpress.com for further details.